Critical Criminological Perspectives

Series Editors
Reece Walters
Faculty of Law
Queensland University of Technology
Brisbane, QLD, Australia

Deborah H. Drake
Social Policy and Criminology Department
The Open University
Milton Keynes, UK

"This book nudges knowledge forward on the relationships between systemic, structural and interpersonal forms of crime and harm. From the scholarly but always heartfelt reflections in the early chapters, to the chapters taking the reader's zemiological gaze in to war, murder, 'extreme' pornography, borders, fashion, rehabilitation and environmental harm-doing, this book takes suffering seriously."
—Pamela Davies, *Professor of Criminology, Northumbria University, UK*

"This superb collection probes points of contact as well as tensions between zemiology and criminology, and between grasping complex patterns of harm and doing something about them. Authors explore the wilful ignorances, silences and omissions that both generate specific contemporary harms and nurture their acceptance. The book can help us better understand exactly what we are up to as critical criminologists in these times."
—Lois Presser, *Professor of Sociology, University of Tennessee, USA*

"This book offers a refreshing new way of understanding the relationship between crime and social harm and between criminology and zemiology. Each chapter is thought provoking and timely. Much can be learned from reading this original anthology, and it is destined to stimulate meaningful debates within international critical criminological circles."
—Walter S. DeKeseredy is *Anna Deane Carlson Endowed Chair of Social Sciences, Director of the Research Center on Violence,* and *Professor of Sociology*

The Palgrave Critical Criminological Perspectives book series aims to showcase the importance of critical criminological thinking when examining problems of crime, social harm and criminal and social justice. Critical perspectives have been instrumental in creating new research agendas and areas of criminological interest. By challenging state defined concepts of crime and rejecting positive analyses of criminality, critical criminological approaches continually push the boundaries and scope of criminology, creating new areas of focus and developing new ways of thinking about, and responding to, issues of social concern at local, national and global levels. Recent years have witnessed a flourishing of critical criminological narratives and this series seeks to capture the original and innovative ways that these discourses are engaging with contemporary issues of crime and justice.

More information about this series at
http://www.palgrave.com/gp/series/14932

Avi Boukli · Justin Kotzé
Editors

Zemiology

Reconnecting Crime and Social Harm

palgrave
macmillan

Editors
Avi Boukli
The Open University
Milton Keynes, UK

Justin Kotzé
Teesside University
Middlesbrough, UK

Critical Criminological Perspectives
ISBN 978-3-319-76311-8   ISBN 978-3-319-76312-5   (eBook)
https://doi.org/10.1007/978-3-319-76312-5

Library of Congress Control Number: 2018933052

© The Editor(s) (if applicable) and The Author(s) 2018
This work is subject to copyright. All rights are solely and exclusively licensed by the Publisher, whether the whole or part of the material is concerned, specifically the rights of translation, reprinting, reuse of illustrations, recitation, broadcasting, reproduction on microfilms or in any other physical way, and transmission or information storage and retrieval, electronic adaptation, computer software, or by similar or dissimilar methodology now known or hereafter developed.
The use of general descriptive names, registered names, trademarks, service marks, etc. in this publication does not imply, even in the absence of a specific statement, that such names are exempt from the relevant protective laws and regulations and therefore free for general use.
The publisher, the authors and the editors are safe to assume that the advice and information in this book are believed to be true and accurate at the date of publication. Neither the publisher nor the authors or the editors give a warranty, express or implied, with respect to the material contained herein or for any errors or omissions that may have been made. The publisher remains neutral with regard to jurisdictional claims in published maps and institutional affiliations.

Cover credit: Paul Daniels/Alamy Stock Photo

Printed on acid-free paper

This Palgrave Macmillan imprint is published by the registered company Springer International Publishing AG part of Springer Nature
The registered company address is: Gewerbestrasse 11, 6330 Cham, Switzerland

To those who cross borders

Acknowledgements

This edited collection is both a collection of ideas and a collective effort involving colleagues, friends, activists, institutions, and families. During challenging times, we began developing this volume in hope that the zemiological spark could light a fire, build bridges, and rejuvenate existing debates.

We both want to thank, first and foremost, the contributors to this volume. They have stuck with us through the process of publishing this book. For their trust, time, and engagement, we are most grateful. We hope this is the beginning of sharing ideas and challenging policies. The series editors, Deb Drake and Reece Walters, as well as the editorial-authorial process have been wonderfully supportive of our efforts to bring this book to life. Thank you all. For their dedication to this work, we are indebted to Josie Taylor, Jananee Murugan, and Stephanie Carey at Palgrave.

Beyond the collective energy, Avi Boukli is grateful to current and previous colleagues and friends from The Open University, the London School of Economics, Birkbeck College, Teesside University, and Panteion University. Avi's deepest thanks go to their family, Flora and Chrysa.

Justin Kotzé would like to thank his colleagues at Teesside University both past and present for their support and encouragement. Special thanks to Prof. Philip Whitehead for his friendship, guidance, and many intellectually stimulating conversations. Finally, Justin sincerely thanks his wife Claire for her invaluable support, love, and patience.

Contents

Introduction   1
Avi Boukli and Justin Kotzé

Part I   Reconsidering Crime and Social Harm

For Pragmatism and Politics: Crime, Social Harm and Zemiology   11
Steve Tombs

Beyond 'Criminology vs. Zemiology': Reconciling Crime with Social Harm   33
Lynne Copson

Harm: A Substitute for Crime or Central to It?   57
Letizia Paoli and Victoria A. Greenfield

Criminology or Zemiology? Yes, Please! On the Refusal
of Choice Between False Alternatives   85
Justin Kotzé

Big Trouble or Little Evils: The Ideological Struggle
Over the Concept of Harm   107
Steve Hall and Simon Winlow

Part II   Contextualising Harm

Whose Harm Counts? Exploring the Intersections
of War and Gendered Violence(s)   129
Sandra Walklate

Gender Murder: Anti-Trans Rhetoric, Zemia,
and Telemorphosis   145
Avi Boukli and Flora Renz

A Doubling of the Offence? 'Extreme' Pornography
and Cultural Harm   165
Alex Dymock

Zemiology at the Border   183
Victoria Canning

Green Criminology, Zemiology, and Comparative
and Inter-Relational Justice in the Anthropocene Era   203
Avi Brisman and Nigel South

Spot the Fashion Victim(s): The Importance of Rethinking
Harm Within the Context of Fashion Counterfeiting   223
Jo Large

**Serving Up Harm: Systemic Violence, Transitions
to Adulthood and the Service Economy** 245
Anthony Lloyd

Harm and Transforming Rehabilitation 265
David Temple

Index 283

List of Tables

Harm: A Substitute for Crime or Central to It?
Table 1   Harm taxonomy (*Source* Authors' adaptation of Greenfield and Paoli (2013) and Paoli et al. (2013))   70
Table 2   Matrix for prioritising harms (*Sources* Authors' adaptation of Greenfield and Camm (2005, 48), drawing from Department of the Army et al. (2001) and other military doctrine, Greenfield and Paoli (2013), and Paoli et. (2013))   71

Introduction

Avi Boukli and Justin Kotzé

The emergence of the zemiological movement during the late 1990s (Pemberton 2016) marked a crucial moment for scholars who sought to move beyond the boundaries of the mainstream criminological canon. Complete with a new vocabulary and the discursive space to articulate a multiplicity of harms, which lay outside the conventional discourse of crime, of criminality and criminalisation, areas of harm generation became legitimate focal concerns (Tombs, Chapter 'For Pragmatism and Politics: Crime, Social Harm and Zemiology', this volume; Hillyard and Tombs 2017). Some years later, the landmark edited collection *Beyond Criminology: Taking Harm Seriously* (Hillyard et al. 2004) was published. Ostensibly grounded upon the Greek term *zemia*, *Beyond Criminology* became the basis upon which future zemiological scholarship would build. To further expand the field, this introduction

A. Boukli (✉)
The Open University, Milton Keynes, UK
e-mail: avi.boukli@open.ac.uk

J. Kotzé
Teesside University, Middlesbrough, UK
e-mail: j.kotze@tees.ac.uk

briefly attempts a clearer—than has hitherto been offered—delineation of zemia, the organising concept around which zemiology is built. Subsequently, we make a case for the organising theme of this current volume; namely, a re-examination of the relationship between both crime and harm, and criminology and zemiology.

As a word originating from Ancient Greece, *zemia* carries numerous connotations. Rather than simply meaning 'harm', as is so often intimated, the word actually denotes, among other things, loss, damage as well as various forms of punishment of deviant and/or legal transgressions (Allen 2000; Boukli 2017). To operationalise this term further, disentangling the concept from its identification and coded equivalence with social harm is necessary. This is achieved by excavating from historical discourses of zemia a deeper range of imbedded meanings. An initial analytical reading reveals that zemia can be approached in at least four different ways (see also Boukli 2019, forthcoming):

1. It can be taken to denote a communicative idea, thought, feeling or emotion.
2. Its meaning may be understood in relation to performative speech acts conveying wear, decay, attrition, wastage, lack, loss, disadvantage, bodily harm, damage, disaster, spoiling and debt.
3. It may be seen as being directly connected to criminal jurisprudence.
4. It may be seen as being directly connected to the practice or institution of punishment of (a) crimes; and (b) deviant transgressions, as well as to informal 'punishment' in a less literal sense.

Immediately it becomes strikingly clear that the English word 'harm' is not as conspicuously ambiguous as 'zemia'.

Nevertheless, even with this ambiguity, a few points of clarity can be teased out. For instance, aligned with what is conveyed in approach two above, zemia, according to the Greek Neohellenic Lexicon by Aulos, denotes not only damage but also financial loss or deficit due to a 'wearing down' or 'decline' of some kind. Similarly, Aristotle distinguishes between *kerdos* (gain) and *zemia* (loss), and, in doing so, identifies the mean between these two poles as *dikaion* (the just) (Balot 2001; Hardie 1980). To transgress this mean, thus, constitutes injustice in as much as by 'trying to get or take more than one's share' one breaches an external standard of distributive fairness (Balot 2001, 27). In this context then, Aristotle asserts that gaining (*kerdainein*) more than one's own share while causing another to have less (*elatton*) than before, and thereby suffering a loss (*zemiousthai*), is to commit an injustice (Balot 2001). This is both contemporarily important and particularly pertinent considering our current socio-economic and politico-cultural immersion within an inherently exploitative capitalist system (Fisher 2009; Miéville 2015). Within a capitalist system increasingly saturated with immense inequality, requiring only twenty percent of the global population to perform all the necessary functions to ensure its continuation (Žižek 2011), and with just one percent of the global population owning more wealth than the other ninety nine percent (Hardoon 2017), there is certainly a great deal of *kerdainein* at the expense of those suffering zemia (*zemiousthai*).

As alluded to in points three and four above, zemia is but one of a number of words utilised in the golden age, fifth century BCE, of Athens to denote punishment (Plato 2007; Allen 2000). Collectively, zemia along with a wider vocabulary that stood for certain types of punishment encapsulated the diverse conceptualisations, rationale and practice of punishment (Allen 2000; Solon 2002; Plato 2007). Zemia is also frequently taken to mean 'make worse' as well as to denote 'hurt'. However, the two are not necessarily contingent upon each other, in that the infliction of the latter does not automatically determine the former as an outcome.

Indeed, we may hurt someone without making them worse. For instance, punishment could take the remedial form of treatment, which may actually do some good (e.g. by preventing drunk driving). That is, if zemia is used in this latter sense, it is inflicted upon someone in order to achieve an arguably beneficial outcome (Cross and Woozley 1994). It is perhaps for this reason that Plato argues for the utilitarian efficacy of zemia (in the context of punishment) by highlighting its seemingly reformative and preventative utility (Saunders 1991). Briefly stated, the fundamental upshot is that the word zemia should be understood to contain a broad range of meanings rather than simply pertaining to contemporary notions of social harm. Accordingly, it cannot, nor should it, be trimmed of its numerous connotations.

Reflecting this broader reading of the meaning of zemia, the current book explores the relationship between crime and harm, and between criminology and zemiology. Through various contributions, the book brings together and analyses various structurally induced harms and the harms endured and perpetrated by those victimised by the capitalist system and its hegemonic vicissitudes. The connecting thread running through the book is thus an effort to help rethink the relationship between systemic or structural and interpersonal forms of crime and harm. The current volume does this by interweaving crucial components of zemiology with critical voices in criminology, and with an empirically grounded application of zemia, social harm and crime.

Zemiology is seen here as both a response to mainstream administrative criminology and an attempt to reiterate key priories for social justice. Indeed, through its fresh and invaluable perspective, zemiology both compliments and strengthens the workings of critical criminology, 'in the sense of being able to more fully grasp the nature and significance of current world transformations and their effects on various aspects of contemporary social meaning' (Hil and Robertson 2003, 97). However, so far abstract understandings of zemia as social harm have served to limit the range of relevant debates and fall short of providing a clear vision that would facilitate a different vocabulary. A vocabulary that takes us beyond simple discourses of duality, opposition and alternatives, beyond the confines of criminal law and the cultures of crime control, away from targeting certain populations through regulation and discipline. By training its analytical and empirical lens upon social injury, caused by nation states, organisations, corporations and individuals, this volume takes the opportunity to reconsider the challenging relationship between concrete applications of zemia and diverse ways of thinking about harm. At its core is the idea that zemiology can help reprioritise harms in the social justice system and push for interpersonal, community and structural actions.

Based on the various contributions to this volume, zemiology *seems* to be emerging in four discernible ways: (a) in direct opposition to criminology, opposing the straightjacket imposed by 'crime' and the criminal justice system, so that the recalibrated focus remains on diverse harms that people experience 'from the cradle to the grave' (Hillyard et al. 2004, 1); (b) in parallel to but separate from criminology, animating a rigorous exploration of the concept of harm, which impels a normative anchorage of harm analogous to the normative anchorage of crime in criminology; (c) working in tandem with criminology, and finding ways to recalibrate the shared foci; (d) dismantling the barriers between crime and harm, and between criminology and zemiology.

Structure and Content

This book is comprised of two parts. Part 1 explores the relationship between crime and harm and between criminology and zemiology. Here the current tendency to separate the study of crime and harm, alongside the disciplines ostensibly charged with their investigation, is questioned and challenged. Impetus is thus provided for movement beyond the contemporary discourse of duality, opposition and alternatives. Part 2 begins to put this impetus to work. The intersections of crime and harm are explored through various lenses, including those trained on war and gendered violence; sexuality and gender; fashion counterfeiting; and the harms of the service economy.

Starting with the first part of the book Chapter 'For Pragmatism and Politics: Crime, Social Harm and Zemiology', by Steve Tombs, sets off the discussion by teasing out some critical points that emerged from the responses to *Beyond Criminology* and posits a number of theoretical differences between critical criminology, social harm and zemiology. In Chapter 'Beyond 'Criminology vs. Zemiology': Reconciling Crime with Social Harm' Lynne Copson seeks to reconcile criminology and zemiology, not by collapsing the one perspective into the other, but by identifying some shared goals towards meaningful change. Chapters 'Harm: A Substitute for Crime or Central to It?' and 'Criminology or Zemiology? Yes, Please! On the Refusal of Choice between False Alternatives' then follow on from these. Firstly, Letizia Paoli and Victoria Greenfield present a solid attempt to operationalize 'harm' without abandoning criminology through the creation of a harm assessment framework. Then, in Chapter 'Criminology or Zemiology? Yes, Please! On the Refusal of Choice between False Alternatives', Justin

Kotzé questions the efficacy of the current drive to force an artificial wedge between criminology and zemiology and between the study of crime and harm based upon partial interpretations of zemia. In Chapter 'Big Trouble or Little Evils: The Ideological Struggle Over the Concept of Harm' Steve Hall and Simon Winlow explore, through a transcendental materialist lens, criminogenic and zemiogenic tendencies that are diffused throughout the social order, and unveil how dominant ideology operates at the core of criminalisation processes, compelling us to regard specific harms as the 'price of freedom'.

The second part of the book begins with Chapter 'Whose Harm Counts? Exploring the Intersections of War and Gendered Violence(s)' within which Sandra Walklate explores the intersections of war and gendered violence and poses a set of crucial questions for both criminology and zemiology. Picking up these insights on gender, Avi Boukli and Flora Renz, in Chapter 'Gender Murder: Anti-Trans Rhetoric, Zemia, and Telemorphosis', draw on international audiovisual examples of harm against trans people and utilise the concept of zemia to investigate what a more just future could look like. In Chapter 'A Doubling of the Offence? 'Extreme' Pornography and Cultural Harm', Alex Dymock offers a critical reading of current legislative efforts to target so-called 'extreme' pornography through the concept of cultural harm. Chapter 'Zemiology at the Border' by Victoria Canning continues the discussion by focusing on the harms of asylum procedures, border controls and 'crimmigration', in order to highlight new directions for zemiology. Chapter 'Green Criminology, Zemiology, and Comparative and Inter-relational Justice in the Anthropocene Era' then builds on these contributions, with Avi Brisman and Nigel South exploring green criminology and the potential of mobilising a zemiological approach to reconsider the adverse human impacts on the environment. Focusing on the fashion industry, Jo Large in Chapter 'Spot the Fashion Victim(s): The Importance of Rethinking Harm within the Context of Fashion Counterfeiting' challenges the traditional criminological boundaries by exploring diverse notions of harm, and, in doing so, further expands the applicability of a zemiological lens. From the fashion industry, Anthony Lloyd, in Chapter 'Serving Up Harm: Systemic Violence, Transitions to Adulthood and the Service Economy', leads the thread to the service economy and offers a recalibrated focus on the systemic and subjective harms experienced by those in late capitalist service economy jobs. Finally, Chapter 'Harm and Transforming Rehabilitation' by David Temple concludes this part, and the book as a whole, by noting how the privatisation of probation in England and Wales can be critically considered within a collaborative zemiological framework.

The discussions in these chapters can only scratch the surface of these issues and give a glimpse of the powerful, exploratory and provocative undercurrents that shape this field, while offering a handful of examples of what becomes possible when critical criminology and zemiological scholarship are brought together. It is hoped that collectively this volume has made some strides towards reconsidering the relationship between crime and harm and, thus, arresting the deep running tensions between criminology and zemiology. The work contained herein will no doubt provoke reinvigorated debates within the academic community. However, in doing so, we hope it will encourage a timely reconsideration of prevailing trends in both academic thought and policy.

References

Allen, Danielle S. 2000. *The World of Prometheus: The Politics of Punishing in Democratic Athens*. Princeton: Princeton University Press.

Balot, Ryan K. 2001. *Greed and Injustice in Classical Athens*. Princeton: Princeton University Press.

Boukli, Avi. 2017. Defining Zemia. *Harm Evidence & Research Collaborative*. Available at https://oucriminology.wordpress.com/2017/05/08/defining-zemia/. Accessed 20 Sept 2017.

Boukli, Avi. 2019. *Zemiology and Human Trafficking*. London: Routledge. Forthcoming.

Cross, R.C., and A.D. Woozley. 1994. *Plato's Republic: A Philosophical Commentary*. Basingstoke: Macmillan.

Fisher, Mark. 2009. *Capitalist Realism: Is There No Alternative?* Winchester: Zero Books.

Hardie, William Francis Ross. 1980. *Aristotle's Ethical Theory*, 2nd ed. Oxford: Oxford University Press.

Hardoon, Deborah. 2017. *An Economy for the 99%*. Oxfam International. Available at https://policy-practice.oxfam.org.uk/publications/an-economy-for-the-99-its-time-to-build-a-human-economy-that-benefits-everyone-620170. Accessed 1 Sept 2017.

Hil, Richard, and Rob Robertson. 2003. What Sort of Future for Critical Criminology? *Crime, Law & Social Change* 39: 91–115.

Hillyard, Paddy, and Steve Tombs. 2017. Social Harm and Zemiology. In *The Oxford Handbook of Criminology*, 6th ed, ed. Alison Liebling, Shadd Maruna, and Lesley McAra, 284–305. Oxford: Oxford University Press.

Hillyard, Paddy, Christina Pantazis, Steve Tombs, and Dave Gordon (eds.). 2004. *Beyond Criminology: Taking Harm Seriously*. London: Pluto.

Miéville, China. 2015. On Social Sadism. *Salvage*. Available at http://salvage.zone/in-print/on-social-sadism/. Accessed 20 May 2016.

Pemberton, Simon. 2016. *Harmful Societies: Understanding Social Harm*. Bristol: Policy Press.

Plato. 2007. *The Republic*. London and New York: Penguin Classics.

Saunders, Trevor J. 1991. *Plato's Penal Code: Tradition, Controversy, and Reform in Greek Penology*. Oxford: Oxford University Press.

Solon. 2002. *Solonos Nomoi: Arhaio Elliniko Dikaio* [Solonos Laws: Ancient Greek Legal System]. Athens: Politeia [in Greek].

Žižek, Slavoj. 2011. *Living in the End Times*. London: Verso.

Part I

Reconsidering Crime and Social Harm

For Pragmatism and Politics: Crime, Social Harm and Zemiology

Steve Tombs

Introduction

In the late 1990s, a group of academics began a series of conversations about how a concept of social harm could be more progressively developed as an alternative to crime. It is at once important to emphasise that the motivations, or routes, via which individuals joined these conversations were various. Some were pursuing long-standing struggles to operationalise a concept of crime in their respective areas of work. Others approached this enterprise on the basis of a concern with the marked expansion of criminology as a discipline and the concomitant increase in the number of degree courses in British and Irish universities, while older subjects, such as social policy and sociology, were declining. Others still felt that the notion of social harm could be developed at the margins of criminology, through challenging the discursive power of concepts of crime, 'criminal' and 'criminal justice'. But for some, given the integral nature of these latter

S. Tombs (✉)
The Open University, Milton Keynes, UK
e-mail: Steve.Tombs@open.ac.uk

© The Author(s) 2018
A. Boukli and J. Kotzé (eds.), *Zemiology*, Critical Criminological Perspectives, https://doi.org/10.1007/978-3-319-76312-5_2

concepts to the discipline of criminology itself, any sustained focus on social harm could only be achieved within a new and separate discipline, soon-to-be-named 'zemiology'.

The most tangible outcome of these conversations was an edited collection, *Beyond Criminology: Taking Harm Seriously* (Hillyard et al. 2004). The range of areas covered in, and the diversity of disciplines contributing to, the edited collection was notable. *Beyond Criminology* was an eclectic, somewhat contradictory work reflecting such a wide variety of contributors, theoretical positions, and levels and objects of analysis. It should also be noted that the content—and indeed the title—of the book was deliberately provocative, as well as indicating arguments which were bold (far too bold, as some might say): in other words, many of the book's contributions were couched within the frame not simply of taking social harm seriously, but in terms of abandoning criminology for a new discipline, zemiology. Yet, we were clear within the book that the shift to social harm from criminology was not one endorsed by all of the authors, nor indeed editors. The book was *designed to generate debate*—and indeed it has done so (Hillyard and Tombs 2017).

This chapter returns to some of the issues raised in and by *Beyond Criminology*, albeit from a personal standpoint. I embraced some notion of social harm, and continue to do so, because it allows me to document empirically, to analyse and to theorise forms of corporate activity for which criminology has historically struggled to account. That said, it remains unclear what is meant by a social harm approach. Moreover, is this synonymous with a zemiological approach? If not, what is the latter? And, however one answers these previous questions, must one be a critical criminologist *or* someone utilising a social harm approach *or* a zemiologist? If so, or indeed if not—to what ends?

From Crime to Social Harm

I came to the social harm conversation through my long-standing academic and campaigning interest in corporate crime. More specifically, workplace death, injury and illness are phenomena which are undoubtedly equated with a great deal of harm, harm with economic, physical, financial, emotional, and psychological dimensions.

Notwithstanding that these harms obviously represented a significant social problem, in an attempt to pursue this work within and around the discipline of criminology, I had long struggled to represent these as a *crime* problem, and in so doing had engaged in a number of (entirely unoriginal) strategies, which included, but were not restricted to:

- expanding the use of the term crime to cover violations of non-criminal law (Pearce and Tombs 1998);
- using Sutherland's distinction between what is punished and what is punishable to expand the ambit of 'crime' and thus criminology (Tombs and Whyte 2009);
- reconstructing specific incidents and groups of incidents to indicate how the essential ingredients of 'real' crime were clearly present therein (Pearce and Tombs 2012), and thus making invisible crimes visible (Tombs 1999);
- challenging and reconstructing some of the assumptions within popular, political, academic and legal constructions of 'real' crime either to indicate how these were logically or conceptually unsustainable, or could in fact be applied to corporate activity which produces death, injury and illness or, indeed, both (Tombs 2007).

In these ways, and through what felt like a series of intellectual gymnastics, I was constantly seeking to legitimate the area of harm-producing social life with which I was concerned as the proper stuff for criminology and, indeed, for the Criminal Justice System (CJS). At the same time, at least in the latter context, we sought to be cognizant of the contradictions and dangers of so doing (see Alvesalo and Tombs 2002), and always to challenge the 'illusions of law' (Tombs 2004). In these contexts, the idea of 'social harm' felt liberating, and had progressive potential.

In not dissimilar ways, contributors to *Beyond Criminology*, and those working in a similar vein since its publication, minimally urged that we go at least beyond 'crime' if not beyond criminology. This might be a relatively short or somewhat long journey, and I wish here to indicate the range of intellectual distance that a commitment to going 'beyond' might, and does, take us—some of which guided the 'intellectual gymnastics' to which I have summarised in bullet-points above. I wish here to suggest several ways in which criminologists can or do go 'beyond' crime and criminology, albeit that these are certainly not mutually exclusive.

One most obvious resort to moving beyond crime is to focus upon violations of law other than the criminal law. Without entering into a definitional debate here regarding the appropriate use of the term 'crime' (one which has been tirelessly rehearsed since the exchanges between Sutherland and Tappan over seventy years ago), it has become common-place to use the term 'crime' to encompass violations of law other than criminal law, notably civil, administrative and regulatory law (Pearce and Tombs 1998). Indeed, if perhaps more latterly, 'crime' has also been used to refer to violations of soft law such as 'standards' or 'codes of conduct' (typically as these apply to corporate actors, not least in their multinational forms; Bittle and Snider 2013). Such efforts have considerable legitimacy, at least in critical criminological circles.

Moving slightly further are those who wish to embrace within their intellectual ambit those harms which are punish*able* but not punish*ed*. This commitment can, again, be traced back notably to the work of Edwin Sutherland, who sought to bring to centre-stage those acts and omissions by corporations and their senior executives which could and should in principle be incorporated within criminal justice processes and within the discipline of criminology—but which remain at best relatively marginal, at worst absent. Thus, in terms of the CJS, he argued that most such violations of law remained non-criminalised, whilst his work during the 1940s was a 'call to arms' to criminologists to focus not simply on the crimes and incivilities of the relatively powerless, but equally to shift their gaze upwards, to focus on the crimes committed by the powerful, within corporate contexts (Tombs and Whyte 2009).

A somewhat different approach to incorporating harms within the criminological purview is represented by long-standing and heterogeneous attempts to focus upon the harms produced by the activities of the CJS itself or, indeed, in a related variation, upon the harms associated with non-criminalisation, that is, the omissions of the CJS.

The latter is increasingly signalled by the use of the phrase 'crime and harm' (Corteen et al. 2016; Quality Assurance Agency 2014). Somewhat differently, it involves substituting the term 'social harm' for crime completely to encompass the legal and illegal (Ruggiero 2015), or via an implicit or explicit reference to immorality, that is, that which is self-evidently harmful if not proscribed by law (Monaghan and Prideaux 2016). The general aim of such efforts is to render invisible crimes visible (typified in Davies et al. 2014), or to name 'new' forms of crime—notable examples here being the emergence of hate- (Jenness and Grattet 2004) and eco- (Ellefsen et al. 2012) crimes. Characterising much of what have become 'critical criminologies', the over-arching focus tends to be on the harms associated with a variety of processes of non/criminalisation, usually in ways which emphasise the maintenance or exacerbation of existing structures of power, whether these be viewed through the lens of class, gender and/or sexuality, ethnicity and race, age or, indeed, via some form of intersectionality. Generally, such attempts are couched in a version of equity or social justice or both, albeit the bases for either or both claims vary significantly, and may be well or barely articulated.

A further, distinct approach to embracing the production of 'harm' within criminology has been a focus upon the generation of harms through legitimate markets which, through the goods or services produced therein, are associated with consequences resembling those produced through acts or omissions which are in fact criminalised. Here, I have particularly in mind the edited collections of Hills (1987), Freudenberg (2014), and Passas and Goodwin (2004) as exemplars. Each of these collections describes a series of markets—created and maintained by the state, not least through law—for essentially legal products despite the fact that they are either designed to, or necessarily generate in their use, wide scale social harms, including, typically, agrochemicals, arms, food, gambling, pharmaceuticals and tobacco (see also Tombs and Hillyard 2004, 44–51).

To be clear, to say that the production, distribution and sale of these goods are legal is not to claim that criminal law in particular, and legal regulation in general, does not intervene in such markets. If we take the international arms trade, for example, it is clear that the market in such goods is regulated by international agreements and national states themselves. Moreover, while these are market regulations, it is also clear that this is a context in which criminal law, both nationally and internationally, can and occasionally does intervene—whether this is in the case of bribery and/or corruption to secure contracts, or as a result of abuse of internationally agreed conventions which results in actual or potential violations of international human rights standards. So this is not a sphere from which law, let alone criminal law, is absent—yet it is a sphere which is relatively far removed from the concerns of much of what passes for criminology.

From Social Harm to Zemiology?

By the point reached at the end of the previous section, the journey from crime to social harm has become a lengthy and significant one—albeit each of the specific steps 'beyond' criminology are, I suspect, quite familiar to readers. And, I would go further: each seems to me to be a perfectly defensible, plausible and indeed productive way in which we can move from 'crime' to 'social harm'. But for some, not least some of the contributors to *Beyond Criminology*, the journey should not and does not stop here.

By way of shorthand, each of the above shifts revolves around the issues of the existence or level of criminalisation or non-criminalisation. But *Beyond Criminology* encompassed a series of harms associated with phenomena far from criminological and criminal justice agendas—including poverty, childhood, inequality, heterosexism, migration, gender, unemployment—and it is here I think that a new discipline of zemiology, the study of social harms *per se*, was being broached, however unconsciously in some specific cases. This is not to deny that many of these phenomena are relevant in understanding the definition and distribution of 'crime' and 'criminalisation', but it *is* to emphasise that many of the considerations around these in *Beyond Criminology* were not much or even at all about such issues. Criminology had, effectively, been abandoned.

By way of illustration of the distinction being drawn here, a useful reference point is some data which Paddy Hillyard and I recently presented on a range of social harms (Hillyard and Tombs 2017). Alongside data on work-related deaths and food poisoning, we addressed what are rather prosaically labelled 'Excess Winter Deaths'. Each year, the UK's Office for National Statistics calculates the number of such deaths—namely, the additional number of deaths, in England and Wales, occurring from December to March compared with the average number of deaths occurring in the preceding and following four month periods. The most recently (November 2015) published figure estimates 43,900 such deaths occurred in 2014/15, the highest number since 1999/2000. Most of these (36,000) occurred among those 75 and over, with 7700 deaths of people aged under 75 (Office for National Statistics 2015).

Now, both work-related deaths and deaths associated with food poisoning have proximate relationships to 'crime', criminalisation and criminal justice processes, in that they are regulated by criminal law, are subject to enforcement (albeit by regulatory bodies rather than, for the most part, police forces) and in any one year attract a number of criminal prosecutions; moreover, the offences so prosecuted may revolve around intent or negligence or both, thus meeting standards of guilt in criminal law. Finally, it is worth noting that there are existent, if small, literatures around each in criminology.

Excess winter deaths are quite distinct in all of these respects. These are not people killed by the cold *per se*—countries with very low winter temperatures in Scandinavia and Northern Europe have very low rates of such deaths. Instead, most deaths result from lack of access to affordable heating, or suitably insulated, warm and dry accommodation, or most likely both (Office for National Statistics 2015). In other words, their routine occurrence is a product of generations of decisions, actions and omissions regarding housing, energy, welfare and social services, healthcare and probably pensions policy, at the very least. Moreover, while each occurrence—a death—is an event, this event can only be understood in the context of the combination of a series of long-term *processes*. Little or none of these characteristics, and their inter-relationships, of what clearly amounts to a significant form of social harm, is *or can be* at all explicable via reference to criminal law—albeit some are clearly affected by regulatory law, not least in the creation then maintenance through and by states of complex markets in energy supply as well as in the regulation of some aspects of private provision of housing, some welfare services and pension provision.

Thus, harms such as excess winter deaths are nowhere near the terrain of crime, nor mainstream criminology, nor encountered on the journey from 'crime' to 'social harm' as sketched out above. They are neither explicable nor preventable through criminal law, which seeks to view or reduce harm to intention, to the inter-personal, to one or a series of discrete events, to victim-offender relationships which have some proximity in time and space (Hillyard and Tombs 2017). A focus on excess winter deaths takes us far beyond crime, criminalisation and criminal justice, far from criminal law and the orbit of mainstream criminology.

It is at this point that it seems to me the epistemological and ontological break with criminology is made—albeit a break that I have only illustrated rather than attempted to theorise. And it is here at which the terrain is crossed into a new discipline. Of course, whether this discipline can be something called 'zemiology' is a moot point. I shall return to that question shortly. But, for now, the above is enough to outline a claim, at least, that zemiology is or should be seen as something distinct from a 'social harm' perspective or approach—a claim never clearly asserted let alone established in *Beyond Criminology* nor, indeed, in some of the work which has followed and which has explicitly sought to develop the epistemological and ontological terrain very sketchily suggested in parts of that text.

The lacunae, tensions and indeed disagreements across the contributions to *Beyond Criminology* may do much to explain why an increasing number of criminological texts make explicit reference to the term 'zemiology' as simply synonymous with 'social harm'—the latter being a concept which has long been part of criminology, albeit one which has recently received greater attention (Muncie 2013). Hence, the term zemiology has been happily embraced by some in the discipline as 'The branch of criminology studying the social harm caused by actions' (Gooch and Williams 2007, 391) rather than the impetus for a separate discipline. The first two editions of *The Sage Dictionary of Criminology* (2001, 2006) each had entries for 'Social Harm', albeit neither contained any reference to the work associated with editors nor contributors to *Beyond Criminology*, a fact which changed in the third edition with an expanded definition of 'Social Harm' which appeared therein. That most recent edition also contained an entry for 'Zemiology', which reads thus: 'See: Social harm' (McLaughlin and Muncie 2013, 496). More generally, the embrace of 'social harm' has been identified in the context of 'critical' criminology. For example, the second edition of *Introduction to Criminological Theory* by Hopkins Burke contains the section 'Critical Criminology and the Challenge of Zemiology', which makes no references to the origins of or debates around the term, but simply begins, 'A significant and fast expanding contemporary variant of critical criminology has been Zemiology or the study of social harm' (Hopkins Burke 2005, 179; see also Hil and Robertson 2003). Tim Newburn's *Criminology* includes 'Zemiology' as a short sub-section within a chapter constituting a whistle-stop tour of 'Radical and critical criminology' (Newburn 2007, 258).

Such claims merely reproduce, perhaps exacerbate, the contradictions, confusions and disagreements that were present in *Beyond Criminology*. It is absolutely clear that in that collection, there was neither agreement on abandoning criminology for zemiology, nor what this might entail or might look like, nor on the relationship between criminology, zemiology and a focus on 'social harm'. For example Paddy Hillyard and myself proposed at least the consideration of abandoning the discipline in favour of zemiology—even though we took different positions on this consideration. For Paddy, I am fairly clear that he viewed the study of social harms as an independent set of phenomena, whatever their relationships to crime, criminal justice or criminology—that is, as a new, if not 'replacement', discourse, to be conducted within the rubric of zemiology. My own position, as reflected in my work if not the statements of social harm and zemiology, has been much more ambivalent—a point discussed earlier and to which I shall return briefly, below.

If at best we set out some of the possible epistemological, theoretical and substantive commitments of zemiology as an alternative discipline, we did not attempt to set out in detail what that discipline might look like—a point which has been rehearsed in critical commentaries of *Beyond Criminology*. Thus, for example, Loader and Sparks (2011) argue that we spend too long critiquing criminology and not enough time describing what will replace it. Hughes (2007, 198) concludes that we fail to offer 'a viable critical project for criminology, intellectually or politically'. Reiman, in particular, notes that taking 'the next step ... from a provocative kaleidoscope to a coherent disciplinary perspective', entails at least two tasks: first, being 'clear on the harm perspective's relationship to criminology' (Reiman 2006, 363); and, second, since 'so much of the harm discussed in *Beyond Criminology* is attributed to social groups or structures, the harm perspective will need to spell out a plausible doctrine of social or structural responsibility' (Reiman 2006, 364). These points are well made, and represent a significant challenge to those who would either develop a social harm perspective or an alternative discipline of zemiology.

From Rights to Needs?

Thus I want to suggest that there are a number of theoretical differences between critical criminology, social harm, and zemiology, which pertain to the question of whether zemiology should be considered as a separate discipline or simply a branch of critical criminology, perhaps with a social-harm-approach twist.

One of the central, indeed motivating, concerns for some of those involved in *Beyond Criminology* was the observation that criminology, and in particular critical criminology, has long struggled over the boundaries of the discipline in an attempt to shake off the limitations of the straightjacket of the legal definitions of crime and thus to expand the discipline to study a whole range of harms not captured by the criminal law. And within these efforts, a significant body of literature has emerged which encompasses a range of criminaliseable harms, from ethnic and religious intolerance to ecocide and genocide.

Conceptually, within the vast terrain of critical criminological work, conduct norms, social aberrance, social deviance, social injury *and* social harm are just a few of the intellectual attempts to mark out a more inclusive set of harmful behaviours. Kramer (2013) provides a comprehensive overview of these attempts and argues that 'international law in all of its forms can still provide a rhetorical touchstone for criminologists to frame judgments about what is and is not criminal. It can allow us to "expand the core" of the discipline to better take into account corporate and state crimes' (Kramer 2013, 33). This is a claim rather similar to that famously made by the Schwendingers (1970) some four decades ago. For some of the contributors to *Beyond Criminology*, the 'expanding … core' of the discipline was the very problem that produced their motivation for engaging with the project—not part of any solution to the deleterious effects of a discipline organised around a concept of 'crime'.

Somewhat differently, Yar (2012, 59), in a thoughtful analysis of the potential of zemiology, argues that the lack of specificity in our analysis 'leaves the concept of harm lacking the very same ontological reality that is postulated as grounds for rejecting the concept of crime'. In short, we fail to define what makes something 'a harm' or harmful and how harmful acts differ from non-harmful ones. He suggests that the concept of 'recognition' can deal with this deficit in our theorization and that it is possible to establish the basic needs that form human integrity and well-being. Harm occurs when there is no recognition of these basic needs. Harms, in this sense, reflect disrespect. While acknowledging that the criminal law can be conceived as 'a coercive instrument legitimated by the power of the capitalist state', Yar argues that it is possible to adopt a different view of the law using a recognition-based theoretical standpoint. From this position, law's attempt, however 'partial, flawed or misguided', to enshrine formal codes and prohibitions to protect people from harm assists in securing their basic rights.

Yar, then, concludes with a clear appeal to the law in defining harm. On this basis he considers zemiology as a promising orientation but one to be pursued *within* critical criminology. Similarly, much critical criminology, for all of its significance, originality and sophistication, ends up in attempts to redefine the legitimate area of criminology and is based in an implicit or explicit call for law, not least criminal law, to be more effectively developed or enforced, in ways that promote greater social justice through criminal justice, and in ways that uphold or extend various rights.[1]

---

[1] Including much of my own work; though, see Alvesalo and Tombs (2002).

In short, much critical criminological work, whether it appeals to social harm or not, proceeds, at least implicitly, on the basis of a rights-based framework. Indeed, protecting or furthering such rights is often central to the social justice orientation of such work. But for me this focus on rights is ultimately problematic (see Hillyard and Tombs 2017). Notwithstanding that some people may secure their basic rights through the criminal law and that many more will buy into the notion of the idea of justice, even define this, in terms of the recognition of such rights, either substantively or procedurally, the majority of those affected by social harms will have little or no recognition by the legal system, particularly those victims of harms which are not captured by the criminal law. In other words, for many of the social harms upon which we and others have focussed, law and rights, and the definitions of procedural and substantive justice which they imply, are likely to be of very little relevance at all. This is one of the key ways in which we can locate the relationships between critical criminology, social harm and zemiology. It is only the latter which potentially breaks from (actual or potential) legal definitions of harm, not least those linked to apparently progressive—but ultimately flawed (Fudge and Glasbeek 1992)—rights-based frameworks.

In a somewhat analogous way, Copson (2011, 2012) has analysed the fundamental differences which exist between the conceptualisations of harm within criminology, critical criminology and zemiology, reflecting different ideas and assumptions around issues of justice and liberty in the context of the fulfilment of human need. Criminology, she argues, deploys a liberal individualistic notion of harm as embraced by conventional jurisprudence. In contrast, zemiology situates harm in the context of human needs. Thus harm occurs when people are prevented by either the social structures or individual actions from meeting their needs (see Tifft and Sullivan 2001). Harm, in this sense, is linked to positive liberty in contrast to the negative liberties which law claims to protect and to which all forms of criminology are inevitably drawn. Critical criminology's notion of harm, she suggests, falls somewhere between the two positions.

While increasingly recognising socially structured harm, nevertheless, it continues to embrace individualistic notions of harms articulated in rights or conventional jurisprudence.

On the distinction between social harm and zemiology, Pemberton has sought to provide some clarity. 'The existing literature', he writes, 'confusingly makes reference to both social harm and zemiology, and at times these terms have been used interchangeably. For some, including myself, social harm represents the study of socially mediated harms, whereas zemiology, derived from the Greek *xemia* for harm, denotes the study of harm' (Pemberton 2015, 6). This is, he continues:

> more than an issue of semantics. Zemiology is preferable, insofar as a by-product of *Beyond Criminology* has been the co-option of the language of social harm into criminological discourse ... Thus, zemiology would serve to demarcate those critical scholars whose interest lies 'beyond criminology' from criminologists using the notion of social harm, to establish an alternative field of study. Social harm therefore becomes the organising concept for zemiology as a field of study. When these distinctions are drawn, the emergent characteristics of zemiology can be more clearly articulated. (Pemberton 2015, 6–7)

Thus he goes on to note five such 'emergent characteristics'. First, following Hillyard and Tombs (2004), he notes that zemiology seeks 'to provide an alternative "lens" that captures the vicissitudes of contemporary life'. Second, it requires a shift in emphasis from 'individual level harms' to those associated with states and corporations (7); third is a recognition that most widespread social harms 'are not caused by intentional acts, but rather, result from the omission to act or societal indifference to suffering' (8), and, fourth, that such harms are preventable, that is, products of social and economic organisation. This leads him, finally, to espouse for zemiology a reformist commitment to identifying 'less harmful forms of capitalism' (Pemberton 2015, 8).

This still begs the question, of course, of what is to be the basis for identifying a phenomenon as 'harmful' or a 'social harm', and thus falling within the legitimate ambit of zemiology? For Pemberton, the answer is to be found in a theory of human needs. Using Doyal and Gough's (1991) classic work, Pemberton (2007; Pantazis and Pemberton, 2009) argue that harm is perpetuated when specified needs are not fulfilled. It is not clear, however, how invoking a theory of 'needs' gets potential zemiologists out of the theoretical woods. While personally I am sympathetic to Doyal and Gough's conceptualisation of needs, it is hardly unproblematic. Indeed, one of the oft-raised objections to any attempt to identify a theory of human need is that once this shifts from the most abstract universal statements to the level of adding greater specificity to identifying such needs, then any such exercise almost inevitably descends into relativism. This was one of the central topics of the celebrated exchange between Kate Soper in response to Doyal and Gough's formulation (Soper 1993; Doyal 1993), it was also raised more recently by Lasslett (2010) in response to Pemberton's (and others') centring of a theory of social harm or zemiology around needs.

More recently, Pemberton (2015) has attempted to operationalise a needs approach to harm. While in so doing he provides insightful and persuasive analyses of the performance of a number of selected states and regimes in relation to a range of harms, the theoretical work of grounding the latter in the context of needs is rather over-looked. There is no doubt that he advances our empirical understanding of the distribution of social harm considerably, while his text demonstrates the potential of a paradigm within which social harm is central but which is neither linked to, nor reliant upon, law, jurisprudence or some other legal framework. But at the same time his work underscores the fact that a *zemiology* of social harm is very much in its infancy, a work in progress at best (Tombs 2015).

In this respect, the challenge indicated by Richard Garside, in one of the more careful and critical analyses of the ideas within *Beyond Criminology* to date, remains to be taken up:

> A critical challenge for social harm scholarship is to apply its insights on the social and relational nature of social harm – the fact that its mediations are concrete and material, not natural nor merely political or ideological – and its connection to human need, through the development of a clear and coherent understanding of the social production and reproduction of harm in the material processes of capital accumulation. (Garside 2013, 257)

For Pragmatism and for Politics

In a thoughtful, critical response to *Beyond Criminology*, John Muncie commented that, 'the abandonment of crime in favour of "harm" is ultimately a political project' (Muncie 2005, 201). In very similar fashion, Paddy Hillyard and myself had concluded one of the contributions to that book thus:

> whether or not a new disciplinary focus is to emerge, we must accept that raising issues of social harm does not entail making a simple, once-and-for-all choice between representing these as *either* crimes *or* harms; each may form part of an effective political strategy. What we would add is that it is crucial that whether/when we speak of crime or harm, we must be clear about which we are speaking on particular occasions, that is, description and analysis must not slide between the two … . (Hillyard and Tombs 2004, 29)

For my part, these comments are as valid (or otherwise) as they were over a decade ago. Two elaborations follow, which are a fitting way to conclude the considerations of this chapter.

First, there is no necessary 'antagonism' (Lasslett 2010) nor 'innate duality' between 'crime' and 'harm' (Boukli and Kotzé this volume), and we should avoid the false alternative of a commitment to one or the other (ibid.). It seems at least reasonable to assert that since law attempts to define a subset of harms as crimes, however contestable specific definitions of such may be (for example, Weait 2005), then 'crime' and 'social harm' may often exist on a logically connected ontological terrain as, indeed, some of the earlier sections of this chapter have claimed.

That said, it remains the case that what social harm *is*, what zemiology might be, and in what relationships each exists to critical criminology are issues that require a great deal of theoretical, conceptual and empirical labour, to which I expect this present volume to make a significant contribution. Moreover, as indicated in the quotation above, even on the part of those of us who might eschew such sustained labour, then greater conceptual clarity will be achieved if those of us who use the terms 'social harm' and 'zemiology' provide some context-specific clarity or clarification of such usage—recognising, at least, that these terms are hardly unproblematic.

Second, it matters politically whether we speak of crime or harm—which takes me back to how I initially came to the conversation about social harm. One of the common themes of my academic career has been to work with victims of corporate crime, most notably those who have been bereaved by workplace death, and, more recently, by deaths at the hand of the state. Notwithstanding variations in their experiences, typically such victims experience what has been commonly referred to as 'double-victimisation'—first, the avoidable death of a loved one at the hands of an employing organisation or state institution and, second, the consistent inabilities of the CJS to treat, which generally means adequately investigate let alone consider any formal response to, such a death as if it were potentially analogous to a 'real' killing, and in so doing deny the dead and the bereaved their status as actual or potential victims (Snell and Tombs 2011). In their campaigns, organisations such as *Families Against Corporate Killers* (FACK)[2] seek not vengeance, but rather, and of course to generalise, they want an investigation of the circumstances of their loved ones' deaths, recognition—if appropriate—that their loved one has died as a result of legal violation, and then for an appropriate formal sanction to be imposed following due process—in short, and following other organisations which campaign against corporate and state injustice, they seek 'truth, justice and accountability',[3] where the law, criminal justice and judicial systems legitimate themselves on promises for such.

In a society which uses the discursive and material power of 'crime' and the CJS to denote the seriousness of certain categories of harms over others, these seem understandable and modest aims. Far from challenging, I have actively supported such families, such as I can, and will continue to do so—a very non-social harm, non-zemiological position. Yet at the same time, however, it seems absolutely obvious to me that a criminal justice response to work-related deaths, injuries or illness, or other forms of corporate and state crimes will not and cannot significantly mitigate their relentless toll in terms of lives lost and

---

[2] http://www.hazardscampaign.org.uk/fack/about/index.htm.
[3] The 'strapline' of INQUEST; see http://www.inquest.org.uk/.

lives devastated. Indeed, this much is painfully obvious to the families such as those who constitute FACK. For while the criminal law may (albeit very rarely) provide them with a formal recognition of a criminally-defined harm against their loved one, this does not begin to touch the harm to which they are subject as a result of the death. This harm might include a loss of income; mental health problems which manifest themselves in a variety of ways; the loss of friends, who do not know how to speak about or deal with the death; problems of alcohol or drug dependency, in turn creating problems for gaining or seeking employment, or parenting, or of maintaining relationships—many of which, in turn, generate significant costs for society. These, then, are matters of social and public policy well beyond the criminal law or CJS. They are harms associated with a crime. This implies, again, that harm and crime are not located in an antagonistic dualism.

Meanwhile, we need to be clear that ultimately addressing corporate and state crime requires far more radical, even utopian (Tombs 2015; Tombs and Whyte 2015) solutions, far beyond the realms of the CJS. But if political and academic work can and must be seen as mutually supportive, rather than alternative, paths which critical social scientists might pursue, then so too must be our use and deployment of 'crime' and 'harm'. Only on the basis of a politics of context-specific pragmatism can we challenge power and domination as it confronts us, whilst keeping in sight the vision of less harmful ways of organising social life—a post-imperial, post-patriarchal, post-capitalist society of equality and social justice.

References

Alvesalo, Anne, and Steve Tombs. 2002. Working for Criminalisation of Economic Offending: Contradictions for Critical Criminology? *Critical Criminology: An International Journal* 11: 21–40.
Bittle, Steven, and Laureen Snider. 2013. Examining the Ruggie Report: Can Voluntary Guidelines Tame Global Capitalism? *Critical Criminology* 21: 177–192.

Copson, Lynne. 2011. *Archaeologies of Harm: Criminology, Critical Criminology, Zemiology*. Unpublished PhD thesis, Faculty of Social Sciences and Law, School of Sociology, University of Bristol.

———. 2012. Zemiology: At the Edge of Criminology or Beyond Its Borders? Paper presented at the British Society of Criminology Annual Conference, University of Portsmouth.

Corteen, Karen, Sharon Morley, Paul Taylor, and Joanne Turner (eds.). 2016. *A Companion to Crime, Harm and Victimisation*. Bristol: Policy Press.

Davies, Pamela, Peter Francis, and Tanya Wyatt (eds.). 2014. *Invisible Crimes and Social Harms*. Basingstoke: Palgrave Macmillan.

Doyal, Len. 1993. Thinking About Human Need. *New Left Review* I/201 (September–October): 113–128.

Doyal, Len, and Ian Gough. 1991. *A Theory of Human Need*. Basingstoke: Palgrave Macmillan.

Ellefsen, Rune, Ragnhild Sollund, and Guri Larsen (eds.). 2012. *Eco-global Crimes: Contemporary Problems and Future Challenges*. London: Routledge.

Freudenberg, Nicholas. 2014. *Lethal but Legal: Corporations, Consumption, and Protecting Public Health*. Oxford: Oxford University Press.

Fudge, Judy, and Harry Glasbeek. 1992. The Politics of Rights: A Politics with Little Class. *Social & Legal Studies* 1: 45–70.

Garside, Richard. 2013. Addressing Social Harm: Better Regulation Versus Social Transformation. *Revista Crítica Penal y Poder* 5: 247–265.

Gooch, Graham, and Michael Williams. 2007. *A Dictionary of Law Enforcement*. Oxford: Oxford University Press.

Hil, Richard, and Rob Robertson. 2003. What Sort of Future for Critical Criminology. *Crime, Law and Social Change* 39: 91–115.

Hills, Stuart L. (ed.). 1987. *Corporate Violence: Injury and Death for Profit*. New Jersey: Rowman & Littlefield.

Hillyard, Paddy, and Steve Tombs. 2004. Beyond Criminology? In *Beyond Criminology: Taking Harm Seriously*, ed. Paddy Hillyard, Christina Pantazis, Steve Tombs, and Dave Gordon, 10–29. London: Pluto Press.

———. 2017. Social Harm and Zemiology. In *The Oxford Handbook of Criminology*, 6th ed., ed. Alison Liebling, Shadd Maruna, and Lesley McAra, 284–305. Oxford: Oxford University Press.

Hillyard, Paddy, Christina Pantazis, Steve Tombs, and Dave Gordon (eds.). 2004. *Beyond Criminology: Taking Harm Seriously*. London: Pluto Press.

Hopkins Burke, Roger. 2005. *An Introduction to Criminological Theory*. Cullompton: Willan Publishing.

Hughes, Gordon. 2007. *The Politics of Crime and Community*. London: Palgrave Macmillan.
Jenness, Valerie, and Ryken Grattet. 2004. *Making Hate a Crime: From Social Movement to Law Enforcement*. New York: Russell Sage Foundation.
Kramer, Ronald C. 2013. Expanding the Core: Blameworthy Harms, International Law and State-Corporate Crimes. Paper presented at the Presidential Panel, "Reconsidering the Legal Definition of Crime," at the Annual Meeting of the American Society of Criminology, Atlanta, November 21.
Lasslett, Kristian. 2010. Crime or Social Harm? A Dialectical Perspective. *Crime, Law and Social Change* 54: 1–19.
Loader, Ian, and Richard Sparks. 2011. *Public Criminology?* London: Routledge.
McLaughlin, Eugene, and John Muncie (eds.). 2001. *The SAGE Dictionary of Criminology*. London: Sage.
———. 2006. *The SAGE Dictionary of Criminology*, 2nd ed. London: Sage.
———. 2013. *The SAGE Dictionary of Criminology*, 3rd ed. London: Sage.
Monaghan, Mark, and Simon Prideaux. 2016. *State Crime and Immorality: The Corrupting Influence of the Powerful*. Bristol: Policy Press.
Muncie, John. 2005. Book Review of *Beyond Criminology: Taking Harm Seriously. Crime, Law and Social Change* 43: 199–201.
———. 2013. Social Harm. In *The Sage Dictionary of Criminology*, 3rd ed., ed. Eugene McLaughlin and John Muncie, 430–432. London: Sage.
Newburn, Tim. 2007. *Criminology*. Cullompton: Willan Publishing.
Office for National Statistics. 2015. *Excess Winter Mortality in England and Wales 2014/15 (Provisional) and 2013/14 (Final)*. London: Office for National Statistics.
Pantazis, Christina, and Simon Pemberton. 2009. Nation States and the Production of Social Harm: Resisting the Hegemony of 'TINA'. In *State, Crime, Power*, ed. Roy Coleman, Joe Sim, Steve Tombs, and David Whyte, 214–233. London: Sage.
Passas, Nikos, and Neva Goodwin (eds.). 2004. *It's Legal but It Ain't Right: Harmful Social Consequences of Legal Industries*. Michigan: University of Michigan Press.
Pearce, Frank, and Steve Tombs. 1998. *Toxic Capitalism: Corporate Crime and the Chemical Industry*. Aldershot: Ashgate.
———. 2012. *Bhopal: Flowers at the Altar of Profit and Power*. North Somercotes: CrimeTalk Books.

Pemberton, Simon. 2007. Social Harm Future(s): Exploring the Potential of the Social Harm Approach. *Crime, Law and Social Change* 48: 27–41.

———. 2015. *Harmful Societies*. Bristol: Policy Press.

Quality Assurance Agency. 2014. Subject Benchmark Statement, Criminology. http://www.qaa.ac.uk/en/Publications/Documents/SBS-criminology-14.pdf. Accessed 30 Aug 2017.

Reiman, Jeffrey. 2006. Book Review of Beyond Criminology: Taking Harm Seriously. *British Journal of Criminology* 46: 362–364.

Ruggiero, Vincenzo. 2015. Social Harm and the Vagaries of Financial Regulation in the UK. *International Journal for Crime, Justice and Social Democracy* 4: 91–105.

Schwendinger, Herman, and Julia Schwendinger. 1970. Defenders of Order or Guardians of Human Rights? *Issues in Criminology* 5: 123–157.

Snell, Katy, and Steve Tombs. 2011. 'How Do You Get Your Voice Heard When No-One Will Let You?' Victimisation at Work. *Criminology & Criminal Justice* 11: 207–223.

Soper, Kate. 1993. A Theory of Human Need. *New Left Review* 1 (197): 113–128.

Tifft, Larry L., and Dennis R. Sullivan. 2001. A Needs-Based, Social Harms Definition of Crime. In *What is Crime? Controversies over the Nature of Crime and What to Do About It*, ed. Stuart Henry and Mark M. Lanier, 179–203. Lanham: Rowman and Littlefield.

Tombs, Steve. 1999. Health and Safety Crimes: (In)visibility and the Problems of 'Knowing'. In *Invisible Crimes: Their Victims and Their Regulation*, ed. Pamela Davies, Peter Francis, and Victor Jupp, 77–104. London: Macmillan.

———. 2004. Workplace Injury and Death: Social Harm and the Illusions of Law. In *Beyond Criminology: Taking Harm Seriously*, ed. Paddy Hillyard, Christina Pantazis, Steve Tombs, and Dave Gordon, 156–177. London: Pluto.

———. 2007. 'Violence', Safety Crimes and Criminology. *British Journal of Criminology* 47: 531–550.

———. 2015. Harmful Societies. *Criminal Justice Matters* 101: 36–37.

Tombs, Steve, and Paddy Hillyard. 2004. Towards a Political Economy of Harm: States, Corporations and the Production of Inequality. In *Beyond Criminology: Taking Harm Seriously*, ed. Paddy Hillyard, Christina Pantazis, Steve Tombs, and Dave Gordon, 30–54. London: Pluto Press.

Tombs, Steve, and David Whyte. 2009. Crime, Harm and Corporate Power. In *Crime: Local and Global*, ed. John Muncie, Deborah Talbot, and Reece Walters, 137–172. Cullompton: Willan Publishing.
———. 2015. *The Corporate Criminal: Why Corporations Must Be Abolished*. London: Routledge.
Weait, Matthew. 2005. Harm, Consent and the Limits of Privacy. *Feminist Legal Studies* 13: 97–122.
Yar, Majid. 2012. Critical Criminology, Critical Theory and Social Harm. In *New Directions in Criminological Theory*, ed. Steve Hall, and Simon Winlow, 52–65. London: Routledge.

Author Biography

Steve Tombs is Professor of Criminology at The Open University. He has long worked with the Hazards movement in the UK, and is a Trustee and Board member of Inquest.

Beyond 'Criminology vs. Zemiology': Reconciling Crime with Social Harm

Lynne Copson

Introduction

Recently, zemiology and the field of social harm studies have emerged as part of a project concerned to move 'beyond criminology' (Hillyard et al. 2004a). Central to this endeavour is a commitment to the idea of 'harm' as a fundamentally more useful concept than 'crime' for understanding and addressing a whole host of harmful social phenomena that we experience 'from the cradle to the grave' (Hillyard and Tombs 2004, 18). In its emergence, zemiology has also constituted a site of tension and ambiguity for criminology, raising questions about the very project of criminology and its relationship to power. In particular, in terms of its initial reception, questions have arisen as to whether zemiology is best understood as an extension or supplement to existing criminological theory, thereby constituting a new theoretical contribution *within* contemporary criminology or a radical *alternative* to it.

Taking the emergence of zemiology and its apparent tension with criminology as a starting point, this chapter explores the relationship

L. Copson (✉)
The Open University, Milton Keynes, UK
e-mail: lynne.copson@open.ac.uk

© The Author(s) 2018
A. Boukli and J. Kotzé (eds.), *Zemiology*, Critical Criminological Perspectives,
https://doi.org/10.1007/978-3-319-76312-5_3

between zemiology and criminology. Whilst early indications appeared to suggest an ambiguous relationship between zemiology and criminology, increasingly it appears that, at least for those invested in them, these perspectives risk either becoming polarised into competing projects or harmonised to the point that issues of social harm are simply, and apparently unproblematically, co-opted into the *raison d'être* of criminology. However, it is the central argument of this chapter that either approach: polarisation or harmonisation (at least in their current form), risks impoverishing both the criminological and zemiological projects, as well as their capacity to effect meaningful social change.

Specifically, I argue that a central theme within early sociological and, more explicitly, critical and radical criminologies has been to raise awareness of the problematic use of the criminal justice system as a means of recognising and responding to what are, properly speaking, *social* problems. As such, both zemiology and criminology are animated by a concern to appropriately apportion responsibility for, and address the causes of, harm. Likewise, zemiology does not necessarily commit its proponents to the abolition of crime or the criminal justice system per se, but rather suggests its reservation for responding to genuinely culpable acts of individual harm, which can only be identified once broader structural harms have been recognised and addressed. As such, the aim of this chapter is to suggest that what is at stake in the tension between zemiology and criminology is not a question of ultimate *ends* (e.g. addressing or at least reducing harm) but about the more effective *means*, and the appropriate starting point for realising these ends. However, so long as the projects of criminology and zemiology are seen as being in tension, the contribution of each is in danger of being undermined, with a risk of academic infighting and navel-gazing between different 'disciplines' and fields of study overshadowing the development of constructive and meaningful policy responses to social problems.

Criminology, Zemiology and Social Harm

Since its emergence as a distinct field of study at the start of the twenty-first century, zemiology has borne a somewhat ambiguous and at times problematic relationship to criminology. Variously described as 'a **new** field of study' (Kauzlarich and Matthews 2006, 17 [emphasis added]), a 'significant and fast expanding contemporary **variant of critical criminology**' (Burke 2005, 179 [emphasis added]) and 'a new perspective from which to approach the study of crime and criminal justice' (Whyte 2005, 488), zemiology arguably occupies a contested position in terms of its relationship to criminology (see Reiman 2006). This is reflected in questions as to whether zemiology presents a development *within* critical criminology or an *alternative* to it. For example, from Whyte's review of *Beyond Criminology*, it is not altogether clear the extent to which zemiology is identified as an alternative to, rather than a continuation of, criminology. The characterisation of the text as 'truly groundbreaking' (Whyte 2005, 488) suggests it is in some ways importantly divergent from all that has preceded it, whilst the designation of zemiology as proposing 'a new perspective from which to approach the study of crime and criminal justice' (Whyte 2005, 488) reasserts its primary locus as residing in the subject matter typically identified as the territory of criminology. By contrast, other interpretations (such as that of Burke 2005) explicitly characterise zemiology as a type of criminology, suggesting, perhaps, it is akin to other variants within criminology such as abolitionism or feminist criminology.

At the same time, it also seems that there is growing recognition that zemiology might not be so simply or unproblematically subsumed within criminology. The significance of zemiology and its critique of contemporary approaches to tackling problems of crime and justice, reflected in the growing visibility of zemiology and/or social harm references in criminology subject benchmarks and curricula (Hillyard and Tombs 2017, 293–294) suggests awareness that the identification of zemiology with criminology cannot necessarily be assumed. However, this has only resulted in further confusion over, and problematisation of their relationship (see Hillyard and Tombs 2017). This includes, more recently, not only a questioning of the relationship between zemiology and criminology but also, in attempting to further clarify (or perhaps establish) a distinction between the two, raising questions as to whether zemiology is also best understood as distinct from 'social harm' more generally (Hillyard and Tombs 2017, 298–301; see also Pemberton 2008, 84). This subsequent distinction (between zemiology and 'social harm') appears to stem from a recognition of the legacy of the concept of social harm *within* criminology (see, e.g., Hulsman 1986; Muncie 2000; Tifft and Sullivan 2001), and subsequent concern to distinguish the zemiological project from the critical criminological one by some of the former's most prominent architects (e.g., Hillyard and Tombs 2017).

Criminology vs. Zemiology

Whilst space precludes a more detailed analysis, a reciprocal tension between zemiology and criminology can thus be identified. Without wishing to deny the variety of perspectives and positions occupied by those engaged in the criminological and zemiological enterprises, respectively, nor to essentialise these perspectives, to generalise, from a zemiological standpoint, criminology is seen as problematic insofar as it:

i. constructs harm in particular problematic ways
ii. reifies the criminal justice system
iii. reinforces existing (liberal individualist) models of causation and responsibility (see, e.g., Hillyard and Tombs 2004, 2017; Copson 2016).

Alternatively, from a criminological standpoint, zemiology is seen as problematic insofar as it:

i. colonises existing approaches or themes *within* critical criminology and re-presents them as 'novel' and peculiar to zemiology
ii. denies the role of the criminal justice system (and, by extension, criminology) in effecting meaningful social change
iii. fails to articulate a clear alternative basis for its own theorising of and response to, social problems (see, e.g., Zedner 2011).

The result of this apparent tension between zemiology and more established modes of criminological thought has been an increasing polarisation of criminology and zemiology into seemingly opposing hostile camps. Consequently, on the one hand, key proponents of the zemiological or social harm perspective have explicitly sought to distance their work from that of 'criminology'. Simon Pemberton, for example, identifies his project as helping to develop social harm as an 'oppositional' discourse to that of crime, maintaining that:

> if the social harm debate remained within the confines of criminology, it would be stuck within a conceptual cul-de-sac, whereby the individualising tendencies of the criminal law would constrain the possibility of producing systematic and holistic analyses of harm. (Pemberton 2015, 6)

On the other hand, equal antipathy has been shown by critical criminologists who have argued that zemiologists' claims to offer harm as an *alternative* to crime essentially amounts to a repackaging of pre-existing criminological theorising under a new name, thereby denying the way in which harm has provided a key site of investigation and critique within criminology. In particular, they challenge the extent to which zemiology presents a radical break with the established critical tradition within criminology (see Muncie 2005; Hughes 2006). Indeed, the notion of social harm has been used in direct conjunction with that of crime, with crime often presented as one form of social harm within a wider range of socially injurious behaviours (see, e.g., Room 2000; Nutt et al. 2007; Cain and Howe 2008). This usage arguably reflects a long-established critical criminological project of expanding the object of criminological study away from crime as legally defined (whilst avoiding the problems of designating such behaviours as criminal in the absence of a violation of criminal law). Primarily, this aims to decouple the study of crime and criminal justice from the operations of state power and control. This is reflected in a litany of criminological studies seeking to develop the concept of crime and thus provide a means of addressing harmful behaviours not currently included in or prosecuted by the criminal justice apparatus (albeit, at times, implicitly through the presumption of such areas as proper for criminological interrogation in the first place). This includes attempts to recognise as criminal (or rather *better recognise* as criminal): harmful actions of states and corporations, human rights violations, environmental and ecological harms, poverty and homelessness (see, e.g., Schwendinger and Schwendinger (1975); Barak and Bohm (1989); Cohen (1993); Green and Ward (2004);

Walters (2006); Whyte (2007); Felices-Luna (2010)). Essential to such endeavours is a resistance on the part of criminologists to becoming simply a 'scientific "alibi"' (Garland 1992, 404) for the existing social order, maintained and legitimated through the criminal justice apparatus. As a result, questions arise as to whether the emphasis on social harm advanced by proponents of the zemiological perspective necessarily requires 'the abandonment of criminology' (Muncie 2005, 200), or whether zemiology should instead operate alongside, thereby supplementing existing approaches towards harm and justice (see Muncie 2005; Reiman 2006).

If zemiology's claims to offer harm as an *alternative* to crime is considered, essentially, at best, a repackaging of pre-existing criminological theorising under a new name, at worst, it stands accused of denying the centrality of the concept of harm to the notion of crime. It also risks reinforcing the compartmentalisation of knowledge production and the suppression of normative theorising in twenty-first century academic thought (see Zedner 2011, 277–278; Copson 2013, 2014).

For example, Lucia Zedner has questioned the social harm perspective's 'central claim [...] that it makes no sense to distinguish between criminal and other harms' (2011, 273), arguing that:

> [t]his assertion fails to recognize that the construction of crime is necessarily a normative exercise and one in which criminology, alongside criminal law, has an important role to play in determining which principles should underpin its definition, policing and punishment. (Zedner 2011, 274)

Moreover, Zedner contends, '[i]n a legal system grounded on individual autonomy there are good reasons to identify criminal wrongdoing and to punish those who perpetrate it. Failure to do so constitutes a denial of individual autonomy' (2011, 274). In addition, central to Zedner's account is a view of the criminal law and its application as a fundamentally normative endeavour concerned not only to hold individuals accountable but also, and crucially, to limit the power of the state to interfere with individuals' conduct and to protect them from its excesses in a way that does not apply in other areas of policy or law. As such, she concludes, before criminologists capitulate to the call to abandon crime (and with it criminology) they might think more critically about the claims made for alternative approaches and consider the positive restraints and protections entailed in criminal law and procedure. (Zedner 2011, 276)

Reconciling Crime with Harm

Just as there has been an apparent growing antipathy between some scholars of crime and justice, on the one hand, and advocates of social harm, on the other, (most notably social harm theorists who explicitly reject any affiliation of their project with that of criminology (see Pemberton 2015; Hillyard and Tombs 2017)), there also appear increasing numbers of other critical scholars who talk about 'crimes and harms' collectively, that is, under the same umbrella. This is reflected in the growing incorporation of issues of social harm into criminology curricula noted above, as well as in the inclusion of issues of social harm/zemiology in mainstream criminology conferences noted by Hillyard and Tombs (2017, 295). Resisting any tendency towards polarisation between zemiology and criminology, these scholars seek to add social harm/zemiology to the criminological *raison d'être*—to which some of the arguments included in this edition themselves bear witness.

Whilst recognising the apparent tensions between zemiology and criminology, instead of polarisation here one finds a project of harmonisation with attempts made to reconcile zemiology and criminology. Of particular note are Yar's (2012a, b) recent attempts to resolve the tensions between zemiology and criminology through the use of critical theory and the concept of recognition. Attributing much of the ambiguity in the relationship between zemiology and criminology to an 'ontological deficit' (Yar 2012a, 59) in that which 'distinguishes the harmful from the non-harmful' (2012a, 59), for Yar (2012a, 59), the problem stems from the fact that a 'lack of specificity leaves the concept of harm lacking the very same ontological reality that is postulated as grounds for rejecting the concept of crime'. Thus, whilst 'harm' is lauded by advocates of the social harm perspective for its independence from formal legal apparatus for establishing its *raison d'être*, without more rigorous definition '[t]he appeal to social harm is sustained by its intuitive moral-political appeal and "commonsense" purchase, but no more' (2012a, 59).

As a remedy, Yar offers 'recognition' as both the solution to this 'ontological deficit' of the social harm perspective, and also the means by which 'to dissolve the juxtaposition of "harm" and "crime" into competing conceptual alternatives' (Yar 2012b, 116). Drawing on critical theory, and particularly on the work of Axel Honneth, the concept of 'recognition' is related to the capacity for self-realisation based on a view of human beings as living in, and formed by, an intersubjective and mutually dependent social world. This is opposed to the liberal view of humanity as formed of pre-existent individuals who enter the world with a fully formed sense of self. Based on the idea that '[t]he individual comes to know himself, to recognise himself as a being with particular attributes or properties, through the acknowledgement conferred by an "other"' (Yar 2012a, 57), recognition is identified as a central component in 'the forging of a coherent sense of selfhood (self-esteem)'. Three key modes of recognition are identified: respect, esteem and love, which serve as 'critical yardsticks [...] to identify existing social, political, economic and cultural arrangements that *deny* recognition to human beings' (Yar 2012a, 58). Against this backdrop, Yar suggests a conceptualisation of social harm as 'nothing other than *the inter-subjective experience of being refused recognition with respect to any or all of these dimensions of need*' (2012a, 59).

It is important to note that here Yar is employing a particular Hegelian notion of 'recognition' as a site of self-realisation or identification in relation to others. This is distinct from the more general idea of the formal recognition of particular rights in law. However, in terms of resolving the tension between criminology and zemiology, Yar maintains that, via this account of harm as non-recognition (in the Hegelian sense), social harm and crime can be reconciled as mutually compatible since the role and function of criminal law *should* be to ensure protection of individual rights to recognition (notwithstanding that this may not always be realised in practice). In this way, Yar argues, 'making recourse to recognition as the grounds of a theory of harms can help resolve the conflict by bringing "crime" critically into the ambit of social inquiry' (2012b, 116). Moreover, reflecting a commitment to normative evaluation to which critical theory is tied avowedly, Yar (2012a, 62) claims that:

> [b]y using recognition as a benchmark or litmus test, we can [also] evaluate the common categories of crime as legitimate (or illegitimate) with reference to the basic needs of social subjects. This enables us to discriminate between formally constituted categories of crime according to their consistency with the principle of promoting recognition, and whether they offer protection from social harm.

Accordingly, we can then still make sense of the social harm perspective's commitment to decoupling definitions of crime and applications of the criminal justice system from sites of power without necessarily identifying social harm and crime as mutually incompatible: rather, the problems lie in the way in which the concept of 'crime' may have been illegitimately applied. Therefore, *this* should be the focus of evaluation.

However, even these attempts at reconciliation can be seen as problematic. Whilst Pemberton (2015, 19) credits Yar's work inasmuch as it 'correctly [...] focuses our attention on the relational nature of harm, allowing us to consider the injuries of social isolation, as well as misrecognition as harm', he also suggests that 'the needs Yar identifies are inevitably highly subjective in nature' (2015, 19). Therefore, in terms of its capacity to offer an ontological account of what, exactly, harm is, the approach is perhaps less satisfying than it initially purports, with questions of 'how emotional needs such as love and esteem are operationalised in empirical study' left 'for future social harm analyses to resolve' (Pemberton 2015, 19).

However, this criticism does not challenge Yar's position or his aim per se (namely to reconcile crime and social harm): rather, it simply highlights a limitation as to what it provides as an account of social harm. That said, whilst Pemberton perhaps (understandably) overlooks Yar's commitment to the language of crime in favour of his contribution to the development of social harm, in a field where, as Pemberton (2015) highlights, such contributions are often lacking, for Hillyard and Tombs (2017, 299), Yar's approach is more fundamentally problematic.

They point out that 'for many of the social harms upon which [they] and others have focussed, law and rights are likely to be of very little relevance at all' (Hillyard and Tombs 2017, 299).

Indeed, recognition of the basic rights we all have simply by virtue of our existence as humans has been important for affording individuals protections from violations and excesses of power. However, as has often been seen (most notably, with the formal enshrinement of human rights in international law), the language of rights remains saturated by the undercurrent of individualism, taking from the outset the individual as the primary unit to whom such rights are both attributable and attributed. Not only has it been suggested that discussions of rights violations tend to focus on particular individuals or groups, who can be identified as violating these rights, neglecting the way in which such violations might be located in broader systems of harm (see Sjoberg et al. 2001; Kennedy 2002, 124–125), but, more fundamentally, that doctrines of human rights 'undergird the individualism of the capitalist system' (Sjoberg et al. 2001, 18).

Moreover, in acknowledging rights violations (whether of formally enshrined human rights or informal rights, such as Yar's suggested right to recognition), there seems a general orientation towards recognising the active causation of harm, through, for example, direct acts, arguably at the expense of a recognition of harm as something that might equally arise, from more apparently passive, 'benign neglect'. This is reflected in the absence of the imposition of positive duties to assist those experiencing any form of difficulty, hardship or suffering, where such experiences do not arise from identifiable events or active interventions. Obligations reside primarily in duties not to exacerbate or impose such experiences, rather than to alleviate pre-existing ones. This is not to say that measures to create positive duties to alleviate suffering are not recognised (for example, the United Nations Convention on the Elimination of All Forms of Discrimination Against Women 1981), but to suggest their limited effectiveness as long as they reside in a system which, it has been argued, is ultimately situated in the tradition of liberal individualism. Indeed, this is a limitation reflected in Yar's (2012b, 115) own approach to reconciling crime with harm, insofar as he identifies as 'concrete examples' of harm:

actions such as inter-personal physical, sexual, and emotional violence within the family [which] acquire their specifically *harmful* character because they violate the necessary conditions for a person to establish basic self-confidence through the experience of love. Public (including state-sanctioned) **practices** of torture and abuse, theft, and appropriation [which] amount to a denial of those rights that meet the need for dignity and equality amongst others as citizens. **Practices** such as market discrimination or symbolic denigration on the basis of gender, ethnicity, or sexual orientation are harms in that they deny to subjects a recognition of the distinctive worth of their identities and ways of life. (Yar 2012b, 115 [emphasis added])

Whilst undoubtedly instructive in its capacity to recognise the way in which social structures can conspire to bring about individual harm (in terms of non-recognition), through recognition of, in particular, 'market discrimination or symbolic denigration' on the basis of particular social identities, Yar's account of harm nevertheless does not entail a positive duty to realise equality in the first place. More specifically, whilst it might entail a duty to ensure what has traditionally been termed 'formal equality' (see Barnard and Hepple 2000, 562–563) in terms of social structures, institutions and processes, it is neither clear that it goes so far as to impose a requirement for more 'substantive equality' (see Barnard and Hepple 2000, 564–567), nor that it recognises the absence of *this* as a basis for harm. However, this is an element that appears to be supported, at least, by some of the strongest proponents of the zemiological perspective.

For example, whilst it might be considered harmful to deny equal access to employment opportunities or respect for family life based on gender, ethnicity, sexual orientation and so on, on a recognition-based conception of social harm, it does not necessarily entail that inequalities in the basic structures of society are necessarily recognised as 'harms', nor, subsequently, that they will be suitable candidates for legal intervention. In a society based on social stratification, one may argue that we all are afforded the same formal recognition, irrespective of social position, but that our abilities to realise our own projects or sense of self is nevertheless unequal. One can argue that we can all enjoy the same formal recognition insofar as we all have the same *right* to education, legal representation, sexual autonomy, employment, etc., irrespective of gender or social class, for example. However, our ability to exercise those rights may be shaped by our social position: poorer people are less likely to have the opportunity to exercise those rights in the same way as wealthier people, but there is no person or agency barring their doing so, so it is not clear to what extent such people are suffering from 'non-recognition' and, hence, 'harm'.

That Yar's account is limited in this respect perhaps stems from his commitment to focus on the criminal law. Indeed, it is interesting and important to note in relation to Yar's (2012a, b) arguments about the normative role of the *criminal* law, that the recognition and enshrinement of such rights, is typically concentrated in other areas of law. This is because, as Zedner (2011, 282) notes, the criminal law is concerned to protect individuals from the violation of particular rights by the state. It is not concerned with the positive formulation or recognition of rights by the state or society more generally in the first place.

On this closer reading, therefore, Yar's approach appears perhaps more a continuation of existing legal discourses for identifying harm, echoing those of critical criminologists with which proponents of zemiology have taken issue (see, e.g., Hillyard and Tombs 2004). For example, the title of one of Yar's articles explicitly indicates that he is seeking to provide 'a general theory of crime **as** social harm' (Yar 2012b, 109 [emphasis added]). That Pemberton's criticism of Yar (2012a) does not extend further, therefore, is perhaps less a reflection of Yar's theory, than of Pemberton's own project: to study social harm in its own right, without recourse to criminology or the language to crime. Pemberton states:

> A key challenge for those wishing to establish zemiology as a distinct field of study is the absence of an established definition of social harm […]. With few exceptions this literature has developed on the margins of criminology, where social harm is used as a means to expand the notion of crime. […] this book seeks to develop a definition of social harm as an organising concept for zemiology, a distinct field of study to that of criminology. Disregarding the attempts to extend the notion of crime, this literature offers an important departure point from which the concept of social harm may be developed. (Pemberton 2015, 14)

It is important to situate Pemberton's response to Yar in this context. His disattending to Yar's attempts to synthesise social harm with crime arguably stems from his primary interest in the use and definition of social harm per se, without recourse to crime. Indeed, Pemberton (2015, 14) states that he explicitly excludes 'literature relating to "criminal harm"' in his analysis of the concept of social harm and its various uses, 'as it represents a distinct criminological enterprise to remedy the neglect of "harm" within discussions of "crime"'. Clearly, then, Pemberton either does not see Yar's enterprise as part of this project or is willing to overlook this aspect of his work because Pemberton is more concerned with understanding and developing the concept of social harm itself, in abstraction from the role it has played in criminology.

In either case, it certainly seems important to distinguish Yar's efforts from more 'traditional' approaches within criminology to expand the notion of crime to incorporate other harmful acts, typically through recourse to other (often legal) standards such as human rights abuses (Schwendinger and Schwendinger 1975) or civil law or administrative requirements (Sutherland [1949] 1983). Yar is clearly not straightforwardly seeking to expand the notion of crime via the provision of some alternative yardstick for defining crime in the same vein as these previous attempts. Rather, he is seeking to render compatible the projects of criminology and zemiology by identifying a shared ontological basis upon which they are founded. As Hillyard and Tombs (2017, 299) summarise:

> While acknowledging that the criminal law can be conceived as 'a coercive instrument legitimated by the power of the capitalist state', Yar argues that it is possible to adopt a different view of the law using a recognition theoretical standpoint. From this position, the law's attempt, however 'partial, flawed or misguided', to enshrine formal codes and prohibitions to protect people from harm assists in securing their basic rights.

However, insofar as it focuses on the right of recognition as the locus for identifying social harm and seeking to provide a synthesis of social harm with crime, Yar's approach is 'ultimately problematic, notwithstanding that some people may secure their basic rights through the criminal law and many more will buy into the notion of this possibility of justice' (Hillyard and Tombs 2017, 299). This is due to its continued unreflective commitment to the discursive framework of crime.

Beyond 'Criminology vs. Zemiology'?

Thus, notwithstanding the important contribution that attempts such as Yar's have made in terms of trying to reconcile zemiology with criminology, the challenge for resolving the ambiguity between zemiology and criminology remains. The temptation easily could be to dismiss this as an interesting but irrelevant footnote to academic infighting and jostling for intellectual esteem, and there is certainly a concern that such debates risk accusation of academic navel-gazing without a stronger account of why such issues matter. For many, the question of the terminology we use, or whether we identify as criminologists or zemiologists, surely will seem a luxury of academics in their ivory tower, detached from the lived reality of the social problems such intellectual theorising claims to seek to address. In a time when the relevance of 'expert knowledge' is increasingly being called into question (see, e.g., Loader and Sparks 2011), there is a very real danger that such academic infighting only serves to reinforce its irrelevance to public life.

This is not helped by the contemporary climate of knowledge production, of which the apparent ambiguity concerning the relationship between zemiology and criminology is arguably indicative, particularly, the opposing tendencies towards, on the one hand, hostile polarisation between these perspectives and, on the other hand, the (often unreflective) co-option of zemiology within criminology. As increasing pressures upon academics to secure funding and growing insecurities regarding position and ensuring contemporary relevance result in increasing specialisation within, and schisms between, different sites of disciplinary knowledge (see Copson 2014, 63), there is a danger that important normative debates are recast all too easily as academic squabbles and jostling for position.

However, the resolution of this ambiguity between criminology and zemiology is important because, whilst cast as minor disputes about abstract issues, at its heart, it taps into normative questions about how critical scholars imagine their role *vis-à-vis* effecting meaningful social interventions that address social problems. The reduction of these tensions to seemingly abstract and often dry debates regarding terminology, reflects the increasing suppression of normative theorising within social research (see Copson 2013, 2016) and increasing consignment of such research to playing a technical 'supporting' role in the administration of public policy (see Zedner 2011; Loader and Sparks 2011). Consequently, perhaps a more fruitful starting point for understanding the relationship between criminology and zemiology resides in delineating their respective normative projects in order to ascertain their compatibility and/or sites of divergence.

To this extent, the argument put forward here echoes that of Yar: that theoretical accounts require normative engagement, starting with a more rigorous exploration and definition of the concept of harm by proponents of the zemiological perspective. It is arguably the absence of this which threatens to raise the hackles of those criminological and legal scholars who (understandably) reject the apparent implication that they are simply operating to legitimate the criminal justice system and existing structures of power, in abstract from normative theorising.

However, the problem with foregoing attempts to reconcile zemiology with criminology (such as Yar's) is a presumption that there is or must be a universal definition of harm that is implicit within *both* the work of critical criminologists and proponents of the zemiological perspective (e.g. harm as non-recognition). What is not considered is the notion that harm itself is an 'essentially contested concept' (Gallie 1956), nor that whilst in many respects looking very similar, the projects of zemiology and critical criminology might be, in some important way, distinct. As an 'essentially contested concept', rather than reflecting an intrinsic quality of experience, 'harm' may be considered from a sociological perspective to be a discursively constructed and applied label, embedded in particular normative assumptions, and articulated and utilised in varying ways with varying implications. The danger of the harmonisation approach taken by Yar and others is an assumption that when talking about 'social harm', proponents of the zemiological perspective are necessarily invoking the same concept that has, indeed, long been drawn upon by critical criminologists, to the same ends.

So whilst there does need to be a more rigorous and robust exploration of the concept of harm, the starting point for this analysis should not be an assumption of the compatibility of 'criminal harm' with 'social harm' as Yar's recognition-based account seems to suggest.

Considered thus, we can see that whilst critical criminologists and zemiologists may envision similar projects in terms of seeking to address social inequalities and to recognise and reduce the harms of the criminal justice system, the divergence between the perspectives lies largely in a disagreement about the means of achieving this. For proponents of the zemiological perspective, the recourse to the language of harm can be considered a deliberate strategy—a form of *transpraxis* (Henry and Milovanovic 1991, 295; see Copson 2016, 90–91)—deliberately used to disrupt and challenge dominant ways of framing social problems without which we can only ever reify existing structures of thought and dominant (e.g. criminal justice) paradigms of conceptualising and responding to social problems. Understood thus, any attempts to subsume social harm within criminology or to incorporate the study of social harm under a broad umbrella of 'crimes and harms' unreflectively as some have sought, risks undermining this strategy. This is particularly so given a general failure (as noted in the foregoing analysis of Yar's (2012a, b) work, and as highlighted by the work of Pemberton (2015)), to unpack and define 'harm' in the first place and to distinguish 'social harm' from 'harm' more generally.

It is worth noting that the concept of 'harm' itself has long played a key normative role in criminal law (see Zedner 2011; Feinberg 1984), with the focus typically on identifying the causation of harm to others as a basis for restricting individual conduct, and for protecting individual rights *vis-à-vis* the state. This is in stark contrast to the account of social harm proposed by proponents of the zemiological perspective, who seek to emphasise the social determinants of (as opposed to individual culpability for) harms. To talk of 'crimes and harms' unreflectively, however, risks an implicit reification of the particular conceptualisation of harm implicit within criminal law, even if it does not necessarily intend this. In this context, therefore, the rejection of their alliance to criminology by some key proponents of zemiology can be understood as a deliberate political strategy, which aims to subvert the dominant criminological paradigm and challenge its particular (if implicit) conceptualisation of harm, rather than either a denial of existing critical work within criminology or a cynical claim to originality for the purposes of securing academic status and funding.

Equally, for proponents of a criminological perspective that advocate the studying of 'crimes and harms', the recourse to the language of 'crime' might equally be considered a more useful strategy for engaging key stakeholders and bringing about meaningful reform than the language of 'harm' alone. In the twenty-first century, 'crime' has political and public currency as a focus for policy intervention in a way that 'harm' does not. As a strategic end, it might be argued, a clear focus on, say reducing the harms wrought by the criminal justice system, or recognising the (often non-criminalised) harms of the powerful as analogously harmful to or more harmful than already criminalised harms, might be a more clearly defined and realistic site for enacting social change than addressing 'harm' in its more nebulous and less tangible forms. In terms of challenging the practices of the powerful, it is undeniable that the use of alternative measures of 'harm' has provided an important means for disrupting and challenging the organisation and justification of inequalities in society perpetuated by the notion of 'crime' and the criminal justice system.

In some respects, the tensions between criminology and zemiology and the various attempts to polarise or harmonise these perspectives can simply be seen as a contemporary rehashing of age-old debates that have occupied social theorists. These have concerned the relative weightings given by critical scholars to structure vs. agency in understanding and responding to human behaviour and the most effective routes to effecting meaningful social change. However, these are also debates that have long featured in criminology, long before zemiology emerged. As such, to reduce the tension between zemiology and criminology to simply these long-standing theoretical questions fails to recognise that there is, perhaps, something more at stake. The problem is, however, that contemporary infighting between academics as to the 'proper' relationship between criminology and zemiology risks overshadowing this.

For example, Zedner's criticisms of social harm noted above reflect a relatively common theme amongst those resistant to zemiology's claims to offer a preferable alternative to the discourse of crime. Anecdotal personal experience suggests a common fear arising in discussions around zemiology is that, through its emphasis on harm rather than crime, and, in particular, its commitment to exploring the social determinants of harm, zemiology ultimately serves to, at best, neglect crime. At worst, it excuses crime as a product of society, thereby absolving culpable individuals from their role in enacting harm on the victims of crime. However, this is arguably to misunderstand the project of zemiology. The zemiological focus on harm is not intended to deny individual culpability for individual acts that result in harm, but rather to beg questions as to where responsibility for those harms should fall. As its key proponents have highlighted:

> to utilise the social as a departure for explanation and theorising need not, and for us does not, entail a rejection of the need to account for human agency. But it is to accept a view of the world that sees human agency as highly delimited by structures, structures which must be known and of which we must provide accurate accounts. (Hillyard et al. 2004b, 271)

Therefore, the systematic analysis of harm advocated by proponents of the zemiological perspective is arguably intended to ensure that, when we are holding individuals responsible for harmful behaviours, we are genuinely holding them responsible for their deliberate, intentional acts, *all other things being equal*. It is not necessarily seeking to provide an alibi for criminality, but seeking to ensure that when we hold people responsible for their behaviours, we hold them responsible only for their behaviours, and not for the circumstances upon which such behaviours are predicated. At present, the problem, for proponents of the zemiological perspective, is that too often 'crime' and the criminal justice system are used to deal with what are, ultimately, social problems. It is, however, only by addressing those social problems and ensuring substantive equality across society that we can hope to legitimately make such a distinction. Arguably, the logical conclusion of the social harm perspective is not necessarily an abolition of crime nor of the criminal justice system (though it would entail its radical reform so as not to exist as a site of 'pain delivery' (Christie 1981) and harm in and of itself), but rather its significant reduction to ensure that we only punish individuals for their *culpable acts*. We can only ensure this, however, once the structures of harm and inequality that permeate our society and too often predicate the application of our criminal justice system, are eradicated.

In short, the contemporary context of knowledge production only adds to the confusion as to what the relationship between zemiology and criminology is, can, or should be and there is a need for clarification if we are to move beyond simple academic infighting and demonstrate relevance to the contemporary social world. The danger is that the current tendencies to either co-option of zemiology within criminology or polarisation between zemiology and criminology, respectively, risk impoverishing both zemiology and criminology, whilst such apparently abstract theoretical debates also risk occluding what is really at stake. For example, Hillyard and Tombs (2017, 295–298) note the tendency of criminologists to overlook the important contributions zemiology has made for the sake of demonstrating the superiority of criminology over zemiology.

Instead, were we to engage with other perspectives with more 'intellectual ambition, political humility' (Loader and Sparks 2011, 132), we might see that the distinction between zemiology and criminology fundamentally lies not in their critical assessment of either the criminal justice system nor their analysis of the best way of understanding the causes of social problems. With perhaps the exception of genuinely 'administrative' criminologies, criminologists and zemiologists alike have shown themselves to be concerned to critique the criminal justice system as a means of responding to social problems. They are also equally concerned to properly recognise and address the causes of those social problems, seeking to situate individual behaviour in broader social structures. The tension that arises seems largely to be a normative disagreement about the most effective means for recognising and addressing these problems, not that these are problems that need addressing. Rather than denying this debate through the collapsing of one perspective into the other, or polarising them into hostile camps of mutual antipathy, it is, perhaps, incumbent upon all critical scholars to act as 'democratic under-labourers' (Locke [1690] 1975 cited in Loader and Sparks 2011, 124), recognising our sites of divergence, and fostering dialogue *between* them if we are to achieve our shared goals and effect meaningful change.

Conclusion

In conclusion, as this discussion has sought to highlight, the danger is that existing debates around the relationship between criminology and zemiology, tend to take place in the abstract—missing the extent to which such theoretical perspectives can and should be understood as normative projects. In this respect, Zedner (2011) is right to highlight the suppression of normativity within criminology and the danger this poses for turning criminology into a technical discipline for administering criminal justice. However, this is a threat that is facing contemporary social research more generally (see Copson 2013). Within these normative projects, there are sites of agreement—most notably, the shared goal for both critical criminologists and proponents of zemiology that the role of their intellectual endeavours is to challenge dominant power structures and address contemporary inequalities. But there are also sites of divergence, and understanding the commitment to the language of 'harm' as part of a strategy or *transpraxis* for disrupting dominant ways of thinking is central to understanding the project of zemiology. As such, attempts to simply reconcile zemiology with criminology (such as Yar's 2012a, b) arguably miss the point of zemiology and threaten to reduce what are bold normative questions about how to effect change into conceptual problems in need of resolution.

Whilst such issues may be of interest to the social theorist, their wider significance is less obvious. If we want to move beyond accusations of academic navel-gazing and infighting, we need to connect our theoretical interests with the real world. And in this respect, one might well question whether it really matters what we call ourselves—zemiologists, criminologists, academics or activists: what is more important is what we seek to achieve and how best we might do this. By doing so, the hope is that we can move beyond what may amount to little more than academic identity politics towards what are, ultimately, political and normative debates about how better we might achieve the ends to which we are committed.

References

Barak, Gregg, and Robert M. Bohm. 1989. The Crimes of the Homeless or the Crime of Homelessness? On Dialectics of Criminalization, Decriminalization and Victimization. *Contemporary Crises* 13: 275–288.
Barnard, Catherine, and Bob Hepple. 2000. Substantive Equality. *Cambridge Law Journal* 59: 562–585.
Burke, Roger H. 2005. *An Introduction to Criminological Theory*, 2nd ed. Devon: Willan Publishing.
Cain, Maureen, and Adrian Howe (eds.). 2008. *Women, Crime and Social Harm*. Oxford: Hart Publishing.
Christie, Nils. 1981. *Limits to Pain*. Oxford: Martin Robertson.
Cohen, Stanley. 1993. Human Rights and Crimes of the State: The Culture of Denial. *Australian and New Zealand Journal of Criminology* 26: 97–115.
Copson, Lynne. 2013. Towards a Utopian Criminology. In *Crime, Critique, and Utopia*, ed. Margaret Malloch and Bill Munro, 114–135. Basingstoke: Palgrave Macmillan.
———. 2014. Penal Populism and the Problem of Mass Incarceration: The Promise of Utopian Thinking. *The Good Society* 23: 55–72.
———. 2016. Realistic Utopianism and Alternatives to Imprisonment: The Ideology of Crime and the Utopia of Harm. *Justice, Power and Resistance* 1: 73–96.
Feinberg, Joel. 1984. *The Moral Limits of the Criminal Law: Volume One Harm to Others*. Oxford: Oxford University Press.
Felices-Luna, Maritza. 2010. Rethinking Criminology(ies) Through the Inclusion of Political Violence and Conflict as Legitimate Objects of Inquiry. *Canadian Journal of Criminology and Criminal Justice* 52: 249–269.
Gallie, W.B. 1956. Essentially Contested Concepts. *Proceedings of the Aristotelian Society New Series* 56 (1955–1956): 167–198.
Garland, David. 1992. Criminological Knowledge and Its Relation to Power: Foucault's Genealogy and Criminology Today. *British Journal of Criminology* 32: 403–422.

Green, Penny, and Tony Ward. 2004. *State Crime: Governments, Violence and Corruption*. London: Pluto Press.

Henry, Stuart, and Dragan Milovanovic. 1991. Constitutive Criminology: The Maturation of Critical Theory. *Criminoloy* 29 (2): 293–316.

Hillyard, Paddy, Christina Pantazis, Steve Tombs, and Dave Gordon (eds.). 2004a. *Beyond Criminology: Taking Harm Seriously*. London: Pluto Press.

———. 2004b. Conclusion: 'Social Harm' and Its Limits. In *Beyond Criminology: Taking Harm Seriously*, ed. Paddy Hillyard, Christina Pantazis, Steve Tombs, and Dave Gordon, 267–275. London: Pluto Press.

Hillyard, Paddy, and Steve Tombs. 2004. Beyond Criminology? In *Beyond Criminology: Taking Harm Seriously*, ed. Paddy Hillyard, Christina Pantazis, Steve Tombs, and Dave Gordon, 10–29. London: Pluto Press.

———. 2017. Social Harm and Zemiology. In *The Oxford Handbook of Criminology*, 6th ed., ed. Alison Liebling, Shadd Maruna, and Lesley McAra, 284–305. Oxford: Oxford University Press.

Hughes, Gordon. 2006. Book Reviews: Paddy Hillyard, Christina Pantazis, Steve Tombs, and David Gordon (eds.), *Beyond Criminology: Taking Harm Seriously*. London: Pluto Press, 2004, 332 pp. *Social and Legal Studies* 15: 157–159.

Hulsman, Louk. 1986. Critical Criminology and the Concept of Crime. *Contemporary Crises* 10: 63–80.

Kauzlarich, David, and Rick Matthews. 2006. Lakoff's Framing Theory and Teaching About the Criminality of the U.S. War on Iraq. *The Critical Criminologist* 16: 4–25.

Kennedy, David. 2002. The International Human Rights Movement: Part of the Problem? *Harvard Human Rights Journal* 15: 101–125.

Loader, Ian, and Richard Sparks. 2011. *Public Criminology?* London: Routledge.

Muncie, John. 2000. Decriminalising Criminology. In *British Criminology Conference: Selected Proceedings*, vol. 3. Available at http://britsoccrim.org/volume3/010.pdf. Accessed 3 Mar 2017.

———. 2005. Book Review: Paddy Hillyard, Christina Pantazis, Steve Tombs, and Dave Gordon (eds.), *Beyond Criminology: Taking Harm Seriously*. London, Pluto; Nova Scotia, Fernwood, 2004. *Crime, Law and Social Change* 43: 199–201.

Nutt, David, Leslie King, William Saulsbury, and Colin Blakemore. 2007. Development of a Rational Scale to Assess the Harm of Drugs of Potential Misuse. *The Lancet* 369: 1047–1053.

Pemberton, Simon. 2008. Where Next? The Future of the Social Harm Perspective. In *Criminal Obsessions: Why Harm Matters More than Crime*, 2nd ed., ed. Danny Dorling, Dave Gordon, Paddy Hillyard, Christina Pantazis, Simon Pemberton, and Steve Tombs, 70–90. London: Centre for Crime and Justice Studies.

———. 2015. *Harmful Societies*. Bristol: Policy Press.

Reiman, Jeffrey. 2006. Reviews: Paddy Hillyard, Christina Pantazis, Steve Tombs, and Dave Gordon (eds.), *Beyond Criminology: Taking Harm Seriously*. London: Pluto Press, 2004, x + 332 pp. £17.99 pb. £55.00 hb. *British Journal of Criminology* 46: 362–364.

Room, Robin. 2000. Concepts and Items in Measuring Social Harm from Drinking. *Journal of Substance Abuse* 12: 93–111.

Schwendinger, Herman, and Julia Schwendinger. 1975. Defenders of Order or Guardians of Human Rights? In *Critical Criminology*, ed. Ian Taylor, Paul Walton, and Jock Young, 113–146. London: Routledge and Kegan Paul.

Sjoberg, Gideon, Elizabeth Gill, and Norma Williams. 2001. A Sociology of Human Rights. *Social Problems* 48: 11–47.

Sutherland, Edwin. [1949] 1983. *White Collar Crime: The Uncut Version*. New Haven: Yale University Press.

Tifft, Larry L., and Dennis C. Sullivan. 2001. A Needs-Based, Social Harms Definition of Crime. In *What is Crime? Controversies over the Nature of Crime and What to Do About It*, ed. Stuart Henry and Mark M. Lanier, 179–203. Lanham: Rowman and Littlefield.

Walters, Reece. 2006. Crime, Bio-Agriculture and the Exploitation of Hunger. *British Journal of Criminology* 46: 26–45.

Whyte, Dave. 2005. Book Review: P. Hillyard, C. Pantazis, S. Tombs, and D. Gordon (eds.), *Beyond Criminology: Taking Harm Seriously*. London: Pluto, 2004. 332 pp. ISBN 1-55266-148-2. *Punishment and Society* 7: 488–490.

———. 2007. The Crimes of Neo-Liberal Rule in Occupied Iraq. *British Journal of Criminology* 47: 177–195.

Yar, Majid. 2012a. Critical Criminology, Critical Theory and Social Harm. In *New Directions in Criminological Theory*, ed. Steve Hall and Simon Winlow, 52–65. London: Routledge.

———. 2012b. Recognition as the Grounds for a General Theory of Crime a Social Harm? In *Recognition Theory as Social Research: Investigating the Dynamics of Social Conflict*, ed. Shane O'Neill and Nicholas Smith, 109–126. Basingstoke: Palgrave Macmillan.

Zedner, Lucia. 2011. Putting Crime Back on the Criminological Agenda. In *What is Criminology?* ed. Mary Bosworth and Carolyn Hoyle, 271–285. Oxford: Oxford University Press.

Author Biography

Lynne Copson is Lecturer in Criminology at the Open University. Her research focuses on zemiology and its relationship to criminology particularly in terms of their respective implications for understanding 'harm' and realising 'justice', and utopianism (particularly the idea of using utopia as a method), and the intersections between academic research and public engagement.

Harm: A Substitute for Crime or Central to It?

Letizia Paoli and Victoria A. Greenfield

Introduction

Building on the tradition of critical criminology (e.g., Hulsman 1986; Christie 2000), Hillyard, Tombs, and their colleagues have probed the limits and unintended consequences of much contemporary criminological research and have responded audaciously by conventional academic standards. They have proposed replacing the notion of 'crime' with that of 'social harm' and orienting social policy toward harm reduction (see, e.g., Hillyard et al. 2004; Hillyard and Tombs 2007; Yar 2012) and they have founded an alternative discipline, 'zemiology', which is dedicated to the study of social harm.

Although we share many of their concerns about research and policy, our perspective and intentions are less radical. We agree that

---

L. Paoli (✉)
University of Leuven, Leuven, Belgium
e-mail: Letizia.Paoli@kuleuven.be

V. A. Greenfield
George Mason University, Fairfax, VA, USA

criminalisation and prosecution are just one possible strategy for dealing with harm and not necessarily the best, but we do not advocate replacing crime with harm. Rather, we advocate acknowledging the centrality of harm to crime—as reflected in early legal doctrine, ongoing scholarly debate, and contemporary criminal policy—and drawing out the implications for criminal policy.

We also contend that proper acknowledgement of harm requires a means of operationalisation. It is one thing to claim the centrality of a concept; it is another thing to put it to effective use. To that end, we offer a methodology, the 'harm assessment framework', that the policy community, including scholars and practitioners, can use to identify harms and gauge their significance, both systematically and empirically. The framework is evolving, but we take encouragement from an anonymous reviewer of Greenfield and Paoli (2013), who asserted that the framework can do much to move zemiology 'towards rigorous social scientific analysis'.[1]

Lastly, we push back against the long-standing focus of positivist criminology on the causes of crime and argue that 'starting at the end', by making the systematic, empirical assessment of the consequences of crime a new branch of criminology, would benefit criminal policy and the discipline. The emphasis on consequences and assessment could provide crucial evidence for supporting deliberations on criminalisation and establishing priorities in crime control and sentencing; for evaluating policy and improving accountability across interventions; and, ultimately, for helping to advance social justice or at least remove manifest cases of injustice. In addition, it could allow criminology to better connect to broader social goals, including, but not limited to, those of justice.

The organisation of our chapter parallels that of our arguments. We demonstrate the centrality of harm to crime; describe our harm assessment framework; and discuss how assessment can serve criminal policy and criminology.

---

[1]After publication, we learned that the reviewer was Gordon Hughes.

Harm's Place in the Theory and Practice of Criminal Policy

Evidence of harm's association with crime dates at least as far back as Roman and Old Germanic law, even if neither body of law defined 'crime' per se. The literature disagrees on whether they distinguished between what would now be called tort and crime, that is, between purely private wrongs and public wrongs (see, e.g., Weber 1960; Mueller 1955; Waelkens 2015). Nonetheless, each body of law, through tort claims or public prosecutions, meant to restore or prevent injuries done to certain goods, interests or rights of individuals or the community.[2] The main reason for these claims and prosecutions was not the breach of law, but the harm to a valuable interest, such as life, body or property; religion or morality; or statehood (Eser 1966, 349–359).

Eventually, focus shifted from harms to individuals or communities to harms to the interests of ruling or governing authorities, the king or the state, and to acts of insubordination: 'the disobedience against the king or the state emerged as the substance of crime' (Eser 1966, 351). Accordingly, formal definitions of crime surfaced that embraced that perspective and, today, statutory definitions in common and civil-law countries tend to speak of crime as an act or omission in violation of a law with an associated punishment (ibid.).

With the shift in focus from individuals to kings, states, and insubordination, 'harm' lost some visibility, but it did not cede its part in the theory or practice of criminal policy. Here, we demonstrate harm's persistence through a brief exploration of its role in criminal policy, beginning with criminalisation and proceeding to crime control and policing, sentencing, and programmes for victims of crime and restorative justice.

---

[2]Mueller (1955) distinguishes between *delicta privata* and *crimina publica*.

Criminalisation

Harm represents a major, if not the exclusive, criterion for justifying criminalisation in academic discourse and as a matter of policy. Taking an extreme consequentialist position, John Stuart Mill ([1859] 1978, 9) famously claimed that 'the only purpose for which power can be rightfully exercised over any member of a civilised community, against his will, is to prevent harms to others'. Most contemporary scholars (e.g., Feinberg 1985; Simester and von Hirsch 2011) take a broader view than Mill (for an exception, see Husak 2007) and advocate for consideration of additional factors (e.g., Hart [1968] 2008, 1).

The non-consequentialist, i.e., moralist, conception of criminal law suggests additional factors for that 'broader view'. The moralist conception makes the immorality of the conduct and the moral culpability of the offender the focal concerns of criminal law (e.g., Duff 2013). In its extreme formulation, legal moralism leaves no room for consideration of the consequences of crime. According to Moore (1997, 35), for example, the only function of criminal law is to achieve retributive justice by punishing 'all and only those who are morally culpable in the doing of some morally wrongful action'. More typically, however, scholars propose combinations of harmfulness and wrongfulness (see Duff 2013). Requirements of justice, for example, might temper or constrain a consequentialist approach to criminal law and preclude some practices, such as the criminalisation of faultless conduct, even if those practices would further a goal of harm prevention (Hart 2008). Others, such as Feinberg (1984, 1985), accept immorality as a reason for criminalisation, but emphasise harm prevention as a major purpose of criminal law, drawing on and revising Mill's Harm Principle. Qualifying simple legal moralism, Duff (2007, 140–141) defines crimes as 'public wrongs' that injure collective goods or 'properly concern… the public, i.e. the polity as a whole'.

In contemporary legal theory, though, the term 'Harm Principle' lacks a precise, commonly accepted definition. Duff and Marshall (2014) identify three formulations (Mill [1859] 1978; Feinberg 1984; Simester and von Hirsch 2011), from which they derive two different principles, namely a 'harm prevention principle' and a 'harmful conduct principle'. In its strictest 'Millian' version the former designates harm prevention as 'the only good reason for criminalisation' and in its 'Feinbergian' version it places harm prevention as 'one among other sources of good reason to criminalise' behaviour (Duff and Marshall 2014, 206). The latter, which they associate with Simester and von Hirsch (2011), calls for criminalising acts that elicit harm. The two principles can coincide when, for example, criminalising a conduct that is inherently harmful serves to prevent harm, but can diverge when prevention justifies criminalising conduct that is not in itself harmful.

Despite ambiguities in the doctrine, harm prevention has long served as a main goal of criminal law in the United States (US), Europe, and elsewhere. Until the surge of retributivism (see infra) that began in the 1980s, 'punishment theories, institutions, policies, and practices in the English-speaking countries were based largely on consequentialist ideas' (Tonry 2011, 6), with offender rehabilitation presented as the leading tool for achieving crime prevention (Tonry 2011, 6; see also Garland 2001, 27–52). The American Model Penal Code, which was first published by the American Law Institute in 1962, was shaped by consequentialist ideas. The Code, for instance, declares that the first general purpose of the provisions governing the definition of offences is 'to forbid and prevent conduct that unjustifiably and inexcusably inflicts or threatens substantial harms to individual or public interests' (s.1.01(1) quoted in Duff 2013).

German criminal law theory posits a similar starting point, with the notion of *Rechtsgüter* or individual and collective interests, which is embedded in Germany's criminal law-making. In this tradition, criminal law is meant to protect specific individual and collective interests against conduct that seriously threatens them (see Roxin 2006, 8–47).

The legal-interests approach—and attendant concerns for harm—has spread to other European and non-European jurisdictions and contributed to criminal law deliberations at the level of the European Union (EU). For example, in 2009, the Council of the European Union (2009a) adopted model provisions on criminal law, stressing the link between legal interest and harm: 'The criminal provisions should focus on conduct causing actual harm or seriously threatening the right or essential interest which is the object of protection....' (Council 2009a, 3). In addition, the Council called for consideration of 'how serious and/or widespread and frequent the harmful conduct is, both regionally and locally within the EU' (Council 2009a, 2) before adopting new criminal provisions.[3]

Crime Control

Contemporary scholars (e.g., Rubin 1999; Sherman 2007; Sherman et al. 2016) and policy-makers (e.g., Radcliffe 2015; *The Economist* 2016) have proposed harm as a benchmark for priority-setting in crime control and, specifically, policing. Since the 1970s, Finland, a country often regarded as a model for its humane criminal policy and low imprisonment rates, has established the minimisation of the costs and harmful effects of crime and crime control as the main goal of its penal policies (Lappi-Seppälä 2007). In other countries and at the EU level, the concept of 'serious crime' epitomises the growing relevance of harm as a benchmark for crime control and has recently become an organising framework in the crime-control policies of the EU and a number of EU and non-EU states. Europol, for example, claims the fight against serious crime as its mission (Council 2009a, b) and, in 2007 and 2015, the UK adopted the Serious Crime Acts.[4] In addition, Australia allocates substantial resources to serious crime units.

Although serious crime is not defined univocally, EU policy documents, including treaties, highlight 'the nature and impact ... of the offences' (TFEU 2008, Art. 83(1)), which can be interpreted as encompassing harm, as the main substantive criterion for identifying serious crime.[5] Scholars also emphasise the link between serious crime and harm. Dorn (2009, 284), for example, welcomes the policy community's growing attention to serious crime because 'it opens up the possibility of Europol priorities being defined in terms of the seriousness

---

[3]This was the second of three factors for consideration (Council 2009a, 2).
[4]Available online at http://www.legislation.gov.uk/ukpga/2007/27/contents and http://www.legislation.gov.uk/ukpga/2015/9/introduction/enacted.
[5]The other criterion is the 'special need to combat them on common basis'.

of the harms impacting on individual collective or corporate victim' (see also Sheptycki et al. 2011, 18; Paoli et al. 2017). Europol, with its 2013 Serious and Organised Crime Threat Assessment (Europol 2013),[6] as well as several national police and governmental agencies, such as the UK Metropolitan Police Service and the Australian Crime Commission, have begun developing indicators of consequences to implement the idea of serious and/or organised crime (Tusikov 2012).

Some scholars and practitioners also suggest using harm-related metrics to monitor crime trends, to measure change in the severity of crimes being committed and, ultimately, to improve resource allocation and accountability of policy. In 2007 Sherman (2007, 312) proposed the creation of a total harm index based on the public opinion and Sherman et al. (2016) have developed a 'Crime Harm Index' that relates crimes to penalties, specifically the number of prison days that crimes of that type would incur. In their first application, Sherman, Neyroud, and Neyroud work with the Sentencing Guidelines of England and Wales. Along similar lines, statistical agencies from Canada (Statistics Canada 2009), New Zealand (Sullivan and Su-Wuen 2013) and the UK (Office for National Statistics 2016) have developed crime severity or seriousness scores, multiplying police recorded crime data by actual sentencing data. Ignatans and Pease (2015) have constructed another index, using victims' judgements of offences committed against them as weights of crime counts.

Although it is doubtful that these indexes can account fully for the harms of crime,[7] they testify to a collective, emerging realisation that all crimes cannot be treated equally in policy making or implementation and that the consequences of crime must be monitored and considered more systematically in policy deliberations. By comparison, the policy community treats crimes equally and with little introspection when it works with crime counts.

---

[6]In its second SOCTA, Europol (2017) all but expunges 'harm' and adopts the terms 'threat' and 'impact'.
[7]We discuss some of our concerns, below.

Sentencing

Hall (1960, 213) describes harm as 'the fulcrum between criminal conduct and the punitive sanction', but harm plays its part in sentencing through 'seriousness'. Influenced by retributivist and 'just desert' theories (e.g., Von Hirsch 1986), Ashworth (2006, 30–39) and others hold that appropriate sanctions should be proportional to the seriousness of an offence, which, in turn, depends on a combination of the harm done or risked through the commission of a criminal act and the offender's culpability.

The requirement of proportionality goes back to Cesare Beccaria ([1764] 1995, 14), who in his seminal work, *On Crimes and Punishment*, stressed the need to develop a scale of the seriousness of crimes for setting sanctions. His vision remains unfulfilled—indices built from sentencing guidelines cannot be used to create sentencing guidelines—and, according to Lippke (2012, 464), the lack of 'anchoring points' for a sentencing scheme remains 'one of the unsolved, and seemingly insoluble, problems of sentencing theory'.

Despite the empirical deficit, modern society has not given up on the link between sentencing and seriousness, and thus harm, either implicitly or explicitly. Penal codes and sentencing policies in Western countries tend to reflect the presumed seriousness of offences. For example, penal codes might set maximum sentences for particular offenses or appellate courts regard sentences that are grossly excessive in relation to the gravity of the offence as unfair. Finland, Sweden, the UK, and several US states have adopted statutory guiding principles or sentencing guidelines that require proportionality between the severity of the penalty and the seriousness of the offence. In addition, Canada and New Zealand have enacted statements of desert-oriented sentencing aims (Von Hirsch 2011).

Harm is central not only to crime but also to punishment. Whereas the retributivist tradition emphasises that punishment must be burdensome to achieve the communicative aim of censure on harms and wrongs (Duff 2011), retributivist scholars, themselves, admit that the excesses and inhumanity of current correctional systems give credibility to the abolitionists' portrayal of punishment as 'delivering pain' (Duff 2011, 66, quoting Christie 1981). Empirical studies (e.g., Clear 2007; Wacquant 2009; Travis et al. 2014) document the serious harms to offenders, their families, and entire communities, generated by the unprecedented expansion of prison systems especially in the US. This body of literature has contributed to initial attempts to reduce mass imprisonment in the US.

Programmes for Victims of Crime and Restorative Justice

Since the 1970s, concern has risen on both sides of the Atlantic about the individuals who are harmed by crime, as evidenced by the extensive media coverage of victims and their experiences, the great expansion of victimology, and the wide range of victim initiatives, programmes, and legislation (e.g., Walklate 2007). The victims' movement calls for a reform of the criminal justice systems across the world to serve the interests of those directly harmed by crime besides or even before those of the state. A landmark for the global reform movement was the United Nations (1985) Declaration on the Basic Principles of Justice for Victims of Crime and Abuse of Power adopted by the UN General Assembly in 1985. This declaration recognises the centrality of harm to the very concept of victim of crime:

> "Victims" means persons who, individually or collectively, have suffered harm, including physical or mental injury, emotional suffering, economic loss or substantial impairment of their fundamental rights, through acts or omissions that are in violation of criminal laws operative within Member States.

The declaration also calls on countries to grant victims access to justice and fair treatment, restitution and compensation for the harm suffered as well as material, medical, psychological and social assistance. Many such policies have since been introduced, at least in developed countries, for victims of 'ordinary' crimes (e.g., Office for the Victims of Crime 2017). However, even these countries are, according to Letschert and van Dijk (2011), still struggling to address the growing number of victims of international crimes. According to some scholars (e.g., Whyte 2007; Fattah 2010, 54–57), neither victimology nor policy has paid enough attention to non-individual bearers of harm or to offences that lack immediate individual victims, such as corporate crimes.

The restorative justice movement, as manifest in global initiatives and programmes, also centres on matters of harm and repair.[8] Whether presented as an alternative or complement to conventional criminal justice measures, the main purpose of these initiatives and programmes is to repair harm through 'conversations with those who have been hurt and with those who have inflicted the harm' (Braithwaite 2004, 28). Whereas current programs consist mostly of victim-offender mediation and family conferencing that targets juvenile offenders, Walgrave (2003) and other scholars stress that some existing criminal sanctions, such as compensation or community work, can entail a restorative component and that other criminal sanctions, such as fines or even imprisonment, could be reformed to fulfil a restorative aim. In a 'maximalist version of restorative justice', Bazemore and Walgrave (1999), alongside others, appeal for the development of a fully-fledged justice system that is oriented towards doing justice through restoration, which, with time, would replace the existing punitive and rehabilitative justice systems.

The worldwide growth of restorative justice initiatives has been recognised by the UN Economic and Social Council (ECOSOC 2002), which adopted a resolution entailing Basic Principles on the Use of Restorative Justice Programmes in Criminal Matters.

The Harm Assessment Framework

If one accepts the premise that harm is central to crime, then one might also see a need for operationalisation; more specifically, a means of identifying and gauging harm. Although it might be reasonable to

---

[8]For an overview of initiatives and programmes, see, e.g., Restorative Justice International at http://www.restorativejusticeinternational.com/ and Walgrave (2011).

expect to find guidance in a literature replete with debates on theoretical foundations, empirical challenges, and policy implications, that literature has yet to emerge. Perhaps surprisingly, we have not found a methodological cornucopia.

Over the past decade, critical criminologists have begun applying the concept of harm to state crimes, mass atrocities, and a variety of environmentally detrimental and inhumane activities, not all of which are 'criminal' (e.g., Presser 2013; Rothe and Kauzlarich 2014; White 2011). However, neither these critical criminologists nor the broader policy community, including scholarly advocates of harm-based approaches to criminal policy, have developed rigorous typologies or assessment tools.

Here, we offer a brief introduction to the literature and its limitations, before turning to our own contributions.[9] Among the scholarly advocates of 'harm', Rubin (1999, 1) proposes 'minimizing harm as a solution to the crime policy conundrum', but without further specification, and Hillyard and Tombs (2007) suggest the scope of a broader 'social harm' approach, but consider its contours only briefly. In pursuit of specification, Maltz (1990), Von Hirsch and Jareborg (1991), and Dorn and van de Bunt (2010) attempt to categorise the harms of crimes, but have gained little traction empirically. Kopp and Besson (2009), Levi and Burrows (2008) and others de facto equate harm with social cost and, following the cost-of-crime literature (e.g., Cohen 2005), include the costs of societal reactions, which, as we discuss below, might serve to overemphasise extant priorities. Europol's (2013) 'Serious and Organised Crime Threat Assessment' is light on methodological insight, but does not appear to distinguish between harms that result from an activity and those that result from the criminalisation of or responses to the activity (Paoli 2014).

Sherman et al. (2016) created the aforementioned 'Crime Harm Index', but, in basing the index on sentencing guidelines, do not distinguish the harms of crime from the factors that came into play in developing those guidelines. The index reflects and codifies prior

---

[9]For a more complete look back, we suggest Paoli and Greenfield (2013).

policy decisions, which, in turn, involved a mix of public perceptions and political imperatives. For that reason, it cannot be used to establish criminality, policy priorities, or sanctions because it already embodies decisions about each. The same is true of the indexes of government agencies that take similar approaches (see, e.g., Office for National Statistics 2016). Arguably, 'the thing that is broken' cannot be used to fix 'the thing that is broken'.

In recent years, we, the authors of this chapter, have been developing—and applying—a 'harm assessment framework' (Greenfield and Paoli 2013) that addresses many of the conceptual and technical challenges previously facing proponents of harm assessment (Paoli and Greenfield 2013). To do so, we have reached across policy communities, disciplines, and literature, finding salient references as far afield from criminology as U.S. military doctrine (e.g., Greenfield and Camm 2005). Moreover, we join Ashworth (2006, 30–31), Feinberg (1984, 31–36), and others who treat harm as setbacks to stakeholders' legitimate interests and recognise that the 'dominant political morality' (MacCormick 1982, 30) plays a central part in establishing legitimacy. Thus, we accept—and even embrace—normativity, but our approach and its transparency, including explicit criteria for legitimacy, allow us to circumscribe the normative and proceed analytically.[10]

Our framework consists of a set of analytical tools woven together in a multistep process (Fig. 1) that can be used to identify, evaluate, rank, and prioritise harms. The tools, in order of application, include a template for constructing the narrative or 'business model' of a criminal activity, a taxonomy for identifying the particular harms associated with the activity, scales for evaluating the severity and incidence of those harms, and a matrix for combining that information to rank and prioritise them across society. The assessment process, which uses quantitative and qualitative evidence gleaned from official records, interviews, press reports, etc., does not produce point estimates or fuel an index; rather, it yields rankings of harms that can, among other things, be exploited to establish priorities for criminal policy and inform resource allocation decisions.

---

[10]For example, in tallying harms, we exclude losses of ill-gotten property, such as stolen weapons, from consideration, but we include physical and psychological injuries to perpetrators.

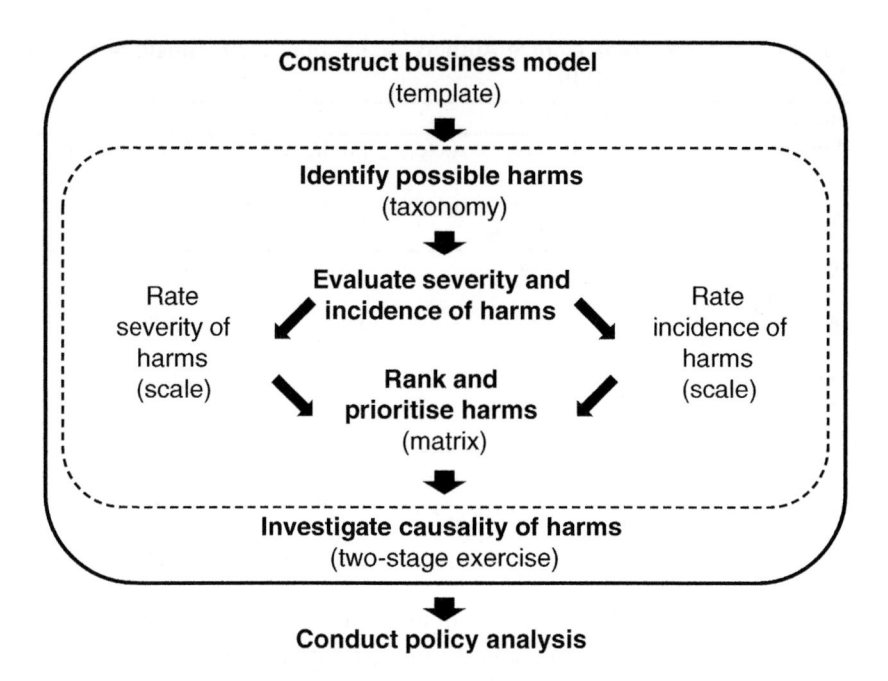

```
┌─────────────────────────────────────────────┐
│            Construct business model          │
│                  (template)                  │
│                      ↓                       │
│ ┌ ─ ─ ─ ─ ─ ─ ─ ─ ─ ─ ─ ─ ─ ─ ─ ─ ─ ─ ─ ─ ┐ │
│            Identify possible harms           │
│                  (taxonomy)                  │
│                      ↓                       │
│    Rate        Evaluate severity and   Rate  │
│  severity of  ↙ incidence of harms ↘  incidence of │
│    harms                                harms │
│   (scale)          Rank and           (scale)│
│              ↘   prioritise harms   ↙        │
│                    (matrix)                  │
│                      ↓                       │
│ └ ─ ─ ─ ─ ─ ─ ─ ─ ─ ─ ─ ─ ─ ─ ─ ─ ─ ─ ─ ─ ┘ │
│           Investigate causality of harms     │
│                (two-stage exercise)          │
└─────────────────────────────────────────────┘
                      ↓
              Conduct policy analysis
```

Fig. 1 Harm assessment process (*Source* Authors' adaptation of Greenfield and Paoli (2012) and Paoli et al. (2013))

The taxonomy gives practical meaning to 'harm' by calling out the potential claimants or 'bearers' of harm and the types of harms they might experience with each criminal activity under consideration (Table 1).

The taxonomy accommodates the possibility of harms to each of four general 'classes' of bearers that, together, might constitute much of a society, namely: individuals; private-sector entities, including businesses and nongovernmental organisations (NGOs); public-sector entities, including government; and the social and physical environment.[11]

Bearers in each class experience harms as damages to one or more 'interest dimensions' (Von Hirsch and Jareborg 1991, 19), consisting

---

[11] We define 'government' as all state entities (executive, legislative, or judicial), ranging from local to national, but could include supranational and other publically-funded or -managed bodies.

Table 1 Harm taxonomy (*Source* Authors' adaptation of Greenfield and Paoli (2013) and Paoli et al. (2013))

Interest dimension	Class of bearer			
	Individuals	Private sector, including businesses and NGOs	Public-sector, including government	Environment, including social and physical
Functional integrity	X[a]	X[b]	X[b]	X[c]
Material support	X	X	X	n/a
Reputation	X	X	X	n/a
Privacy and autonomy	X	X	X	n/a

Notes X = applicable; n/a = not applicable
[a]Functional integrity refers to physical, psychological, and intellectual integrity
[b]Functional integrity refers to operational integrity
[c]Functional integrity refers to physical, operational, and aesthetic integrity

of functional integrity, material support, reputation, and privacy and autonomy. As apparent in Table 1, not all interest dimensions pertain to all classes of bearers and damages to a particular interest dimension, such as functional integrity, can manifest differently across classes. Following Von Hirsch and Jareborg (1991), who build on Sen (1987a, b), we treat these interest dimensions as representing capabilities or pathways to achieving a certain quality of life, referred to as a 'standard of living', or, by analogy, institutional mission.

Our decision to cast a wider net than just individuals and readily quantifiable damages stems largely from our experience working across disciplines.

The severity of a harm depends on the extent to which damages intrude upon either the standard of living or institutional mission; the greater the intrusion, the more severe the harm (Von Hirsch and Jareborg 1991, 17–19). Drawing additionally from Greenfield and Camm (2005, 46–49) and others in the national security community, the framework ranks harms on the basis of both their severity and incidence (Table 2). At one extreme, the damage to an interest could be 'marginal' and occur only 'rarely'; at the other, it could be 'catastrophic' and occur 'continuously'.

Table 2 Matrix for prioritising harms (*Sources* Authors' adaptation of Greenfield and Camm (2005, 48), drawing from Department of the Army et al. (2001) and other military doctrine, Greenfield and Paoli (2013), and Paoli et al. (2013))

Severity	Incidence				
	Continuously	Persistently	Occasionally	Seldom	Rarely
Catastrophic	VH	H	H	H/M	M/H
Grave	H	H	H/M	M/H	M
Serious	H	H/M	M/H	M	L
Moderate	H/M	M/H	M	L	L
Marginal	M/H	M	L	L	L

Notes VH = Very high priority; H = High priority; M = Medium priority; L = Low priority

As shown in Fig. 1, the assessment process begins with the characterisation of the criminal activity and ends with an investigation of causality. Absent a specific tool, we consider causality in two stages. First, we distinguish the harms that result directly from a criminal activity from those that are 'remote'[12] and, second, we examine the extent to which the harms associated with the criminal activity are intrinsic to that activity or arise from the policy environment and related law enforcement practices.

In summary, the framework regards quantitative and qualitative evidence with equal respect and uses it to produce structured narratives and rankings of harms that accrue to individual, institutional, and environmental stakeholders. On that basis, the approach can be used to render a full accounting of harms and comparisons of harms across society, without resorting to the necessary reductionism and generalisations of point estimates or indices. Moreover, by considering individual, institutional, and environmental interests, we acknowledge that the human experience is multidimensional (see, e.g., Nussbaum 1997; Sen 2009) and that the institutions and environmental conditions that help shape the human experience hold value in their own right.

Notwithstanding our interest in casting a wide net, we have set a handful of philosophical and pragmatic bounds on our assessments.

---

[12]Remoteness, in our assessments, refers to the temporal, spatial, or behavioural distance that separates a conduct from its consequences (Greenfield and Paoli 2013).

For example, we exclude law-enforcement and self-protection costs.[13] This decision might go against common practice in the cost-of-crime literature, but it is not without precedent in the criminological literature (e.g., Dorn and van de Bunt 2010). As Levi and Burrows (2008, 294) observe, the inclusion of response costs can yield paradoxical results, 'if one includes the costs of responses to crime as part of the "costs of crime", the less that is done about them, the lower are the "costs of crime"' and vice versa. Moreover, although we aspire to full accounting (see Greenfield and Paoli 2012), we did not tally the benefits of crime, itself, in our analyses of drug and human trafficking. This exclusion was not philosophical, but pragmatic. Were we to assess the harms of other activities (e.g., human smuggling) in other places (e.g., Afghanistan, in the case of opium production), the approach could seriously skew our findings.

With other scholars, we have applied the framework to drug production, drug trafficking, and human trafficking in Belgium and the Netherlands (e.g., Paoli et al. 2013, 2015; Greenfield et al. 2016) and shown that it can be used to produce policy-relevant 'estimates' of harms across crimes, to prioritise particular types of criminal activities relative to their harmfulness, and, potentially, to allocate public resources accordingly.

In the discussion that follows, we broaden the case for harm assessment.

The Case for Harm Assessment

Just as harm permeates matters of criminalisation, crime control and policing, sentencing, and other societal responses to crime, so too can a systematic, empirical harm assessment serve to strengthen related policy making and implementation.

First, taking either a pure or constrained consequentialist perspective, one might use harm assessment to consider whether specific activities

---

[13]We do, however, include medical and reparation costs.

warrant criminalisation, even if a final decision on criminalisation will not be based exclusively on harmfulness. Pursuant to the 'harmful conduct principle', one might use the approach to test whether an activity, criminal or otherwise is sufficiently harmful to be called out as criminal. The assessment could, then, help answer what Duff calls a 'central question about criminalisation' (Duff 2010, 109). To paraphrase, when should we—society—abstain from criminalising some wrongs either because their harms are too trivial or because it is more important to ensure that the harm is repaired or compensated?

In accordance with the 'harm prevention principle', a systematic, empirical harm assessment could be used to establish the extent of harms and investigate the strength of the relationship between a harm and an activity that might not be harmful, in itself. How serious, frequent, and remote are the damages associated with an activity and, if not too distant, could criminalising the activity help prevent substantial harm? In some cases, an assessment might provide solid arguments for avoiding the excessive extension of the harm principle feared by some scholars (e.g., Harcourt 1999). If future applications of the framework were to entail full accounting and include the benefits of activities, they could accommodate any repeated activity that, even if legitimate, is suspected of generating harms (e.g., tobacco production and trade). This is not to say that we advocate criminalisation as an answer to all harms of a particular intensity, but that the approach might provide a means to calibrate the policy response to harm.

Second, the comparison of harms across different types of already-criminal activities can provide initial evidence for setting strategic and tactical priorities for the police and prosecution agencies charged with enforcing criminal (and, possibly, other types of) law. One might, for example, be able to rank activities according to their harmfulness and, without ignoring low hanging fruit, address those activities posing the greatest threats to bearers first. More harmful activities might merit greater attention than less harmful activities, but, as we discuss below, decisions about the implementation of policy measures—and the allocation of resource to them—should also involve consideration of the feasibility and costs of implementation.

Third, the identification of especially 'harmful' perpetrators might suggest particular avenues of policing. For example, the assessment process might reveal that certain types of perpetrators, distinguished by location or criminal affiliations, disproportionally engage in particularly harmful activities. If only implicitly, the High Point, NC, Drug Market Intervention (e.g., Corsaro et al. 2012) took such an approach to reducing violence.

Fourth, an assessment of the severity of the harms of a crime, irrespective of the incidence, could provide evidence to review existing sentencing guidelines and practices. Recalling that 'seriousness' consists of a combination of 'harmfulness' and 'culpability', the assessment might supply an empirical benchmark for judging the former.

Fifth, a systematic, empirical assessment of the harms of crime to different classes of bearers, including businesses, NGOs, government, and the environment, might help programmes for—and research concerning—victims of crime and restorative justice expand their reach beyond traditional crimes and its individual victims (e.g., Fattah 2010, 54–57; Letschert and van Dijk 2011). In particular, the assessment might lead to programmes that more rigorously address the harms of non-individual bearers (e.g., Walgrave 2003, 61; White 2011). Moreover, a systematic, empirical harm assessment could provide a basis for proportionally aligning restoration and harm. Concerns about proportionality have been raised by several restorative justice scholars (e.g., Duff 2013) and groups of practitioners (see Van Ness 2002). They also inform a basic UN principle: 'Agreements … should contain only reasonable and proportionate obligations' (ECOSOC 2002, Art. 7). In addition, an assessment that takes the perspective of an 'impartial spectator' (Sen 2009, 124, citing Smith [1790] 1976) could help policymakers identify and address all the harms of a conduct, even if victims do not report them fully. The assessment might also avoid unduly privileging the harms recounted by the most vocal victims.

Finally, harm assessment could support the evaluation of existing criminal policy interventions and feed into deliberations about future interventions.

A harm-based approach could be used to assess and compare the impact, including the unintended consequences and distributional effects, of different types of policy regimes or of particular policy measures.

The assessment, which might entail a detailed analysis or a well-structured thought exercise, would require repetition to compare the effects of changes in assumptions about the policies or measures in play. A comparison of the status quo with an alternative policy scenario, be it no policy or a newly proposed policy, could support a notional cost-benefit analysis of the status quo in relation to the alternative. However, a full comparison across options, even if only notional, would necessitate consideration of the implementation costs of each of the alternatives. Absent consideration of those costs, one might inadvertently allocate resources at a net loss.

Through such means, systematic, empirical harm assessment can contribute to deliberations on criminalisation, the establishment of priorities in criminal policy, the development of more cost-effective and accountable policy, and, as we discuss below, the advancement of social justice or at least the removal of manifest cases of injustice.

Concluding Remarks

Over the past thirty years, criminology has created an impressive body of evidence on 'what works' and 'what doesn't work' in crime prevention and control (e.g., Sherman et al. 1997; MacKenzie 2006); but, it has had less success in other arenas. It has not yet provided policy makers with a firm analytical foundation for establishing priorities or, even more fundamentally, criminality, and it has devoted little attention to the aims, rather than the means, of criminal policy and the criminal justice system. With the exceptions of critical criminologists (e.g., Hillyard et al. 2004), restorative justice scholars (e.g., Braithwaite 2002; Walgrave 2003) and few mainstream criminologists (e.g., Bottoms 2008), contemporary criminology has largely eschewed normative theorising as unscientific and abstained from 'problematising' the very notions of crime, criminal policy and criminal justice. The dominant positivist criminology also seems to have forgotten that, given the fundamentally constructed nature of crime, criminal policy can only be a means of achieving a higher goal. Both positivist criminology and penal theory, instead, routinely and reductively equate 'criminal justice' with 'retributive justice' and, have become disconnected from broader debates on justice itself (e.g., Brodeur and Shearing 2005).

We see the systematic, empirical assessment of the harms of crime—and criminal policies—as one of the 'ways of judging how to reduce injustice and advance justice' (Sen 2009, ix), thus helping to ensure that criminology does more to enhance justice, not just crime control 'or punishment'. Sen's writings indicate a close association between justice and the enhancement and fair distribution of human capabilities and we have adopted such capabilities as our benchmark for gauging the severity of harms to individuals. Without disregard for the relevance of 'procedural justice' to the legitimacy of criminal justice institutions (Tyler 2006), we agree with Bottoms and Tankebe (2012) that 'distributive justice', defined in terms of the concrete outcomes of criminal policies, matters and does so increasingly, 'the more significant the outcome [is] for the individual's life' (Bottoms and Tankebe 2017) or to others' interests. We do not claim harm as the sole criterion for developing and implementing crime-control policy—or enhancing justice—but, like the mythical Indian prince, Arjuna, who Sen (2009, 213) cites, we argue that 'the results of one's choices and actions must matter in deciding what one should do'.

Almost forty years ago Stanley Cohen ([1979] 2016, 86) advocated for a paradigm shift in criminological thought and research in passionate, if polemical, terms:

> There should be a moratorium on nearly all types of standard criminological research and publication. Absolutely prohibited should be any research about the 'causes' of crime and delinquency or the personal characteristics of criminals and delinquents…. Instead, thought and research should be devoted to such questions as: differential perceptions of the seriousness of various crimes and the level of appropriate punishment, the degree to which certain forms of deviance can be tolerated without invoking the criminal sanction; the extent and nature of harm, victimisation and damage by crime.

Cohen's call for a moratorium on mainstream criminology is extreme, but we are convinced that his proposed research programme is no less urgent now than in 1979 and merits consideration as a new branch of criminology.

Whether labelled 'zemiological' or 'criminological', such research could serve to elevate the debate on crime among policy makers, law enforcement officials, and scholars; clarify and strengthen the normative foundations of research on crime and crime control; benefit concrete policy deliberations and practices; and thus contribute to making our society less unjust.

References

Ashworth, Andrew. 2006. *Principles of Criminal Law*, 5th ed. Oxford: Oxford University Press.

Bazemore, Gordon, and Lode Walgrave. 1999. Restorative Juvenile Justice: In Search of Fundamentals and an Outline for Systemic Reform. In *Restorative Juvenile Justice: Repairing the Harm of Youth Crime*, ed. Gordon Bazemore, and Lode Walgrave, 45–74. Monsey: Criminal Justice Press.

Beccaria, Cesare. [1764] 1995. *On Crimes and Punishments and Other Writings*, ed. Richard Bellamy. Cambridge: Cambridge University Press.

Bottoms, Anthony. 2008. The Relationship Between Theory and Empirical Observations in Criminology. In *Doing Research on Crime and Justice*, 2nd ed., ed. Roy D. King and Emma Wincup, 75–116. Oxford: Oxford University Press.

Bottoms, Anthony, and Justice Tankebe. 2012. Beyond Procedural Justice: A Dialogic Approach to Legitimacy in Criminal Justice. *Journal of Criminal Law and Criminology* 102: 119–170.

———. 2017. Police Legitimacy and the Authority of the State. In *Criminal Law and the Authority of the State*, ed. Antje du Bois-Pedain, Magnus Ulväng, and Petter Asp, 47–88. London: Hart Publishing.

Braithwaite, John. 2002. *Restorative Justice and Responsive Regulation*. Oxford: Oxford University Press.

———. 2004. Restorative Justice and De-professionalization. *Good Society* 13: 28–31.

Brodeur, Jean-Paul, and Clifford Shearing. 2005. Configuring Security and Justice. *European Journal of Criminology* 2: 379–406.

Christie, Nils. 2000. *Crime Control as Industry: Towards Gulags, Western Style*, 3rd ed. London: Routledge.

Clear, Todd R. 2007. *Imprisoning Communities: How Mass Incarceration Makes Disadvantaged Neighborhoods Worse*. New York: Oxford University Press.

Cohen, Mark A. 2005. *The Costs of Crime and Justice*. London: Routledge.

Cohen, Stanley. [1979] 2016. Some Modest and Unrealistic Proposals. *New Society*, March 29: 731–734. Reprinted in *Outside Criminology. Selected Essay by Stanley Cohen*, ed. Tom Daems, 79–87. London: Routledge.

Corsaro, Nicholas, Eleazer D. Hunt, Natalie K. Hipple, and Edmund F. McGarrell. 2012. The Impact of Drug Market Pulling Levers Policing on Neighborhood Violence: An Evaluation of the High Point Drug Market Intervention. *Criminology and Public Policy* 11: 167–199.

Council of the European Union. 2009a. Council Conclusions on Model Provisions, Guiding the Council's Criminal Law Deliberations. *2979th Justice and Home Affairs Council Meeting*. http://www.consilium.europa.eu/uedocs/cms_data/docs/pressdata/en/jha/111543.pdf. Accessed 2 Oct 2017.

———. 2009b. Council Decision Establishing the European Police Office (Europol). *Official Journal of the European Union* L121: 37–66.

Department of the Army, Marine Corps, Navy, and Air Force. 2001. Risk Management: Multiservice Tactics, Techniques, and Procedures. FM 3-100.12, MCRP 5-12.1c, NTTP 5-03.5, and AFTTP(I) 3-2.34. Air Land Sea Application Center.

Dorn, Nicholas. 2009. The End of Organised Crime in the European Union. *Crime, Law and Social Change* 51: 283–295.

Dorn, Nicholas, and Henk van de Bunt. 2010. *Bad Thoughts: Towards an Organised Crime Harm Assessment and Prioritization System*. Rotterdam: Erasmus University.

Duff, R.A. 2007. *Answering for Crime: Responsibility and Liability in the Criminal Law*. London: Hart Publishing.

———. 2010. Perversions and Subversions of Criminal Law. In *The Boundaries of the Criminal Law*, ed. R.A. Duff, Lindsay Farmer, S.E. Marshall, Massimo Renzo, and Victor Tadros, 88–112. Oxford: Oxford University Press.

———. 2011. Responsibility, Restoration and Retribution. In *Retributivism Has a Past: Has It a Future?* ed. Michael Tonry, 63–85. New York: Oxford University Press.

———. 2013. Theories of Criminal Law. In *Stanford Encyclopedia of Philosophy*, ed. Edward N. Zalta. http://plato.stanford.edu/archives/sum2013/entries/criminal-law/. Accessed 2 Oct 2017.

Duff, R.A., and S.E. Marshall. 2014. 'Remote Harms' and the Two Harm Principles. In *Liberal Criminal Theory: Essays for Andreas von Hirsch*, ed. A.P. Simester, Antje du Bois-Pedain, and Ulfrid Neumann, 205–224. London: Hart Publishing.

The Economist. 2016. Bobbies on the Spreadsheet: A New Way to Count Crimes Could Reduce the Amount of Harm They Cause. September 3. https://www.economist.com/news/britain/21706343-new-way-count-crimes-could-reduce-amount-harm-they-cause-bobbies-spreadsheet.

ECOSOC. 2002. *ECOSOC Resolution 2002/12: Basic Principles on the Use of Restorative Justice Programmes in Criminal Matters*. UN Economic and Social Council.

Eser, Albin. 1966. The Principle of Harm in the Concept of Crime: A Comparative Analysis of Criminal Protected Legal Interests. *Duquesne University Law Review* 4: 345–417.

Europol. 2013. *SOCTA 2013: EU Serious and Organised Crime Threat Assessment*. 's-Gravenzande: Deventer.

———. 2017. *SOCTA 2017: Crime in the Age of Technology*. The Hague, the Netherlands.

Fattah, Ezzat A. 2010. The Evolution of a Young and Promising Discipline: Sixty Years of Victimology, a Retrospective and Prospective Look. In *International Handbook of Victimology*, ed. Shlomo G. Shoham, Paul Knepper, and Martin Kett, 43–94. Boca Raton: CRC Press.

Feinberg, Joel. 1984. *Harm to Others*. New York: Oxford University Press.

———. 1985. *Offence to Others: The Moral Limits of the Criminal Law*. New York: Oxford University Press.

Garland, David. 2001. *The Culture of Control: Crime and Social Order in Contemporary Society*. Chicago: University of Chicago Press.

Greenfield, Victoria A., and Frank Camm. 2005. *Risk Management and Performance in the Balkans Support Contract*. Santa Monica, CA: RAND.

Greenfield, Victoria A., and Letizia Paoli. 2012. If Supply-Oriented Drug Policy Is Broken, Can Harm Reduction Help Fix It? Melding Disciplines and Methods to Advance International Drug Control Policy. *International Journal of Drug Policy* 23: 6–15.

———. 2013. A Framework to Assess the Harms of Crime. *British Journal of Criminology* 53: 864–885.

Greenfield, Victoria A., Letizia Paoli, and Andries Zoutendijk. 2016. The Harms of Human Trafficking: Demonstrating the Applicability and Value of a New Framework for Systematic, Empirical Analysis. *Global Crime* 17: 152–180.

Hall, Jerome. 1960. *General Principles of Criminal Law.* Indianapolis: Bobbs-Merill.

Harcourt, Bernard E. 1999. The Collapse of the Harm Principle. *Journal of Criminal Law and Criminology* 90: 109–194.

Hart, H.L.A. [1968] 2008. *Punishment and Responsibility: Essays in the Philosophy of Law.* Oxford: Oxford University Press.

Hillyard, Paddy, and Steve Tombs. 2007. From 'Crime' to Social Harm? *Crime, Law & Social Change* 48: 9–25.

Hillyard, Paddy, Christina Pantazis, Steve Tombs, and Dave Gordon (eds.). 2004. *Beyond Criminology: Taking Harm Seriously.* London: Pluto Press.

Hulsman, Louk H.C. 1986. Critical Criminology and the Concept of *Crime. Contemporary Crises* 10: 63–80.

Husak, Douglas. 2007. *Overcriminalisation: The Limits of the Criminal Law.* New York: Oxford University Press.

Ignatans, Dainis, and Ken Pease. 2015. Taking Crime Seriously: Playing the Weighting Game. *Policing* 10: 184–193.

Kopp, Pierre, and Fabien Besson. 2009. A Methodology to Measure the Impact of Organised Crime Activities at the EU Level. In *Organised Crime in the EU*, ed. E. Savona, 301–320. Rotterdam: Erasmus University.

Lappi-Seppälä, Tapio. 2007. Penal Policy in Scandinavia. In *Crime and Justice: Crime, Punishment, and Politics in Comparative Perspective*, ed. Michael Tonry, 217–295. Chicago: The University of Chicago Press.

Letschert, Rianne, and Jan van Dijk (eds.). 2011. *The New Faces of Victimhood.* Dordrecht: Springer.

Levi, Michael, and John Burrows. 2008. Measuring the Impact of Fraud in the UK. *British Journal of Criminology* 48: 293–318.

Lippke, Richard L. 2012. Anchoring the Sentencing Scale: A Modest Proposal. *Theoretical Criminology* 16: 463–480.

MacCormick, Neil. 1982. *Legal Rights and Social Democracy: Essays in Legal and Political Philosophy.* Oxford: Clarendon Press.

MacKenzie, Doris L. 2006. *What Works in Corrections? Reducing the Criminal Activities of Offenders and Delinquents.* Cambridge: Cambridge University Press.

Maltz, Michael D. 1990. *Measuring the Effectiveness of Organized Crime Control Efforts.* Chicago: Office of International Criminal Justice.

Mill, John S. [1859] 1978. *On Liberty*, ed. Elizabeth Rapaport. Indianapolis: Hackett.

Moore, Michael S. 1997. *Placing Blame: A Theory of Criminal Law.* Oxford: Clarendon.

Mueller, Gerhard O.W. 1955. Tort, Crime and the Primitive. *The Journal of Criminal Law, Criminology, and Police Science* 46: 303–332.

Nussbaum, Martha C. 1997. Capabilities and Human Rights. *Fordham Law Review* 66: 273–300.

Office for National Statistics. 2016. *Research Outputs: Developing a Crime Severity Score for England and Wales Using Data on Crimes Recorded by the Police.* Office for National Statistics. https://www.ons.gov.uk/peoplepopulationandcommunity/crimeandjustice/articles/researchoutputsdevelopingacrimeseverityscoreforenglandandwalesusingdataoncrimesrecordedbythepolice/2016-11-29. Accessed 4 Oct 2017.

Office for the Victims of Crime. 2017. *Overview of Crime Victims' Rights.* Office for the Victims of Crime. https://www.ovc.gov/rights/overview_rights.html. Accessed 4 Oct 2017.

Paoli, Letizia. 2014. How to Tackle (Organized) Crime in Europe? The EU Policy Cycle on Serious and Organized Crime and the New Emphasis on Harm. *European Journal of Crime, Criminal Law and Criminal Justice* 22: 1–12.

Paoli, Letizia, and Victoria A. Greenfield. 2013. Harm: A Neglected Concept in Criminology, A Necessary Benchmark in Crime Policy. *European Journal of Crime, Criminal Law and Criminal Justice* 21: 359–377.

Paoli, Letizia, and Victoria A. Greenfield. 2015. Starting from the End: A Plea for Focusing on the Consequences of Crime. *European Journal of Crime, Criminal Law and Criminal Justice* 23: 87–100.

Paoli, Letizia, Tom Decorte, and Loes Kersten. 2015. Assessing the Harms of Cannabis Cultivation in Belgium. *International Journal of Drug Policy* 26: 277–289.

Paoli, Letizia, Victoria A. Greenfield, and Andries Zoutendijk. 2013. The Harm of Cocaine Trafficking: Applying a New Framework for Assessment. *Journal of Drug Issues* 43: 407–436.

Paoli, Letizia, An Adriaenssen, Victoria A. Greenfield, and Mieke Coninckx. 2017. Exploring Definitions of Serious Crime in EU Policy Documents and Academic Publications: A Content Analysis and Policy Implications. *European Journal on Criminal Policy and Research* 23: 269–285.

Presser, Lois. 2013. *Why We Harm*. New Brunswick: Rutgers University Press.
Radcliffe, Jerry H. 2015. Harm-Focused Policing. *Ideas in American Policing* 19: 3.
Rothe, Dawn, and David Kauzlarich (eds.). 2014. *Towards a Victimology of State Crime*. London: Routledge.
Roxin, Claus. 2006. *Strafrecht Allgemeiner Teil*, 4th ed., vol. 1. Munich: CH Beck.
Rubin, Edward L. 1999. Introduction: Minimizing Harm as a Solution to the Crime Policy Conundrum. In *Minimizing Harm: A New Crime Policy for Modern America*, ed. Edward L. Rubin, 1–33. Boulder: Westview.
Sen, Amartya. 1987a. The Standard of Living: Lecture I, Concepts and Critiques. In *The Standard of Living—The Tanner Lectures, Clare Hall, Cambridge, 1985*, ed. Geoffrey Hawthorn, 1–19. Cambridge: Cambridge University Press.
———. 1987b. The Standard of Living: Lecture II, Lives and Capabilities. In *The Standard of Living—the Tanner Lectures, Clare Hall, Cambridge, 1985*, ed. Geoffrey Hawthorn, 20–38. Cambridge: Cambridge University Press.
———. 2009. *The Idea of Justice*. Cambridge: Harvard University Press.
Sheptycki, James, Hager Jaffel, and Didier Bigo. 2011. International Organized Crime in the European Union. *Note Prepared for the European Parliament Directorate General for Internal Policies, Policy Department C: Citizens' Rights and Constitutional Affairs*. http://www.europarl.europa.eu/document/activities/cont/201206/20120627ATT47775/20120627ATT47775EN.pdf. Accessed 4 Oct 2017.
Sherman, Lawrence W. 2007. The Power Few: Experimental Criminology and the Reduction of Harm. The 2006 Joan McCord Prize Lecture. *Journal of Experimental Criminology* 3: 299–321.
Sherman, Lawrence, Peter W. Neyroud, and Eleanor Neyroud. 2016. The Cambridge Crime Harm Index (CHI): Measuring Total Harm from Crime Based on Sentencing Guidelines. *Policing* 10: 171–183.
Sherman, Lawrence W., Denise C. Gottfredson, Doris L. MacKenzie, John Eck, Peter Reuter, and Shawn D. Bushway. 1997. *Preventing Crime: What Works, What Doesn't, What's Promising*. A Report to the United States Congress. Washington, DC: National Institute of Justice.
Simester, A.P., and Andreas von Hirsch. 2011. *Crimes, Harms, and Wrongs: On the Principles of Criminalisation*. London: Hart Publishing.
Smith, Adam. [1790] 1976. *The Theory of Moral Sentiments*. Oxford: Clarendon Press.
Sullivan, Charles, and Ong Su-Wuen. 2013. Justice Sector Seriousness Score (2012 revision). December 13. https://www.justice.govt.nz/assets/Documents/Publications/justice-sector-offence-seriousness-score-faq.pdf.

Statistics Canada. 2009. *Measuring Crime in Canada: Introducing the Crime Severity Index and Improvements to the Uniform Crime Reporting Survey.* Ottawa: Minister of Industry.

TFEU. 2008. Consolidated Version of the Treaty on the Functioning of the European Union. *Official Journal of the European Union* C115: 47–199.

Tonry, Michael. 2011. Can Twenty-First Century Punishment Policies Be Justified in Principle? In *Retributivism Has a Past: Has It a Future?* ed. Michael Tonry, 3–29. New York: Oxford University Press.

Travis, Jeremy, Bruce Western, and Steve Redburn (eds.). 2014. *The Growth of Incarceration in the United States: Exploring Causes and Consequences.* Washington, DC: National Academies Press.

Tusikov, Natasha. 2012. Measuring Organised Crime-Related Harms: Exploring Five Policing Methods. *Crime, Law and Social Change* 57: 99–115.

Tyler, Tom R. 2006. *Why People Obey the Law.* Princeton: Princeton University Press.

United Nations General Assembly. 1985. Declaration of Basic Principles of Justice for Victims of Crime and Abuse of Power. United Nations A/RES/40/34.

Van Ness, Daniel. 2002. Creating Restorative Systems. In *Restorative Justice and the Law*, ed. Lode Walgrave, 130–149. Cullompton: Willan.

Von Hirsch, Andrew. 1986. *Doing Justice: The Choice of Punishments.* Boston: Northeastern University Press.

———. 2011. Punishment Futures: The Desert-Model Debate and the Importance of Criminal Law Context. In *Retributivism Has a Past: Has It a Future?* ed. Michael Tonry, 256–273. New York: Oxford University Press.

Von Hirsch, Andrew, and Nils Jareborg. 1991. Gauging Criminal Harm: A Living-Standard Analysis. *Oxford Journal of Legal Studies* 11: 1–38.

Wacquant, Loic. 2009. *Punishing the Poor: The Neoliberal Government of Social Insecurity.* Durham: Duke University Press.

Waelkens, Laurent. 2015. *Amne Adverso: Roman Legal Heritage in European Culture.* Leuven: Leuven University Press.

Walgrave, Lode. 2003. Imposing Restoration Instead of Inflicting Pain. In *Restorative Justice and Criminal Justice: Competing or Reconcilable Paradigms?* ed. Andrew von Hirsch, Julian Roberts, Anthony E. Bottoms, Kent Roach, and Mara Schiff, 61–78. London: Hart Publishing.

———. 2011. Investigating the Potentials of Restorative Justice Practice. *Journal of Law & Policy* 36: 91–139.

Walklate, Sandra (ed.). 2007. *Handbook of Victims and Victimology.* Cullompton: Willan.

Weber, Max. 1960. *Rechtssoziologie*, ed. Johannes F. Winckelmann. Neuwied: Luchterhand.
White, Rob. 2011. *Global Environmental Harm: Criminological Perspectives*. Portland: Willan.
Whyte, Dave. 2007. Victims of Corporate Crimes. In *Handbook of Victims and Victimology*, ed. Sandra Walklate, 446–463. Cullompton: Willan.
Yar, Majid. 2012. Critical Criminology, Critical Theory and Social Harm. In *New Directions in Criminological Theory*, ed. Steve Hall and Simon Winlow, 52–65. Oxon: Routledge.

Authors' Biography

Letizia Paoli is since 2006 full professor of criminology at the University of Leuven Faculty of Law. She has published extensively on organised crime, (quasi-)illegal markets and related control policies as well as the assessment of the harms of crime. In 2016 Paoli was awarded the Thorsten Sellin & Sheldon and Eleanor Glueck Award by the American Society of Criminology for her 'contributions to international criminology' and the Distinguished Scholar Award of the International Association for the Study of Organised Crime. She received her PhD in social and political sciences from the European University Institute, Florence.

Victoria A. Greenfield is a visiting scholar in the Department of Criminology, Law and Society at George Mason University. She specialises in national security and international social and economic issues, including transnational crime, and is chairing the National Academies' committee on precursor chemicals and improvised explosive devices. Greenfield has held the positions of Senior Economist, RAND Corporation; Admiral William Crowe Chair, US Naval Academy; and, during the Clinton Administration, Senior Economist for international trade and agriculture, President's Council of Economic Advisers. She received her PhD in agricultural and resource economics from the University of California, Berkeley.

Criminology or Zemiology? Yes, Please! On the Refusal of Choice Between False Alternatives

Justin Kotzé

Introduction

The discipline of criminology has long been beset by a nagging tension that seemingly runs right to its heart. That is, the tension between the concepts of 'crime' and 'harm'. Debates regarding the appropriateness of the terms' conceptual boundaries, range of theoretical efficacy and empirical operationalisation have occupied scholars, particularly those on the margins of criminology's boundaries, for years (Pemberton 2016; Hughes 2006). Indeed, the issues raised by these debates continue to animate scholars who appear determined to settle the issue, to finally put to bed a tension that has in many ways become regarded as innate to the discipline. Certainly one of the most concerted efforts to lay bare the complexities of this long-running tension, albeit from a particular view, can be found in the landmark study *Beyond Criminology: Taking Harm Seriously* (Hillyard et al. 2004a). Authored by a less than

J. Kotzé (✉)
Teesside University, Middlesbrough, UK
e-mail: j.kotze@tees.ac.uk

© The Author(s) 2018
A. Boukli and J. Kotzé (eds.), *Zemiology*, Critical Criminological Perspectives, https://doi.org/10.1007/978-3-319-76312-5_5

unified congregation of scholars (Pemberton 2016; Hillyard 2013), the text draws attention to both conceptual issues and empirical blind spots that pervade and impair the mainstream criminological enterprise. Notwithstanding the broad and diverse range of positions occupied by the contributors, the works that make up this collection take great pains to stress 'the perceived deficiencies of the concept of crime as a lens to capture the full range of harms that impact on our lives' (Pemberton 2016, 4).

Although such deficiencies have been well highlighted before the publication of *Beyond Criminology* (see, e.g., Muncie 2000; Henry and Lanier 1998; Milovanovic and Henry 2001; Henry and Milovanovic 1996; Tifft and Sullivan 2001), students of criminology and zemiology are often encouraged to view the aforementioned text as *the* decisive voice in challenging criminological constraints. This, however, has salient implications. Whilst scholars such as Muncie (2000), for instance, have advocated the utility of reconceptualising criminology's legitimate domain of inquiry so as to decentre 'crime' as the *sole* object of study and broaden its focal concerns beyond myopic understandings of the 'crime problem', some of those associated with the latter movement have been less subtle. Rather than aiming to 'significantly extend the legitimate parameters of criminological study away from a limited focus on those injurious acts defined as such by the criminal law' (Hopkins Burke 2014, 256), the message conveyed by Hillyard et al. (2004b) is to move entirely beyond criminology, as only then, we are told, may we be able to 'take harm seriously'. Essentially, what develops here is a binary between those who wish to extend the legitimate parameters of criminology to incorporate a wider range of un-criminalised and hidden harms as serious focal concerns within its orbit of inquiry, and those who wish to dispense with the discipline entirely. Accordingly, there now exists a palpable tension not only between the concepts of 'crime' and 'harm' but between the disciplines apparently charged with their investigation, criminology and zemiology.

However, we may wish to question the accuracy and efficacy of delimiting strict borders between these subjects. In fact, a closer reading of the term *zemia*, which forms the conceptual basis of zemiology, reveals much in this regard. Much like the Latin origin of the word 'crime', *crimen*, which was heavily imbued with broad notions of harm (Muncie et al. 2010), the Greek term *zemia* denotes much more than harm. Yet despite connoting harm, loss and punishment, amongst other things, the rough translation of zemia as 'the Greek word for harm' permeates the literature (Hillyard et al. 2004b; Hillyard 2013; Pemberton 2016; Loader and Sparks 2011) and reinforces the idea that criminology is for crime and zemiology is for harm. This raises two important questions. Firstly, has the term zemia, as the basis for zemiology, been adequately explored and applied? Secondly, does a more holistic reading of the term substantiate the tendency to position crime and harm, and criminology and zemiology, as diametric opposites? The purpose of this chapter is to explore these questions. By offering both critique and avenues for further development, it is hoped that it may in some way contribute to ongoing discussions relating to the fracture between criminology and zemiology. As Hillyard and Tombs (2017, 296) rightly point out, such dialogical advancement not only signals genuine engagement with previous work but is 'the stuff of healthy academic life'.

Exploring Zemia

Somewhat surprisingly, the nuanced lexical formation of zemia, the central concept around which zemiology has been organised, has received limited attention. Indeed, even in the pioneering work of *Beyond Criminology*, reference to the term zemia occurs only once in a fleeting gesture of explanation. The editors, in an attempt to clarify the naming of this new discipline, note that '[t]he new discipline was termed Zemiology from the Greek Zemia, meaning harm' (Hillyard et al. 2004b, 276). Later, Hillyard (2013, 220) reveals the circumstances surrounding this decision-making process:

> A few of the Bristol Group were chatting in the sun with Professor Vassilis Karydis and I asked him what was the Greek word for harm and he said it was zemia, hence zemiology. The study of harm as a new comprehensive discipline distinct from criminology was therefore born.

This somewhat circumstantial naming process has had profound and lasting effects. Subsequent authors have uncritically adopted this interpretation and continue to advance a seemingly intuitive homology between the term zemia, the concept of harm and the 'zemiological' study of phenomena so conceptualised. For instance, Loader and Sparks (2011, 151) note that the term zemiology 'derives from the Greek word "zemia" meaning harm'. Similarly, Pemberton (2016, 6, original emphasis) states that '…zemiology, derived from the Greek *xemia* for harm, denotes the study of harm'. As a final example, an entry in the third edition of The Sage Dictionary of Criminology adds in parenthesis, following the word 'zemiology', 'from the Greek *zemia*, meaning harm' (Muncie 2013, 430, original emphasis). As a text often recommended to undergraduate criminology students as introductory reading, this vague interpretation of zemia is particularly problematic.

This issue should not be cast aside or rated a second-order concern, a matter of 'mere semantics', since greater semantic analysis is precisely what is required here. As alluded to previously, further development of this line of inquiry is salient for in its current dominant translation/interpretation the term zemia remains devoid of its numerous other connotations and is therefore stilted and rather limiting. Restricted to a single meaning, zemia has become both a limited organising concept of the emerging zemiology and the justification for its sole focus upon 'social harm' and the exclusion of 'criminal harm' (Pemberton 2016). Accordingly, a deeper exploration of *zemia* is needed. This requires an effort to trace with more accuracy the subtle nuances in the lexical formation of zemia (Boukli 2019). In doing so, one is able to register understated interconnections between its various connotations and in turn question the efficacy of the dominant drive to carve out a 'zemiological niche' that focuses only upon a bounded conception of harm, artificially divorced from the broader facets with which the term zemia is concerned.

The word *zemia* is often understood to mean 'hurt', 'damage' (Saunders 1991) and, amongst other things, the imposition of 'harm' or 'loss' upon an individual (Cairns 2015). These understandings are perhaps the closest fit to the dominant reading of zemia currently employed throughout much of the social harm literature. Indeed, within this growing body of work, copious references are made to various forms of financial, physical, psychological and environmental losses and damage which impinge upon basic human needs, rights and planetary well-being. This includes, but is not limited to, poverty, debt, malnutrition, inadequate housing, the proliferation of preventable illness and disease, pollution, habitat destruction, accelerated animal extinction, resource depletion, genocide and numerous other deleterious events or absences, often associated with either too little or too much state intervention (Hillyard and Tombs 2007; Muncie 2000). As an illustration of this 'closeness of fit', Henry and Milovanovic (1996, 103, emphasis added) refer to harms of reduction as constituting '…a *loss* of some quality relative to [one's] present standing'. Moreover, harms of repression are said to occur when one experiences a restriction or *disadvantage*, preventing the achievement of a desired outcome or standing (Henry and Milovanovic 1996). Similarly, Tifft and Sullivan (2001, 198) define social harms as 'actions or arrangements that physically and spiritually *injure* and/or thwart the needs, development, potentiality, health, and dignity of others'; in other words, the perpetuation of social conditions that facilitate the mass production of what Bauman (2004, 5) refers to as '"human waste", or more correctly wasted humans'.

Whilst much of the social harm literature acknowledges the intellectual debt owed to early pioneers such as Sutherland (1945) and the Schwendingers (1975), the debt evidently runs much deeper. For example, Aristotle identifies 'the just' (*to dikaion*) as constituting the mean between gain (*kerdos*) and loss (*zemia*) (O'Connor 1991). Any deviation from this mean is to 'transgress an external standard of distributive fairness' and therefore constitutes injustice (Balot 2001, 27; Boukli 2019). For Aristotle, injustice may also derive from forms of wastefulness that lead to harm to others (O'Connor 1991). Another reading of zemia provided by Allen (2000, 69) indicates that in classical Athenian society 'zemia primarily meant "harmful loss" or "payment"' and understood outside the context of punishment the word 'linked the process of punitive exchange to the process of monetary exchange and to the status of citizens as economic actors'.

Interestingly, the word zemia can also be understood in the context of punishment. According to Saunders (1991, 3), the Greeks historically 'had no single word for "punishment"' but amongst the more notable terms, we find zemia which Saunders (1991, 4) takes to denote '"hurt", "damage", especially loss of money, suffered by offender by way of retaliation, hence "penalty"'. Similarly, its cognate term *zemioun* means '"to damage", "to fine"' (Saunders 1991, 4). Accordingly, the word zemia and its cognate terms describe retaliatory procedures that may naturally be viewed as the enactment of punishment (Saunders 1991). Cairns (2015) highlights the use of the word zemia in Athenian homicide speeches to denote the imposition of a lawful penalty upon an individual who has been convicted, in a legal context, of an offence. Additionally, Versnel (1992) recounts how zemia is also used to convey a kind of ritualised punishment/penalty imposed for the committal of an offence in an attempt to expiate wrongdoings. Allen (2000) also identifies a number of punitive words used in fourth-century Greece to signify punishment, amongst which she notes the word zemia as denoting penalty. In this context, *zemia* and its cognate *zemioo* (to suffer damage) refer to the effect or consequence punishment has on the wrongdoer rather than a 'set of relations between people or their roles in punishment' (Allen 2000, 69). Allen (2000, 174) further demonstrates the punitive tones zemia possesses by referring to Demosthenes' explicit description of laws as a codified delineation of how much anger should be ascribed to various wrongdoings: 'Observe that the laws treat the wilful and hubristic wrongdoer as worthy of greater anger (*orge*) and punishment (*zemia*)'.

From this brief exploration of zemia, we can see that it possesses greater lexical diversity than it is commonly credited with (see also Boukli and Kotzé, this volume; Boukli 2019). Certainly, from this view, there is a discernible relationship between zemia, jurisprudence and the punishment of legal transgression, commonly referred to as 'crime'. Yet the meaning of this relationship is by no means straightforward, for contained within the above paragraph is a complex dyad. On the one hand, we may note the obvious reference in Allen (2000) to the harmful effects and consequences of punishment that animate Hillyard and Tombs' (2007) concern regarding criminalisation and punishment. On the other hand, we may note the equally obvious reference to the notion of proportionality of punishment, a cornerstone of modern-day jurisprudence (Zedner 2004). The crux of the matter is that neither part of this dyad should be elevated or given precedence over the other. Indeed, based upon this revised reading and the clear conceptual linkages that emerge between notions of harm, loss and the punishment of transgression, it seems illogical to force an artificial cleavage between crime and harm. In this context, not to mention the well-established centrality of harm to crime (Paoli and Greenfield 2013), Pemberton (2016) is perhaps inexpedient to separate 'social' and 'criminal' harms in such a way as to perpetuate false dichotomies. Certainly, what we end up with from this bid to carve out a zemiological niche that focusses solely upon the former at the expense of the latter is an unhelpful isolation of two interrelated concepts forcefully corralled into opposing scholarly camps.

Whilst what has been presented thus far is by no means a comprehensive history of zemia's genealogy, it nevertheless opens up a dialogue regarding its lexical scope and underutilised dialectical potential. It is perhaps worth noting that none of this is intended to diminish the contributions made thus far by zemiologists. Rather the intention is to expand, and where necessary reconceptualise, such work by drawing upon the *full range of meaning* contained within the word zemia. When reframed and viewed in this light, the organising theme around which the zemiological movement is built is heir to a broader theoretical and empirical focus than hitherto suspected. Evidently, the upshot is that the current drive to impose strict disciplinary borders between the study of crime and harm is misplaced since an accurate translation of zemia does not support the imposition of such boundaries. To proceed as if zemia simply represents 'the Greek word for harm' is not only conceptually inaccurate, but analytically, theoretically and empirically unproductive. Therefore, instead of divorcing the facet of harm from the broader contexts with which the word zemia is concerned, we must reconceptualise zemia's analytical reach in accordance with its full range of meaning.

Reconceptualising Boundaries

In their drive to establish and develop zemiology as a new and comprehensive discipline distinct from criminology (Hillyard 2013; Pemberton 2016), many of the early zemiologists have been described as resembling quite closely positivist social scientists (Loader and Sparks 2011). This alleged resemblance can arguably be seen in a number of respects but perhaps most clearly in their attempt to secure 'distinct borders and clear demarcations' between crime and harm, and between criminology and zemiology (Young 2007, 9). It may also be seen in the use of official statistics to support the misnomer that '"crime" consists of many petty events' and that such events would not 'score particularly highly on a scale of personal hardship' (Hillyard and Tombs 2007, 11). Such an assertion arguably pays little regard to the experiential reality of crime or the very real consequences for those who experience this reality as harm in the empirical domain of everyday life. It serves no useful purpose to deny that 'crime produces universally discernible and distressing harms to all sorts of victims' (Hall 2012, 160). Nor is it helpful to act as if crime and harm are essentially different currencies in some strange hierarchy of intellectual capital rather than representing two sides of the same coin.

However, this critique must be viewed in context. The principal driving force behind the emergence of the zemiological movement was a desire to 'move beyond the narrow confines of criminology' (Hillyard et al. 2004b, 1). Admirably, the early contributors to this developing programme of study marshalled a movement to fight against the surging tide of a discipline that has historically favoured the investigation and analysis of 'conventional' volume crime. Certainly, it is no secret that politically influential strands of criminology continue to restrict themselves to this crime type and disregard crimes committed by or on behalf of the state, crimes that are technologically sophisticated and/or corporate in nature, and a plethora of un-criminalised harms that emanate from the way in which our current social system is organised. The effect is the obfuscation of the full extent of crime and harm present in today's world. The academic records show quite clearly that paradigmatically dominant strands of criminology have tended to treat crime, deviance and harm as separate yet occasionally overlapping concepts (Smith and Raymen 2016). Rather than view such phenomena through a suitably holistic analytical frame the dominant trend has been towards 'analytical individualism'. This is precisely what the early zemiologists were trying to rectify. Indeed, Hillyard et al. (2004b, 2) make it clear that 'it is a central premise of this book that it makes no sense to separate out harms, which can be defined as criminal, from all other types of harm'.

However, criminology and zemiology continue to be cast in opposing roles, as possessing some innate incompatibility that precludes any hope of collaborative integration. All too often during this casting process criminology is reduced to a 'scarcely recognisable caricature' (Loader and Sparks 2011, 25). What emerges from this reduction is a conflation of diverse and multifaceted criminologies into a singular orthodox 'criminology' indubitably in service of the state and therefore controlled and constrained by governmental agendas and definitions (Hughes 2006, 2007). Whilst such an 'administrative' criminology undoubtedly does exist to some degree, it is *not* indicative of all criminology, or of criminology per se. Rather it is but *one*, albeit influential, form of criminology that emerged in the 1950s (Tierney 2010). Yet, rather than constituting a part of the sum total, this administrative *form* of criminology is often viewed *as* 'criminology *ad totum*'. This simplistic and convenient reading of what criminology is or is not allows the fabrication of a suitable 'straw(wo)man' that is easy to criticise and rally against (Hughes 2006, 2007).

Whilst the pluralistic nature of criminology has to some extent been acknowledged, there is still a tendency to view criminology as a discipline inextricably constrained by the remit of the state and the limits imposed by its drive for pragmatism (Hillyard and Tombs 2017). This is probably true for the most part but not in its entirety. There are a number of important yet understated criminological developments that have undoubtedly taken harm seriously. For example, the increasingly popular *ultra-realism* utilises an advanced conception of harm to explore the reality of our times and explain why individuals inflict harm on others in pursuit of self-interest (Hall and Winlow 2015). In doing so, ultra-realism provides a genuine alternative to the dominant paradigms currently constraining the discipline. This new approach, which has made great strides towards ontologically grounding the concept of harm, represents a discernible break from state-centric approaches and does not attempt simply to extend conceptions of what constitutes 'crime'. In other words, its object of study is not determined by the state. Indeed, ultra-realism has recently formed the basis of numerous stringent critiques of contemporary social issues perhaps thought to be outside the remit of 'traditional' criminological inquiry (Hayward and Smith 2017; Wakeman 2017). For instance, ultra-realism has provided the philosophical and theoretical foundations for the development of a 'deviant leisure' perspective which seeks to explore the harms associated with commodified forms of leisure (Hayward and Smith 2017).

It is salient to emphasise that criminology and zemiology are by no means unified entities. Indeed, both fields are characterised by significant paradigmatic junctures, widely varying views on the nature of 'their' subject matter and the relevancy and legitimacy of content, as well as a fair bit of infighting. Even the most cursory scan through the contents of the voluminous criminology textbooks now available will reveal a scattered history of a discipline very much 'divided amongst itself'. This is also true of zemiology, if perhaps much less evident, for it currently has been unable to pull together all the existing work into a unifying disciplinary perspective (Hillyard 2013). What appears evident throughout the emerging zemiological literature is the presence of long-running tensions between those who wish to abandon and move entirely beyond criminology and those who wish to incorporate the analysis of social harm within the fold of critical criminology (Pemberton 2016). Whilst both criminology and zemiology can of course exist independently from each other, the fundamental upshot is that *both* criminology and zemiology have by and large failed to identify the numerous strands of connective tissue shared by these two social scientific bodies. Rather than celebrating meaningful and productive synergies both bodies are continuously misidentified and often reduced to a series of simplistic signifiers.

Hillyard (2013) has, for example, identified some of the abovementioned tendencies at play in 'criminology's' reaction to the emergence of zemiology. In an admittedly tongue-in-cheek topology, Hillyard identifies five types or forms of reaction that zemiology has received on behalf of 'criminology' which he refers to as colonialists, imperialists, nationalists, reluctant nationalists and misguided nationalists. None of these support an independent zemiology free from the clutches of a 'statecentric' 'criminology'. Quite simply, it appears that influential sections of criminology have not taken the zemiological movement seriously enough. Certainly, this is to some extent reflected in Newburn's (2017) enervations regarding the potential longevity of the movement. However, at the same time that we see criminology's cagy response to zemiology, we witness what might be termed the 'separatist' or 'independent' branch of zemiology offer its own caricatured interpretations of 'criminology'. Interpretations that, as already noted, see 'criminology' as being infinitely confined to an operative view defined by the state and its legal system from which it is seemingly unable to free itself. Yet this ostensibly fails to acknowledge that a great deal of the salient criticisms laid at criminology's door have been immanent. That is to say, they have emerged from within the discipline of criminology itself, emanating largely from the work of various influential critical and radical criminologists who laid much of the groundwork upon which the *Beyond Criminology* project would later tread (Loader and Sparks 2011; Hughes 2006).

In the years since the original publication of *Beyond Criminology*, the simple caricature of criminology noted above has persisted (Hillyard and Tombs 2007; Hillyard 2013; Pemberton 2016). Advances in the realms of critical and radical criminology and the multiplicity of perspectives that have facilitated the expansion of the discipline's intellectual scope (Ross and Richards 2003) have been largely ignored or downplayed. Moreover, there appears to be little acknowledgement that both criminology and zemiology are interdisciplinary rendezvous subjects capable of incorporating and utilising a broad gamut of perspectives to explore and explain pressing social phenomena. There also appears to be little recognition that some of the most significant contemporary advances in both of these disciplines have been made by those willing to expand rather than abandon the criminological imagination by incorporating sophisticated and cutting-edge approaches from cognate fields of study (Hall 2012; Hall and Winlow 2015; Yar 2012; Raymen 2016; Ellis 2016).

Even when some concessions are made regarding criminology's long history of incorporating social harm within its orbit of inquiry, we are often met with yet more confusing distinctions and demarcations. For some, the study of social harm is now firmly and legitimately located within the purview of critical criminology and does not necessarily 'capture the notion of a discipline' (Hillyard 2013, 232–233). Therefore, reference to zemiology is stressed in order to distinguish the emerging new discipline from its criminological counterpart, and more importantly, to demarcate those who wish to 'move beyond' criminology from those who wish to broaden its parameters (Hillyard 2013; Pemberton 2016). For others, however, social harm *is* 'the organising concept for zemiology as a field of study' (Pemberton 2016, 7). There undoubtedly remains some confusion here as to whether or not immutable conceptual differences separate 'zemiology' and the 'social harms' approach. Meanwhile, amidst all the confusion of hastily formed distinctions and demarcations, influential sections of criminology and zemiology continue to jostle for position. Particular schools of thought, which are inaccurately portrayed as being the quintessential face of their discipline *par excellence*, thus continue to overdetermine and trivialise 'conventional' volume crime, and overanalyse and downplay the crimes of the poor and the harms committed by the state. However, amongst all the jostling, these influential strands of criminology and zemiology have missed the point; they have failed to notice the pertinent crossovers that a more collegial approach might otherwise reveal.

Rather than acknowledge that there are numerous patches of common ground to be found between criminology and zemiology, we are instead left with overstated differences predicated upon an inaccurate understanding of what zemia means. Indeed, as has been shown, nowhere in zemia's genealogy is there to be found any innate, natural or inevitable fault lines. Instead, an accurate reading of the meaning of zemia reveals closer connections between harm, crime and the punishment of legal transgression than a number of academics have previously suspected, or have been willing to admit. This is not to suggest that we should reposition the concept of 'crime' at the forefront of our analysis, or that criminal harms represent the most salient dangers facing the social world, or indeed that the answer lays in completely dispensing with 'crime' as an empirical and analytical object of inquiry (Yar 2012). It is simply to note that if we are to attain a more holistic understanding of *both* criminalised and un-criminalised harms and their multifaceted interconnections we must transcend the perpetuation of false dichotomies and artificial disciplinary boundaries. At the very least, it highlights that abstract references to partial notions of zemia cannot be used to support the imposition of false alternatives between crime and harm or between criminology and zemiology.

Instead of facilitating a more holistic exploration of criminalised and un-criminalised harms, the current dominant tendency to force an imaginary dualism between the study of crime and harm results in a failure to consider multiple layers of hidden victimage (Kotzé and Boukli 2016). Indeed, by disconnecting criminal and un-criminalised harm, we risk doing precisely what Hillyard et al. (2004b) explicitly wished to avoid—capturing only isolated strata of contemporary victimisation's multifaceted complexity. This is precisely because 'crime' and 'harm' are interactive and integrative bilateral processes. One may either ignite or emanate from the other in ways that resemble a bilateral implosion or fusion, thereby creating specific yet nuanced and multifaceted phenomena that cannot be subjected to analytical dualism. The early zemiologists undoubtedly recognised and understood part of this complexity for they drew attention to the inadequacy of concentrating solely upon events officially defined as 'crime', which certainly excludes a great many un-criminalised harms (Hillyard and Tombs 2004). However, in a similar move for which they criticise 'mainstream' criminology, some have predominantly trained their analytical lens to focus upon un-criminalised harms to the near exclusion of its criminalised counterpart (Pemberton 2016). This somewhat unilateral focus, generally centred upon state crimes and systemically induced social harms, largely fails to acknowledge 'the second layer of hidden victimage often perpetrated and experienced by the very victims of these state crimes and systemic harms' (Kotzé and Boukli 2016, 820).

In doing so, some sections of zemiology display a tendency to downplay the complex relationship between crime and harm, often labelling the former as 'petty' (Hillyard and Tombs 2004, 2007; Pemberton 2016). However, as criminology has so often reminded us, there is nothing 'trivial', 'petty' or insignificant about persistent offences or incivilities largely perpetrated by and against those in precarious socioeconomic positions (Young 1975, 1988). Indeed, the cumulative effect of such occurrences can have devastating consequences. The tragic case of Fiona Pilkington who, having endured years of abuse from local youths, killed herself and her daughter in October 2007 is a case in point. This, as Chakraborti (2010, 1) notes, undoubtedly 'highlights in no uncertain terms the devastating cumulative impact of so-called "low-level" incidents'. Far from merely representing some unimportant mass of officially defined, discrete and measurable incidents fixed in space and time, 'crime' is fluid (Hall 2005). It ebbs and flows within the broad channels of wider socioeconomic and politico-cultural contexts as it interacts, causally and/or effectually, with serious social harms. Whichever way you cut it, criminalised and un-criminalised harms coexist in a complex relationship characterised by a finely nuanced interplay of harmful absences and events that damage not only individual human subjects but the wider social body.

We cannot therefore continue to arbitrarily separate crime and harm in such a way as to subject one side of the equation to critical analysis only at the expense of the other. To do so evidently results in a rather stilted and incomplete view of such complex social phenomena. Instead, these two facets must be viewed together through a holistic analytical framework developed through a thoroughly integrated approach towards the study of criminalised and un-criminalised harms. This prospect raises a number of pertinent questions as to precisely how we might achieve such a thoroughly integrated approach. Whilst this chapter can offer no definitive blueprint that neatly sketches out the way forward, it can nevertheless be suggested that the first step in this proposed direction must necessarily be to dispense with the unhelpful tendency to cast criminology and zemiology as diametrically opposed entities. Accordingly, when confronted with the increasingly popular question 'criminology or zemiology?' the reply should be an emphatic 'yes, please!', for this is arguably the only logical response.

Towards an Integrated Approach

What is being advocated here is a simple refusal of choice between false alternatives (Žižek 2000). There is no *real* alternative on offer here, for each 'option' simply represents one distorted lens from which to view and make sense of crime and harm. It is akin to being asked to choose between using only your left or right eye, leaving you straining desperately for a broader vision. To choose one over the other is therefore to risk a myopic and limited view of all that ails society, precisely because such ailments are often made up of complex and subtlety interconnected forms of various criminalised and un-criminalised harms. Indeed, the pervasiveness of systemic harms is unquestionable (Hillyard et al. 2004a; Davies et al. 2014), yet such harms, which are subject to intense zemiological, and sporadic critical criminological scrutiny, often precipitate criminal acts that are not always afforded the same attention. In part, this may be due to an entrenched fear that to draw attention to these precipitated criminal acts is to further criminalise the poor. Yet far from protecting the powerless, this equation of analysis with criminalisation serves only to mask the true extent of their plight (Young 1988; Currie 2009; Hall and Winlow 2015). Indeed, not only are the poor subject to numerous social, political and economic injustices, but for many, the path taken to ameliorate such inequitable social circumstances engenders further harm and misery.

For instance, many of those who constitute the indivisible remainder of neoliberalism's wasteful and rejecting logic (Bauman 2000) often have little option than to offset their socioeconomic redundancy by becoming involved in various aspects of the hidden economy (Lea 1999, 2002). Far from constituting 'petty' acts of crime, such involvement is fraught with harm for all those involved. Individuals are forced to flirt dangerously with illegality and risk being absorbed into more dangerous criminal enterprises that carry heavy penalties as they try to negotiate the boundaries between harmful and beneficial criminal activity (Lea 1999, 2002). This should serve as a crucial reminder that the roles of victim and offender are not mutually exclusive but often overlap extensively. Nowhere is this made clearer than in the literature documenting the victimisation of the homeless. This body of literature clearly demonstrates how such individuals suffer 'the ultimate state of victimisation' since they are victimised not only by the state and the general public, but indeed from within the homeless population itself (Fitzpatrick et al. 1993, 366; Garland et al. 2010; Lee and Schreck 2005).

Rather than being viewed as unimportant 'petty' crime undeserving of our attention, such examples should be understood as a corollary of broader systemic harms wrought by neoliberal market capitalism. Accordingly, it makes little sense to view 'crime' as somehow independent of harmful absences or processes that result from the way in which we organise our social system. Instead, it must be acknowledged that 'crime' and 'harm' are two sides of the same coin. Crucially, there are fundamental synergies between criminology and zemiology that, if brought to bear on contemporary academic thought, could facilitate the exploration of a broader range of societal ills than each is capable of achieving alone. Perhaps now more than ever, it is necessary for us to explore with more rigour the interconnected complexities of crime and harm by connecting the dots rather than forcing a wedge between criminology and zemiology. If this is to be achieved, we must dispense with unhelpful dichotomies that incorrectly advance criminology and zemiology as inherently polarised and competing projects based upon a limited understanding of zemia. Not only does such a view show little comprehension of zemia's genealogy, but it encourages both analytical and empirical inertia. As we begin to see ever-growing tensions coupled with increasing levels of visible social dislocation manifest at alarming rates (Žižek 2012), we can afford no disciplinary myopia but require all of our intellectual acuity. Indeed, as Thomas Hardy once noted, 'if a way to the better there be, it lies in taking a *full* look at the worst' (cited in Becker 1975, xi, emphasis added).

This is precisely the point and it bears labouring; a *full* look at the worst necessitates an integrated approach capable of exploring and explaining *both* criminalised and un-criminalised harms. It requires a concerted effort to traverse artificial disciplinary borders and dispel fierce 'topical guardianship'. Instead of ignoring phenomena because they are deemed to be outside of some supposedly predefined remit, or trivialising acts of illegality because they are not deemed 'serious enough', we should have greater cognisance of their complex, multifaceted and nuanced interconnections. Yet despite the desperate need of such an integrated approach, criminology and zemiology continue to be cast as incompatible entities characterised by what are thought to be immutable differences that presuppose a necessary separateness.

Undoubtedly, as Hillyard and Tombs (2017) have recently noted, a great deal more needs to be done in order to explore and establish the relationship between criminology and zemiology. This could perhaps be taken a step further by suggesting that during this process more needs to be done to affirm their compatibility and reciprocity.

Conclusion

Since the emergence of zemiology as a new discipline seemingly distinct from criminology (Hillyard 2013), many of those within its fold have operated under the assumption that zemia, the organising concept around which zemiology is built, simply represents 'the Greek word for harm'. This lingering oversimplification has had profound and lasting effects, not least of all because it has all too often been used as a conceptual hammer to drive an artificial wedge between the study of crime and harm. Having laid the groundwork in the foregoing discussions, it is appropriate to answer the two questions posed in the introduction to this chapter. The answer to both questions is of course a firm 'no'. The meaning of zemia has not been adequately explored or applied; nor does a holistic reading of the meaning of zemia substantiate the tendency to position crime and harm and criminology and zemiology as diametric opposites.

It is clear that there has hitherto been insufficient attention paid to the highly nuanced lexical formation of zemia. Instead, the word has been carved up and trimmed of its numerous other connotations so that it commonly conveys only a portion of its broader meaning. Accordingly, this chapter has sought to trace with more accuracy the semantical complexities of *zemia* and, in doing so, has demonstrated that it possesses a broader range of meaning than previously acknowledged. Far from simply denoting harm, zemia has a clear association with crime and its punishment. In fact, an accurate reading of zemia clearly shows that it denotes closer connections between harm, crime and its punishment than many academics would perhaps care to admit. Nowhere in zemia's genealogy is there to be found any support for the imposition of artificial boundaries or false dichotomies between crime and harm, or between criminology and zemiology. In reality, quite the opposite is true. That is to say that a more thorough examination and application of the word zemia actually implies and facilitates a more integrated approach between criminology and zemiology.

The importance of developing such an integrated approach should not be underestimated for criminalised and un-criminalised harms coexist in a complex relationship and as such cannot be sufficiently explored as isolated phenomena. Indeed, the multifaceted interplay of harmful absences and events or processes that surround both crime and harm cannot be arbitrarily divided and placed into neatly formed categories that 'belong' to certain disciplines. If we are to attain a more holistic understanding of both criminalised and un-criminalised harms, and their highly nuanced and complex interconnections, we must transcend artificially imposed disciplinary boundaries and the perpetuation of false alternatives between criminology and zemiology. Perhaps a good place to start is to acknowledge the speciousness of removing from zemia its clear association with crime and its punishment and forcibly limiting its denotation to various forms of un-criminalised harms. From here, we may begin to analytically reconnect crime and harm and recognise the collaborative potential of criminology and zemiology to provide a stronger lens through which we may take a full look at the worst.

References

Allen, Danielle S. 2000. *The World of Prometheus: The Politics of Punishing in Democratic Athens*. Princeton: Princeton University Press.

Balot, Ryan K. 2001. *Greed and Injustice in Classical Athens*. Princeton: Princeton University Press.

Bauman, Zygmunt. 2000. Social Issues of Law and Order. *British Journal of Criminology* 40: 205–221.

———. 2004. *Wasted Lives: Modernity and Its Outcasts*. Cambridge: Polity Press.

Becker, Ernest. 1975. *Escape from Evil*. New York: The Free Press.

Boukli, Avi. 2019. *Zemiology and Human Trafficking*. London: Routledge.

Cairns, Douglas L. 2015. Revenge, Punishment, and Justice in Athenian Homicide Law. *Journal of Value Inquiry* 49: 645–665.
Chakraborti, Neil. 2010. Future Developments for Hate Crime Thinking: Who, What and Why? In *Hate Crime: Concepts, Policy, Future Directions*, ed. Neil Chakraborti, 1–15. Cullompton: Willan Publishing.
Currie, Elliott. 2009. *The Roots of Danger: Violent Crime in Global Perspective*. Upper Saddle River, NJ: Prentice Hall.
Davies, Pamela, Peter Francis, and Tanya Wyatt (eds.). 2014. *Invisible Crimes and Social Harms*. Basingstoke: Palgrave Macmillan.
Ellis, Anthony. 2016. *Men, Masculinities and Violence: An Ethnographic Study*. London: Routledge.
Fitzpatrick, Kevin M., Mark E. La Gory, and Ferris J. Ritchey. 1993. Criminal Victimization Among the Homeless. *Justice Quarterly* 10: 353–368.
Garland, Tammy S., Tara Richards, and Mikaela Cooney. 2010. Victims Hidden in Plain Sight: The Reality of Victimization Among the Homeless. *Criminal Justice Studies* 23: 285–301.
Hall, Nathan. 2005. *Hate Crime*. Cullompton: Willan Publishing.
Hall, Steve. 2012. *Theorizing Crime and Deviance: A New Perspective*. London: Sage.
Hall, Steve, and Simon Winlow. 2015. *Revitalizing Criminological Theory: Towards a New Ultra-realism*. London: Routledge.
Hayward, Keith, and Oliver Smith. 2017. Crime and Consumer Culture. In *The Oxford Handbook of Criminology*, 6th ed., ed. Alison Liebling, Shadd Maruna, and Lesley McAra, 306–328. Oxford: Oxford University Press.
Henry, Stuart, and Dragan Milovanovic. 1996. *Constitutive Criminology: Beyond Postmodernism*. London: Sage.
Henry, Stuart, and Mark M. Lanier. 1998. The Prism of Crime: Arguments for an Integrated Definition of Crime. *Justice Quarterly* 15: 609–627.
Hillyard, Paddy. 2013. Zemiology Revisited: Fifteen Years On. In *Critique and Dissent: An Anthology to Mark 40 Years of the European Group for the Study of Deviance and Social Control*, ed. Joanna Gilmore, J.M. Moore, and David Scott, 219–233. Ottawa: Red Quill Books.
Hillyard, Paddy, and Steve Tombs. 2004. Beyond Criminology? In *Beyond Criminology: Taking Harm Seriously*, ed. Paddy Hillyard, Christina Pantazis, Steve Tombs, and Dave Gordon, 10–29. London: Pluto Press.
———. 2007. From 'Crime' to Social Harm? *Crime, Law and Social Change* 48: 9–25.

---. 2017. Social Harm and Zemiology. In *The Oxford Handbook of Criminology*, 6th ed., ed. Alison Liebling, Shadd Maruna, and Lesley McAra, 284–305. Oxford: Oxford University Press.

Hillyard, Paddy, Christina Pantazis, Steve Tombs, and Dave Gordon (eds.). 2004a. *Beyond Criminology: Taking Harm Seriously*. London: Pluto Press.

Hillyard, Paddy, Christina Pantazis, Steve Tombs, and Dave Gordon. 2004b. Introduction. In *Beyond Criminology: Taking Harm Seriously*, ed. Paddy Hillyard, Christina Pantazis, Steve Tombs, and Dave Gordon, 1–9. London: Pluto Press.

Hopkins Burke, Roger. 2014. *An Introduction to Criminological Theory*, 4th ed. London: Routledge.

Hughes, Gordon. 2006. Review of Paddy Hillyard, Christine Pantazis, Steve Tombs and David Gordon (eds) Beyond Criminology: Taking Harm Seriously. *Social and Legal Studies* 15: 157–159.

---. 2007. *The Politics of Crime and Community*. Basingstoke: Palgrave Macmillan.

Kotzé, Justin, and Avi Boukli. 2016. Review of Invisible Crimes and Social Harms by Pamela Davies, Peter Francis and Tanya Wyatt. *British Journal of Criminology* 56: 818–820.

Lea, John. 1999. Social Crime Revisited. *Theoretical Criminology* 3: 307–325.

---. 2002. *Crime and Modernity: Continuities in Left Realist Criminology*. London: Sage.

Lee, Barrett A., and Christopher J. Schreck. 2005. Danger on the Streets: Marginality and Victimization Among Homeless People. *American Behavioral Scientist* 48: 1055–1081.

Loader, Ian, and Richard Sparks. 2011. *Public Criminology?* London: Routledge.

Milovanovic, Dragan, and Stuart Henry. 2001. Constitutive Definition of Crime: Power as Harm. In *What Is Crime? Controversies Over the Nature of Crime and What to Do About It*, ed. Stuart Henry and Mark M. Lanier, 165–178. Lanham: Rowman and Littlefield.

Muncie, John. 2000. Decriminalizing Criminology. In *Rethinking Social Policy*, ed. Gail Lewis, Sharon Gewirtz, and John Clarke, 217–228. London: Sage.

---. 2013. Social Harm. In *The Sage Dictionary of Criminology*, 3rd ed., ed. Eugene McLaughlin and John Muncie, 430–432. London: Sage.

Muncie, John, Deborah Talbot, and Reece Walters. 2010. Interrogating Crime. In *Crime: Local and Global*, ed. John Muncie, Deborah Talbot, and Reece Walters, 1–36. Cullompton: Willan Publishing.

Newburn, Tim. 2017. *Criminology*, 3rd ed. London: Routledge.
O'Connor, David K. 1991. The Aetiology of Justice. In *Essays on the Foundations of Aristotelian Political Science*, ed. Carnes Lord and David K. O'Connor, 136–164. Berkeley: University of California Press.
Paoli, Letizia, and Victoria A. Greenfield. 2013. Harm: A Neglected Concept in Criminology, a Necessary Benchmark for Crime-Control Policy. *European Journal of Crime, Criminal Law and Criminal Justice* 21: 359–377.
Pemberton, Simon. 2016. *Harmful Societies: Understanding Social Harm*. Bristol: Policy Press.
Raymen, Thomas. 2016. Designing-in Crime by Designing-out the Social? Situational Crime Prevention and the Intensification of Harmful Subjectivities. *British Journal of Criminology* 56: 497–514.
Ross, Jeffrey I., and Stephen C. Richards. 2003. Introduction: What Is the New School of Convict Criminology? In *Convict Criminology*, ed. Jeffrey I. Ross and Stephen C. Richards, 1–14. Belmont: Wadsworth.
Saunders, Trevor J. 1991. *Plato's Penal Code: Tradition, Controversy, and Reform in Greek Penology*. Oxford: Oxford University Press.
Schwendinger, Herman, and Julia Schwendinger. 1975. Defenders of Order or Guardians of Human Rights? In *Critical Criminology*, ed. Ian Taylor, Paul Walton, and Jock Young, 113–146. London: Routledge and Kegan Paul.
Smith, Oliver, and Thomas Raymen. 2016. Deviant Leisure: A Criminological Perspective. *Theoretical Criminology*. https://doi.org/10.1177/1362480616660188.
Sutherland, Edwin H. 1945. Is "White-Collar Crime" Crime? *American Sociological Review* 10: 132–139.
Tierney, John. 2010. *Criminology: Theory and Context*, 3rd ed. Harlow: Pearson Education.
Tifft, Larry L., and Dennis C. Sullivan. 2001. A Needs-Based, Social Harms Definition of Crime. In *What Is Crime? Controversies Over the Nature of Crime and What to Do About It*, ed. Stuart Henry and Mark M. Lanier, 179–203. Lanham: Rowman and Littlefield.
Versnel, Henk S. 1992. The Festival for Bona Dea and the Thesmophoria. *Greece & Rome* 39: 31–55.
Wakeman, Stephen. 2017. The 'One Who Knocks' and the 'One Who Waits': Gendered Violence in *Breaking Bad*. *Crime, Media, Culture*. https://doi.org/10.1177/1741659016684897.
Yar, Majid. 2012. Critical Criminology, Critical Theory and Social Harm. In *New Directions in Criminological Theory*, ed. Steve Hall and Simon Winlow, 52–65. London: Routledge.

Young, Jock. 1975. Working-Class Criminology. In *Critical Criminology*, ed. Ian Taylor, Paul Walton, and Jock Young, 63–94. London: Routledge and Kegan Paul.
———. 1988. Risk of Crime and Fear of Crime: A Realist Critique of Survey-Based Assumptions. In *Victims of Crime: A New Deal?* ed. Mike Maguire and John Pointing, 164–176. Milton Keynes: Open University Press.
———. 2007. *The Vertigo of Late Modernity*. London: Sage.
Zedner, Lucia. 2004. *Criminal Justice*. Oxford: Oxford University Press.
Žižek, Slavoj. 2000. Class Struggle or Postmodernism? Yes, please! In *Contingency, Hegemony, Universality: Contemporary Dialogues on the Left*, ed. Judith Butler, Ernesto Laclau, and Slavoj Žižek, 90–135. London: Verso.
———. 2012. *The Year of Dreaming Dangerously*. London: Verso.

Author Biography

Justin Kotzé is a Senior Lecturer in Criminology and Criminal Justice at Teesside University. He was awarded his PhD in 2016 and maintains an interest in analysing the 'crime decline', the mutation of crime and social harm. Justin has previously published work in the fields of ex-prisoner reintegration and the historical sublimation of violence.

Big Trouble or Little Evils: The Ideological Struggle Over the Concept of Harm

Steve Hall and Simon Winlow

Introduction

This chapter builds upon the authors' previous work, which suggests that there has never been a 'civilising process' across the course of modernity but an economically functional conversion of harms from physical brutality to socio-symbolic aggression (Horsley et al. 2015). Although harm is integrated into the system's generative core, it appears as morbid symptoms during dysfunctional intervallic periods. The subject's acceptance of core harms and their various manifestations can be best explained in a theoretical framework of transcendental materialism, with a focus on the process of deaptation, which proliferates harms as morbid symptoms appearing in the tension between a changing real world and ossified ideologies. Capitalism can be best explained as a process of managed deaptation,

S. Hall (✉)
Teesside University, Middlesbrough, UK
e-mail: stevehall29@btinternet.com

S. Winlow
Northumbria University, Newcastle Upon Tyne, UK

which constantly puts us at risk of the continuation and unpredictable mutation of a broad spectrum of harms. The criminalisation of harms is maintained in a state of imbalance by the catastrophising negative ideology of capitalist realism, which compels us to legitimise the existing spectrum of harms. Capitalism's conservative and liberal political classes constantly warn us of the far greater harms we would risk should we instigate a process of transformation. Given star billing in an endless cautionary tale, potential transformative harms are condemned as absolute, intolerable and inevitable whilst the system's everyday morbid harms are excused as relative, tolerable and contingent. This dominant ideology operates at the core of the criminalisation process, legitimising negative rights and compelling us to regard specific types of crime as the 'price of freedom' whilst downplaying the harms they cause. As such, this ideology is resistant to the centralisation of zemiology in the criminological discipline.

Harm and the Pseudo-Pacification Process

There has never been a 'civilising process' (Horsley et al. 2015). Rather, a long-running economically functional process, beginning in the late fourteenth century, has moved civil society away from physical brutality and towards socio-symbolic aggression. To explain this historically unique and rather unstable situation, we must understand the basic principles that underlie capitalism's *pseudo-pacification process*. This concept gives us an insight into how liberal permissiveness and conservative repression, often seen to be in opposition, actually operate together as complementary cultural forces in the dynamic psychosocial process that drives forward the capitalist economy. This process has been explicated in greater depth and detail elsewhere (see Hall 2007, 2012a, 2014, 2015), but here we present its primary elements.

From the late fourteenth century, beginning in England and appearing later in Europe, arbitrary interpersonal violence in public space consistently declined up to the mid-1950s (Horsley et al. 2015). This decline in interpersonal violence occurred despite the establishment of a white, patriarchal bourgeois elite as the dominant social group in an unequal social order. However, during the same period, there seems to have been an undulating increase in non-violent acquisitive and abstract crimes throughout the social structure (see Sharpe 1996). The fundamental driver for the decline in violence was not the establishment of a general civilised ethos descending on us from *spiritus mundi* but the emergence of a dual economic need for pacification in an emerging market economy. The two primary interactive functions of this dual need are:

1. The protection of property rights and the reduction of violent interactions between traders to *enhance safer trading activity* throughout the nascent market economy's arteries and nodes—this provided a crucial condition for expanding the *production and circulation of commodities.*
2. The sublimation of destructive and repressive physical aggression into *functionally aggressive* yet physically pacified rule-bound competition for wealth and status represented by the acquisition and display of socio-symbolic objects in a burgeoning consumer culture—this expanded the *demand for commodities.*

Capitalist market economies cannot become efficient and expand under conditions of *arbitrary physical violence*. However, neither can they do so under conditions of *institutionalised altruism*. Mediaeval Distributism regulatory customs and laws institutionalised altruism and a measure of social justice in the economy. For example, restrictions on trading activities, usury, price undercutting, low wages, maximum wages and profits above the level of 'sufficient livelihood' were held in place (Hall 2012a). As urban markets developed, these laws were repealed and new laws and customs were introduced to simultaneously decrease violence and bypass these restrictions. Another important cultural current had already been generated by the introduction of the laws of primogeniture and entail throughout the social structure in twelfth century England (Macfarlane 1978). This atomised the traditional defensive socio-economic units of family and community, creating a *socio-economic tumour*, a process of cell division that cast out anxious individuals to participate in the development of markets as they were forced to fend for themselves by seeking contractual business or employment opportunities.

The combination of resentment, anxiety, ambition and excitement that characterised this new individual was the wellspring of the modern Western competitive individual. It released a powerful current of libidinal energy that was to be harnessed by the supply and demand sides of the emerging market economy. In such a fundamentally competitive culture, the difficult project of dispersing altruistic love outside the parent–child relationship to the external socio-economic world became almost impossible. Fake benevolentism and sentimentalism established the tradition of post hoc charity that masked the functional *obscene Real* at the core of our culture (Eagleton 2009). The modern Western competitive individual's disposition towards maintaining pacified relations became overly dependent on the corresponding expansion of opportunities to obtain material and socio-symbolic rewards. From the Peasant's Revolt through the American and French Revolutions to the present day, this core expectation 'embourgeoisfied' all forms of pacification and rebellion. Projects of political and social solidarity, especially those based on class struggle, became very difficult to establish.

The pseudo-pacification process outlawed arbitrary physical violence for the purpose of pacifying subjects and their relations in such a way that they could compete against each other with more intensity. This major shift in the nature of previously violent competition allowed *relatively safe libidinal energy* to be generated in abundance and supplied to the project of expanding markets. In transcendental materialist terms, the pseudo-pacification process was a complex dualistic form of *permanent managed deaptation*, the systematic disruption of ideologically and culturally coherent subjectivities and socio-economic ways of life and their replacement by symbolic inefficiency, constantly dislocated subjectivities and unstable yet dynamic markets. Liberal-postmodernism's celebration of symbolic inefficiency has contributed to capitalism's final historical dominance in the neoliberal era (Winlow and Hall 2012). Liberals tend to accept capitalism because they think that any attempt to establish a new altruistic order will end up as a totalitarian nightmare replete with variants of the old oppressive order (see for instance Butler 1993; Holloway 2002; see also Hall 2015).

Thus, the stable and just community exists only as a vague and melancholic *memory* of unfinished projects and a *fundamental fantasy* of the general *lost object* (Winlow et al. 2015). Such a fundamental absence constantly creates desire for love and stable community, which supplies immense libidinal energy to the corporate political, media and advertising complex that serves the circulation of today's symbol-rich commodities. Relentless socio-economic disruption and competitive individualism structure reality whilst the market fails to deliver enough in real terms to maintain the credibility of its fantasy. In such a stream of constant failure, diverse *replacement fantasies* of lost collectivism—volkish nationalist groups, fundamentalist religious sects, roots ethnic groups, neo-tribes, bourgeois cosmopolitan networks, street gangs, organised crime families and so on—structure politics and culture in the post-social milieu.

The fundamental harm at the capitalist system's generative core is the constant destruction of the physical and symbolic infrastructure that maintains the individual's integrity and security, a process that liberals of right and left accept as collateral damage necessary for what they hope will be the continuity of progressive social transformation. Neoliberalism's hapless stumble into the recent financial crisis, military interventions and austerity cuts has further disrupted the already broken communities of the politically disunited working class. The recent worrying turn towards the far right in Europe and the USA was a consequence that should have been quite obvious, yet liberalism failed to predict it (Winlow and Hall 2013; Winlow et al. 2017). A zemiological turn in social science could have helped to clarify the situation and provide some early warnings, but the current way we think about harm remains rather incoherent because a clear founding ethical concept has not been formulated.

Yar (2012) suggests that we ground our understanding of harm in Axel Honneth's (1996) revival of Hegelian recognition. In Hegel's famous theory of the master–slave relation, subjects and their identities are always socially interdependent, therefore the dominant is always reliant on the recognition of the subjugated. This ineluctable need for recognition prevents the master from achieving *special liberty* (see Hall 2012a) by breaking free from his/her obligations towards the slave. This is the basis of social recognition, which of course needs to be advanced from its initial source in instrumental interdependency and culturally and legally normalised. For Yar:

The theory of recognition can ground a theory of social harms, firstly, because it seeks to establish at a fundamental anthropological level the 'basic needs' that comprise the conditions of human integrity and well-being (what Aristotelians call 'flourishing'). The theory, as already noted, identifies a differentiated order of such needs through the categories of 'love', 'rights' and 'esteem' (Honneth 1996: 131–9) … [A]ctions such as inter-personal physical, sexual and emotional violence within the family acquire their specifically *harmful* character because they violate the necessary conditions for a person to establish basic self-confidence through the experience of love. Public (including state sanctioned) practices of torture and abuse, theft and appropriation, amounts to a denial of those rights that meet the need for dignity and equality amongst others as citizens. Practices such as market discrimination or symbolic denigration on the basis of gender, ethnicity, sexual orientation and suchlike are properly harms in that they deny those subject to them the experience of self-esteem or recognition of the distinctive worth of their identities and ways of life. Thus for each of the many forms of harm that may be adduced as social problems, we find a corresponding basis in the refusal of that recognition which is the basis of human self-realisation. (Yar 2012, 59–60)

However, Honneth and Yar are assuming that this progressive advance from a social relation in a superseded era has been realised. But this assumption is only a dream at the heart of liberalism's fundamental fantasy. In neoliberal capitalism's harsh socio-economic reality, there has in fact been a regression. Today's capitalists, benefiting from advanced technology, the mobility of capital and the precedence of finance capital, no longer need labour in the numbers and the grounded communities they once did. The masters have escaped responsibility to the extent that they have reached a position of independence, special liberty and narcissistic self-affirmation, a historically unprecedented position where they alone have the right to grant recognition. The fundamental social relation has been severed, politics enervated and dialectical movement suspended. Until the business class can be politically and legally forced into a position where they must attain legitimising rights from the majority before they embark on their potentially disruptive and harmful socio-economic undertakings, the social recognition that Honneth and Yar seek cannot be realised. Making a first move towards mutuality requires a pre-emptive political move that shifts power and authority to an ideologically unaffected and fully informed majority who can grant conditional rights and legitimation on their own terms. It is only one step beyond this to a position where the majority can refuse to grant all rights and legitimation, a structural refusal that Žižek (2008) suggests is the first step towards systemic social change.

Transcendental Materialism, the Subject and the Fundamental Fantasy

Neoliberalism's harms—environmental, social and psychological—continue to mount up (see, e.g., Klare 2012; Hiscock 2012; Smith 2014; Crank and Jacoby 2014; Raymen and Smith 2016). The majority's frustrating acceptance of neoliberalism's plutocratic non-relation and their refusal to make a significant initial political move against neoliberalism can perhaps be best explained in the philosophical framework of transcendental materialism (Johnston 2008; Hall 2012a; Winlow and Hall 2013; Wakeman 2017). As the left realists warned in the early 1980s, critical criminology's tendency to impose a crude comparative structural template on criminology's analyses of harm is an intellectual impediment. Of course, the harms of the comparatively more powerful state and the business class are costlier, but some of the 'little evils' inflicted on everyday people by less politically and economically powerful criminals can be traumatic in ways that are often very difficult to detect, measure and understand as an aggregate. The ultra-realist position (see Hall and Winlow 2015) takes this critique a step further to argue that harms are perpetrated and inflicted on individuals, the social fabric and the physical environment throughout the social structure. Therefore, criminology should broaden its horizon to construct critical analyses of the whole advanced capitalist way of life, from its deep ethics and system dynamics to its cultural forms, subjectivities and everyday practices.

Constructing typologies of harms and arguing about their relative impacts can be useful for lobbying policymakers, but it tells us little about the motivations and justifications behind harmful practices. In the Anthropocene era, the speculative realists warn, not just everyday 'little evils' but most of the large-scale environmental and social harms are the consequences of human actions (Ennis 2011). The transcendental materialist concept of *deaptation* (Johnston 2008) helps us to understand how harms proliferate as morbid symptoms in the tension between a changing real world and obsolete ideologies. Capitalism can be best explained as a process of *managed deaptation* (Hall and Winlow 2015), which constantly puts us at risk of the continuation, unpredictable mutation and deleterious consequences of its broad spectrum of core and peripheral harms (Hall 2012a). The zemiological aspect of managed deaptation is an attendant ideology that categorises and evaluates harms across a spectrum defined at one end by absolute evils and at the other by unfortunate but necessary collateral damage. The political ability to place in the latter category the harms that are the consequences of one's actions allows such actions to be performed, justified and accepted by the actor and the electoral majority of the population, even some of the victims. The problem with critical criminology's structural analyses is that they neglect the fact that some of the more active amongst the powerless accept and act in accordance with these ideological principles (Winlow 2001; Hall 2012a), and therefore make their own relatively small but nevertheless numerous contributions to the overall zemiological aggregate (Hall and Antonopoulos 2016). The harms that are most readily justified and accepted are those associated with 'doing the business' (Hobbs 1988), or in other words clearing the way to outcompete others, make profits and publicly display the trappings of success (Hall et al. 2008).

The negative ideology of *capitalist realism* (Fisher 2009) constantly persuades us to legitimise and accept the whole existing spectrum of harms and their justifications by constantly warning us of the far greater harms we would risk should we instigate a politically driven process of transformation. In a never-ending cautionary tale, potential transformative harms are condemned as absolute, intolerable and inevitable, whilst the system's everyday morbid harms are excused as relative, tolerable and contingent. This dominant ideology operates at the core of the criminalisation process to legitimise negative rights and compel us to regard specific types of harm as the 'price of freedom' or the 'price of progress'. Transcendental materialism suggests that although the forces and processes in the deep system, or what critical realists call the 'intransitive' realm (Bhaskar 2008), seem to act independently of our knowledge and activity, this realm is a product of the historical accumulation of actions that are constantly and systematically fetishistically disavowed and ultimately *made unconscious*. We really know about these actions, and indeed we have always known about them as we perform them or allow others to perform them, but we constantly either deny them or, as we become more knowing and cynical in the communication age, simply accept them as necessary or unavoidable.

In other words, we already know quite a lot about the so-called 'intransitive' systemic realm—the realm of processes and forces that systematise possibilities and restraints in everyday life and operate outside language (see Bhaskar 2008)—and the direct and indirect roles we play in reproducing it. Perhaps we have known for a very long time. Each day we knowingly act to reproduce it, but we fetishistically deny our collusion and thus repress it into our unconscious. The unconscious realm of repressed symbols is not the product of external repressive forces imposed on us by 'power'—the ruling class, patriarchy, biopower, the media or any of these dominant forces of evil in liberal-leftist demonology. We create it ourselves by *choosing to repress* specific aspects of our knowledge and even our experience, which allows us to reproduce the system we inhabit by acting out what we *don't want to know* and have thus convinced ourselves that we *don't know*. In other words, put very simply, we persistently *choose* our own unconscious into being. Constantly deconstructing and changing 'meaning' is of little use when every day we choose to fetishistically disavow the crucial bits of what we know anyway and accept the consequences as unavoidable contingencies with no real causes. 'Well', we say to ourselves every day, 'shit happens'.

Transcendental materialism offers a potent conception of subjectivity (see Johnston 2008; Hall 2012a, b). It draws upon Lacan's three interconnected psychic realms of the Real, the Imaginary and the Symbolic. The Real, which consists of the unnameable irruptions of reality unknown to but experienced by the individual, is the primary neurological source of stimulation, consternation and terror. The Imaginary is the realm of misidentification and self-deception, where, in an attempt to escape the Real's terror, the ego splits and misidentifies itself with spectral objects in the external world. The Imaginary is the primary target of ideology as it is circulated by mass media, consumer culture and the atomised, cynical, ironic and introspective popular culture of neoliberalism's post-political era. The Symbolic is the realm of collective symbols, institutions, customs and laws that allows us to understand and act in the world in ways that are coordinated with other people. A degree of symbolic efficiency, or rough agreement on what important things mean and how we should act in the world, is essential for a civilised existence. Symbolic Orders can be rigid, conservative and hierarchal, but, if they leave gaps in which subjects can freely move, they can be reflexive, egalitarian and progressive. It is the role of science, art and politics to create these gaps and allow forward movement without destroying the whole structure and thus condemning the subject to return through the fragile and temporary comforts of the Imaginary to the terror of the Real.

Žižek (2012), acknowledging the latest neuroscientific research on the plasticity and adaptability of the brain and the neurological system, uses the Lacanian concept of the Real as a void filled with conflicting and disorientated drives and stimuli from internal and external sources, which inflict the proto-subject with terrifying feelings of unexplained uncertainty and fear. Liberals instruct us to celebrate the former and reject the latter, failing to see their unavoidable relation of circular causality. The proto-subject, desperate to escape the Real and the constant misidentifications of the Imaginary, always seeks comprehensible, coherent and substantial meanings in the Symbolic Order. The orthodox notion that dominant forces in the social order *impose* hegemonic signifiers and norms on the subordinate and reluctant individual, which they either internalise to become a subject or resist to become an independent or dissenting non-subject, is completely wrong. Rather, the individual proto-subject has no choice but to *actively solicit* the trap of a coherent Symbolic Order to escape the primary terror of the Real and, when it eventually proves to be insubstantial, the secondary terror of the Imaginary (Hall 2012b). The Symbolic Order is temporarily 'renaturalised' by the subject as it demands the subject's *emotional commitment* to the symbols that constitute its underlying fundamental fantasy. However, these orders can be either closed or dialectical and open. The contradictory gaps that can be dialectically opened up in the symbolic order—the stains on the Lacanian mirror—provide the subject with opportunities to glimpse reality and free itself for the purpose of reflexive revision and progress. These gaps, in which new symbols can be produced, make partial perceptions of reality possible as new knowledge and guides for our actions. A zemiologically informed criminology could open up crucial gaps in which politically important new conceptions of our current reality can be constructed. The Lacanian twist is that, as individuals driven by a primal fear of the void of the Real, before we begin to cut gaps we have no choice but to *first* solicit the ideological trap that the Symbolic Order sets for us.

However, specific Symbolic Orders become ideologically entrenched in specific real historical circumstances. When these circumstances undergo change, the entrenched Symbolic Order becomes obsolete and dysfunctional. Johnston (2008) calls this descent into dysfunctionality *deaptation*, which, ideally, can be counteracted by replacing the once secure but often oppressive and hierarchal conservative order—an oppression that worsens as it tries to return to its fundamentals as it wrestles with an accumulation of fetishistically disavowed knowledge of its own obsolescence—with a reflexive and egalitarian order. But the crucial point is that either order is better than no order at all. Deconstructing and abolishing all coherent symbolism to set ourselves 'free' as detached individuals and relying on spontaneous resistance and renewal from the ruins, as we have been encouraged to do in the liberal-postmodern era, prevents us from overcoming our primal fears. Therefore, this *intensifies rather than transcends* the emotional need for a coherent order of symbols, which can be met temporarily by consumer culture's surrogate order, or—when that mask slips and reality's traumas multiply and bite hard (see Winlow 2014; Ellis 2016) to activate objectless anxiety (Hall 2012a)—more substantially by the return of regressive collective forms such as fundamentalist religion, nationalism and the classical security state. This is how the liberal fantasy and praxis of total individual freedom always descends into oppressive forms of intervention and control.

Because no true individuation can constitute itself without some sort of collective existence to affirm identity (see Simondon 1964), liberal-postmodernism's new post-Kantian cult of indeterminacy, pragmatism, irony and contingency has set us up for permanent insecurity and driven us to *actively solicit* forms of repressive external control. The criminological aspect of transcendental materialism's philosophical framework now becomes clear. For Soper (1995), liberalism's immaterial and disinterested *transcendental subject* constantly dissipates the physical energy needed to activate and sustain ethical and political projects. Draining off this energy into the realm of objectless anxiety has a number of deleterious consequences. It endlessly postpones vital political interventions. It incorporates the subject into a melancholic fantasy of loss in the past and a fearful fantasy of anticipated loss in the future (Winlow et al. 2017). This fantasy intensifies and monopolises culture and the psyche as postmodern liberalism endlessly postpones real political intervention in the capitalist system to produce overwhelming feelings of an impending general loss of wealth, status and security with no means of averting it or receiving some sort of compensation. This propels populations into a generalised dystopian fantasy, a nightmarish vision of an impending fall with no safety net. This acted as the powerful ideological advocate for the ascent of neoliberalism after 1971 when capitalism once again began to descend into recession despite the efforts of the Keynesian stabilisation infrastructure. Now that neoliberalism is failing and an alternative has been accepted as either impossible or contingent on unknown spontaneous processes of organic dissent and subjective renewal, fundamental fantasies from the past return to assert themselves in our midst.

Capitalism's fundamental fantasy is the main contender in this general revivalist effusion. It rests on the celebrated narrative of a socio-economic rags-to-riches situation that never existed for the majority, a world full of opportunities for poor individuals to turn a buck and achieve wealth and status. Now, in the post-political era of capitalist realism, this and all other contending fantasies simply pump a profuse diversity of deaptative ideologies into the air. All are obsolete and none can guarantee the individual's social comfort or economic survival. This places a huge strain on the precarious individual's likelihood of remaining within the law. Criminogenic and zemiogenic tendencies are diffused throughout the social order from the ghetto to the boardroom as individuals bang their heads against a confusing diversity of brick walls blocking off the future. These tendencies are now leading to systemic corruption.

The Truncated Politics of Harm

In the neoliberal era, the quest for symbolic efficiency was systematically abandoned in a flurry of relativistic interpretive paradigms that came to dominate intellectual and political life. All were centrist and quite vacuous. As the quest to represent and intervene in reality was abandoned and the 'passion for the real' (Badiou 2007) fell back and fragmented into the diversity of anachronistic fantasies thrown up by neoliberalism's disintegration, it has become increasingly difficult to tell which criminological and zemiological threats are real and which are constructed: Trump or Clinton, street crime or corporate crime? Neither the neoliberal right's cynical assumption that everything is threatening nor the liberal-left's naïve assumption that nothing is threatening provides any analytical purchase on an increasingly turbulent reality. Recent political events based in a discernible shift to the right in the absence of a traditional left demonstrate quite clearly that populations across Europe and the USA are sensing the need to move beyond post-war liberalism's centrist and politically inactive relativism. Because the politics of harm has been confined to this narrow, relativistic and endlessly procrastinating centre, the intellectual debate, which of course includes criminology, has to a large extent been trapped there too.

When harmful events hit everyday individuals in the face as they experience reality as *concrete universals*, those who control the criminological agenda can choose to either investigate them or ignore them. Centrist pragmatism and the fear of any 'alarmism' that might stir the public's ire and threaten the peace that for the centrists can be indefinitely sustained prevented the criminological gaze from delving too deeply into either capitalism's systemic harms and injustices—environmental destruction, communal disintegration, institutional corruption and so on—or the 'little evils'—violence, fraud, cyber crimes and so on—that some of its less powerful subjects perpetrate in everyday life. Truths that are uncomfortable to dominant or subdominant social groups, truths that might threaten their primary concerns of, respectively, protecting or minimising state power, were systematically ignored, invalidated and marginalised by strictly controlled empirical work. Both groups were determined to avoid the remotest possibility of public alarm. A vast cornucopia of events and complex causal contexts were swept under the carpet. These causal contexts were left to rumble on like the magma chamber and pressure vents inside an active volcano.

The repressed real is currently returning, as it always does, in altered or novel forms—normalised criminal markets in run-down post-industrial areas, drug abuse, proliferating cyber crimes, localised eruptions of homicide, environmental degradation, illegal labour markets, international trafficking, organised child abuse, new types of extreme politics, hidden institutional corruption, deviant leisure and so on—in everyday reality to experience as the morbid symptoms of the interregnum between a disintegrating socio-economic system and an as yet unidentified alternative. Just as Brexit, Trump's election and the rise of a reconstituted far right—or 'alternative right'—across the West have taken liberalism's obsolete radar system by surprise, an unknown proportion of the myriad harms that characterise this difficult interregnum are also entering our lives undetected. The mainstream criminological research industry's recent admission of its own failure to include proliferating cyber crimes in its statistical picture warns us that if our current aggregative representation of the limited category of legally defined crimes is such an understatement, then any honest evaluation of our current representation of harms is likely to reveal a significant zemiological deficit. Whether this deficit is the product of a deliberate political move remains a moot point, but there is little doubt that the now highly questionable narrative of an overall 'international crime decline' has been the perfect foil for post-war liberalism's intellectual and political complacency (Kotzé 2016). There are now sufficient unrepresented zemiological symptoms bubbling up in advanced capitalism's increasingly turbulent magma flow to warrant at least a serious discussion about the need for a thorough re-evaluation of criminology's post-war paradigm.

For Thomas Kuhn (1962), a 'paradigm' is a coordinated set of underlying ethical and ontological assumptions that furnish a scientific discipline with the theoretical concepts that make up its basic framework. All events and phenomena—and, when allowed, systemic structures and dynamic processes studied—are interpreted and explained within this broad framework. Post-war social science's assumptions have been drawn from the various positions that constitute Western political philosophy. Criminology's investigation of its fundamental question of what motivates people to inflict harm on others ended up, after a complex process of censorious filtering (see Hall and Winlow 2015), trapped between the narrow parameters of liberal-left and liberal-right domain assumptions. These are, respectively, social liberalism's take on social deprivation and oppression versus classical liberalism's take on lack of self-control and refusal of social responsibility. Traditional conservative or socialist ideas play only bit parts in this truncated and heavily policed debate. The pre-war attempt to dig to the deepest possible level of systemic socio-economic, cultural and psychological dynamics and construct synthetic theories had produced only crude and often misleading results, some of which fed into pseudo-scientific pathologisation discourses that were used to justify horrific political moves to 'purify' populations. Depth theorisation became caught up in post-war liberalism's perfectly understandable fearful reaction to such horrors and was subsequently abandoned. Analyses of the catastrophic politics that led to World War II seemed to put the issue beyond question, so research and theorisation of the institutional protection of negative liberty represented by what was considered to be a baseline of minimal human rights, or what Badiou (2002) theorised as the 'avoidance of mistreatment', dominated the whole criminological domain. The resulting theoretical frameworks and research programmes only rarely and very tentatively encroach on the field of positive liberties that require political interventions in system dynamics such as investment, employment, mediated representations of truth, everyday ethical behaviour and so on. Thus, the zemiological phenomena that would affirm the necessity of such intervention tend to be ignored and the dominant paradigm remains truncated and tightly closed.

The liberal establishment's refusal to investigate zemiological currents in capitalism's deep structural logic and mainstream culture was energised by this *political catastrophism* (Hall 2012a): the irrational fear that any form of deep political intervention in socio-economic and cultural life, from a socialist or even serious social democratic perspective, will inevitably lead to totalitarian governance and the erosion of negative rights (see Jacoby 2007; Žižek 2001). This grim political health warning has confined zemiological investigation to the field of social and state reactions to crime and harm, which has displaced the investigation of the harmful consequences of capitalism's internal logic and deep structures, processes, cultural currents and subjectivities (see Horsley 2013, 2014a, b). The principal intellectual move here has been the ontological demarcation line drawn between system/structure/process and culture/subjectivity, which of course required the denial that a dominant ideology controls or heavily influences human thought and action (see Abercrombie et al. 1980). Of course, when the dominant ideology of the day is one that denies the existence of a dominant ideology and its connection to systemic structures and processes, the diversion of the population from interventionist politics is complete and the plutocratic establishment, always fixated on its own fetishistic wet dream of *special liberty* (see Hall 2012a), thinks it can virtually do what it likes largely unnoticed, and explain away the consequences as temporary errors, acceptable collateral damage or the fault of its victims. Harms proliferate and too many remain off the radar because right-wing (neo)liberalism doesn't care and left-wing liberalism is terrified of caring too much to the extent that it might have to do something resembling political intervention.

The left's self-inflicted defeat ushered in the post-political era of *capitalist realism*. Now that very few individuals believe that an alternative system is possible, traditional oppositional politics has disappeared to be replaced by arguments about how to construct more just and equal social relations within the system as its stands. Social harms tend to be conceptualised in intersectional terms of identity: usually race, ethnicity, age and gender. So far, reactions to Trump's election have been confined to complaining loudly and organising protests about how his political programme will affect various cultural groups. Where class is included, it is viewed as a stratified yet potentially fluid relation that with the aid of some legislation and attitudinal change can easily be made more meritocratic. It is no longer the antagonistic structural relation to be abolished. The neglect of this structural antagonism and its fundamental systemic harms—economic insecurity, chronic unemployment, disintegrating communities, expanding criminal markets, nihilism, loss of hope and so on—played a major role in the hardening of the working class's sentiments and the drift of most away from the liberal left and an electorally significant minority towards the newly constituted populist right.

Today's biopolitical technicians and human rights technicians are uninterested in the underlying systemic conditions and causes of harms, only in the localised symptoms and how they impact on individuals and various groups of victims. This sets the narrow parameters of the discipline's current research programme. On this restrictive and narrow path, criminology students and the public do not get the best theories capable of explaining the world as it is but those which inform technical strategies solicited by various criminal justice professionals—situational crime prevention, experimental criminology, restorative justice and so on—as they try to combine efficient crime reduction strategies with the protection of minimal negative rights. None of this is driven by curiosity, scientific and philosophical enquiry or the political urgency that our current situation demands. Internal disciplinary pressure will bear down from criminology's dominant right-liberal wing and subdominant left-liberal wing to resist the adoption and development of new philosophical and theoretical frameworks, such as transcendental materialism, critical realism and ultra-realism. This pressure, consisting of permutations of the usual Schopenhauerean tactics of ignoring, mocking, attacking and dissolving by incorporation, will be quite stringent. It is already activated. Unless some genuinely new thinking can assert itself, criminology's zemiological audit and its shift to a more informative and sophisticated zemiological mode, which could inspire and inform new and penetrative research programmes and theoretical frameworks that connect system dynamics with their myriad harmful symptoms, will continue to be a sideshow.

References

Abercrombie, Nicholas, Stephen Hill, and Bryan Turner. 1980. *The Dominant Ideology Thesis*. London: Allen & Unwin.
Badiou, Alain. 2002. *Ethics*. London: Verso.
———. 2007. *The Century*. Oxford: Polity.
Bhaskar, Roy. 2008. *A Realist Theory of Science*. London: Routledge.
Butler, Judith. 1993. *Bodies that Matter*. New York: Routledge.
Crank, John, and Linda Jacoby. 2014. *Crime, Violence and Global Warming*. London: Routledge.

Eagleton, Terry. 2009. *Trouble with Strangers: A Study of Ethics*. Chichester: Wiley-Blackwell.
Ellis, Anthony. 2016. *Men, Masculinities and Violence*. London: Routledge.
Ennis, Paul. 2011. *Continental Realism*. London: Zero Books.
Fisher, Mark. 2009. *Capitalist Realism*. London: Zero Books.
Hall, Steve. 2007. The Emergence and Breakdown of the Pseudo-Pacification Process. In *Assaulting the Past*, ed. Katherine Watson, 77–102. Cambridge: Cambridge Scholars Press.
Hall, Steve. 2012a. *Theorizing Crime and Deviance: A New Perspective*. London: Sage.
Hall, Steve. 2012b. The Solicitation of the Trap: On Transcendence and Transcendental Materialism in Advanced Consumer-Capitalism. *Human Studies* 35: 365–381.
———. 2014. The Socio-economic Function of Evil. In *Violence and Society*, ed. Jane Kilby and Larry Ray, 13–31. Oxford: Wiley and The Sociological Review.
———. 2015. What is Criminology About? The Study of Harm, Special Liberty and Pseudo-Pacification in Late-Capitalism's Libidinal Economy. In *What is Criminology About? Philosophical Reflections*, ed. Don Crewe and Ronnie Lippens, 122–140. London: Routledge.
Hall, Alexandra, and Georgios Antonopoulos. 2016. *Fake Meds Online*. London: Palgrave.
Hall, Steve, and Simon Winlow. 2015. *Revitalizing Criminological Theory: Towards a New Ultra-realism*. London: Routledge.
Hall, Steve, Simon Winlow, and Craig Ancrum. 2008. *Criminal Identities and Consumer Culture: Crime, Exclusion and the New Culture of Narcissism*. Cullompton: Willan.
Hiscock, Geoff. 2012. *Earth Wars*. London: Wiley.
Hobbs, Dick. 1988. *Doing the Business*. Oxford: Oxford University Press.
Holloway, John. 2002. *Change the World Without Taking Power*. London: Pluto.
Honneth, Axel. 1996. *A Struggle for Recognition*. Cambridge: Polity Press.
Horsley, Mark. 2013. Relativizing Universality: Sociological Reactions to Liberal Universalism. *International Journal of Criminology and Sociological Theory* 6: 114–127.
Horsley, Mark. 2014a. *The Dark Side of Prosperity*. Farnham: Ashgate.
Horsley, Mark. 2014b. The 'Death of Deviance' and the Stagnation of Twentieth Century Criminology. In *The Death and Resurrection of Deviance: Current Ideas and Research*, ed. Michael Dellwing, Joseph Kotarba, and Nathan Pino, 85–107. New York: Palgrave Macmillan.

Horsley, Mark, Justin Kotzé, and Steve Hall. 2015. The Maintenance of Orderly Disorder: Law, Markets and the Pseudo-Pacification Process. *Journal on European History of Law* 6: 18–29.

Jacoby, Russell. 2007. *Picture Imperfect*. New York: Columbia University Press.

Johnston, Adrian. 2008. *Žižek's Ontology*. Evanston, IL: Northwestern University Press.

Klare, Michael. 2012. *The Race for What's Left*. New York: Picador.

Kotzé, Justin. 2016. Analysing the 'Crime Decline': Change and Continuity in Crime and Harm. Unpublished PhD thesis, School of Social Sciences, Business and Law, Teesside University, Middlesbrough.

Kuhn, Thomas. 1962. *The Structure of Scientific Revolutions*. Chicago: University of Chicago Press.

Macfarlane, Alan. 1978. *The Origins of English Individualism*. Oxford: Blackwell.

Raymen, Thomas, and Oliver Smith. 2016. What's Deviance Got to Do with It? Black Friday Sales, Violence and Hyper-Conformity. *British Journal of Criminology* 56: 389–405.

Sharpe, James. 1996. *Crime in Early Modern England, 1550–1750*. Harlow: Longman.

Simondon, Gilbert. 1964. *L'Individu et sa genese physico-biologique*. Paris: PUF.

Smith, Oliver. 2014. *Contemporary Adulthood and the Night-Time Economy*. London: Palgrave.

Soper, Kate. 1995. *What is Nature?* Oxford: Blackwell.

Wakeman, Stephen. 2017. The 'One Who Knocks' and the 'One Who Waits': Gendered Violence in Breaking Bad. *Crime, Media, Culture*. https://doi.org/10.1177/1741659016684897.

Winlow, Simon. 2001. *Badfellas: Crime, Tradition and New Masculinities*. Oxford: Berg.

———. 2014. Trauma, Guilt and the Unconscious: Some Theoretical Notes on Violent Subjectivity. In *Violence and Society*, ed. Jane Kilby and Larry Ray, 32–49. Oxford: Wiley and The Sociological Review.

Winlow, Simon, and Steve Hall. 2012. What is an Ethics Committee? Academic Governance in an Era of Belief and Incredulity. *British Journal of Criminology* 52: 400–416.

———. 2013. *Rethinking Social Exclusion: The Death of the Social?* London: Sage.

Winlow, Simon, Steve Hall, and James Treadwell. 2017. *The Rise of the Right: English Nationalism and the Transformation of Working-Class Politics*. Bristol: Policy Press.

Winlow, Simon, Steve Hall, James Treadwell, and Daniel Briggs. 2015. *Riots and Political Protest: Notes from the Post-political Present*. London: Routledge.

Yar, Majid. 2012. Critical Criminology, Critical Theory and Social Harm. In *New Directions in Criminological Theory*, ed. Steve Hall and Simon Winlow, 52–65. London: Routledge.

Žižek, Slavoj. 2001. *Did Somebody Say Totalitarianism?* London: Verso.

———. 2008. *Violence: Six Sideways Reflections*. London: Profile.

———. 2012. *Less Than Nothing*. London: Verso.

Authors' Biography

Steve Hall is Emeritus Professor of Criminology at Teesside University and co-founder of the Teesside Centre for Realist Criminology. He is the author of *Theorizing Crime and Deviance* (Sage, 2012), and co-author of *The Rise of the Right* (Policy, 2017), *Revitalizing Criminological Theory* (Routledge, 2015), *Riots and Political Protest* (Routledge, 2015), *Rethinking Social Exclusion* (Sage, 2013), *Criminal Identities and Consumer Culture* (Routledge, 2008) and *Violent Night* (Berg, 2006). He is also the co-editor of *New Directions in Criminological Theory* (Routledge, 2012).

Simon Winlow is Professor of Criminology at Northumbria University and co-founder of the Teesside Centre for Realist Criminology. He is the author of *Badfellas* (Berg, 2001) and co-author of *The Rise of the Right* (Policy, 2017), *Revitalizing Criminological Theory* (Routledge, 2015), *Riots and Political Protest* (Routledge, 2015), *Rethinking Social Exclusion* (Sage, 2013), *Criminal Identities and Consumer Culture* (Willan, 2008), *Violent Night* (Berg, 2006) and *Bouncers* (Oxford University Press, 2003). He is also the co-editor of *New Directions in Crime and Deviancy* (Routledge, 2012) and *New Directions in Criminological Theory* (Routledge, 2012).

Part II
Contextualising Harm

Whose Harm Counts? Exploring the Intersections of War and Gendered Violence(s)

Sandra Walklate

Introduction

Hagan (2015) suggests criminology has been 'silent' on the 2003 war in Iraq as a 'war of aggression'. The accusation that criminology 'slept' as these events unfolded constitutes only a partial reading of what has transpired within the discipline over the last decade or so. It is beyond question that criminologists have engaged with the international legal and humanitarian implications of this war, the consequences for Iraqi civilians resulting from sectarian violence and state victimisation, and the economic and financial criminal costs of the war in relation to corporate criminality and domestic crimes (see inter alia, Hagan et al. 2012; Whyte 2007). Indeed the discipline has become increasingly aware of the issues generated in policing the borders of 'nation states' impacted by the consequent movement of peoples. Nonetheless, criminology and criminologists, if not asleep, appear to be snoozing in the

---

S. Walklate (✉)
University of Liverpool, Liverpool, UK
e-mail: S.L.Walklate@liverpool.ac.uk

© The Author(s) 2018
A. Boukli and J. Kotzé (eds.), *Zemiology*, Critical Criminological Perspectives,
https://doi.org/10.1007/978-3-319-76312-5_7

face of the *gendered* consequences of war and conflict, particularly as the events in Iraq and Afghanistan have unfolded and resulted in consequences in the Middle East more generally. The 'migration crisis' generated by the events in Syria, in particular, has taken, and continues to take, its toll on those fleeing and on those countries fled to. Arguably the tensions generated by these intersecting events came to a head in Cologne on New Year's Eve 2015 (amongst other locations).

It is against this backcloth that this chapter will explore the questions of, the presence or absence of criminal behaviours notwithstanding, whose harm counts, under what conditions and how a gendered lens might cast some light on how it might be possible for a criminologist, or a zemiologist, to make sense of the presently precarious social conditions across Europe. In order to do this, the chapter falls into three parts. The first will make the case for placing war within the criminological or zemiological domain. Having done this, the second part will consider who and what is included and excluded in that placing when gender is put at the centre of the analysis. The third and final part of the chapter will offer some thoughts on what this centring might imply for our understandings of the relationship between crime and harm.

Placing War Within Criminology

Mullins (2011, 919) has suggested that war has been 'all but avoided' by theoretical criminological analysis. Yet to assume from this that there has been no criminological engagement with war would be wrong. As McGarry and Walklate (2016) have pointed out, Bonger (1916), for example, held the view that 'militarism' served the interests of a hegemonic capitalist economy either to control domestic populations, protect sovereign borders, or exploit 'foreign' territory for capital gain. A similar view was adopted by Park (1941). Writing at the same time, Mannheim's (1941) work documents the criminological implications when war is pursued without just cause. Sutherland (1949) also wrote about corporate crime to include war crimes of profiteering, tax evasion and treason. During the 1970s, the 'metaphor of war' (Steinert 2003) became a key part of the criminological policy lexicon:

the war on drugs, war on crime and war on terror. Such metaphors notwithstanding little of the work done in and on these different issues dealt 'with the reality of war and its sequellae' (Jamieson 2003, 260).

Jamieson (1998, 1999, 2014) has, however, been a voice in this wilderness. She proposed that criminological analysis has the capacity to think about war in a number of different and critically engaged ways. These range from understanding the moral reasoning for violence, the opportunities for a 'school of crime', as an exaggeration of the 'gender order', as generating new crimes and mass victimisation. Yet this agenda has been marginalised by criminology arguably with renewed interest only emerging in the wake of the 'war on terror'. Since that time, a small but significant literature has emerged endeavouring to focus the discipline on war and its consequences. See amongst others, Morrison (2006), Jamieson (2014), Walklate and McGarry (2015) and McGarry and Walklate (2016). Indeed Morrison (2014) argues war, whilst probably under-explored within criminology, has certainly been visible both in form and content. If Morrison (2014) is correct in this view, what shape has this taken?

Arguably Morrison (2014) is alluding to the powerful ways in which wars, particularly post-World War II, served as a conduit for the intellectual imperial influences of American liberal democratic values. Those values have traversed the globe in a different though not dissimilar way to that of colonialism in the nineteenth century. This imperialism is epitomised by the faith in the recourse to liberal law through initiatives like the International Criminal Court intended to tame the excesses of war. From the global to the local the criminological preoccupation with the troubled and the troublesome has easily translated itself into making sense of some of the consequences of war. This has been particularly exemplified in the contemporary policy concerns in England and Wales with the 'deviant soldier' (the returning veteran who finds himself in the criminal justice system). Other concepts emanating from the more conventional criminological canon also lend themselves well to the consequences of war: for example, Braithwaite's considerable body of work deploying restorative justice as a part of peace-building after conflict; Mullins (2009) and Mullins and Visargatnam (2015) documenting sexual violence of war; Hagan and Rymond-Richmond (2009) using a criminal victimisation survey to document the genocide of Dafur and so on.

Neither has critical criminology (nor a zemiological strand therefore) been absent from offering some insight on war and its consequences as some of the work alluded to above more than illustrates. Yet the point of Morrison's (2014) intervention is to encourage a reflection on the nomos of these interventions. To be more specific, such reflection demands a consideration of why these interventions take the shape and form that they do and asks what is taken for granted in their very nature?

Morrison (2014) is particularly concerned with the bounded intellectual imperial imperatives lying behind much of this criminological informed work. This concern is not too dissimilar from Young's (2011) distillation of the 'nomothetic impulse' that for him also curtails the criminological imagination. Both of these writers are alluding to the ways in which the contemporary shape and form of criminology as a discipline operates both theoretically and methodologically in such a bounded way that other ways of thinking and doing become marginalised: lying outside these boundaries they become 'othered'. For the purposes of this chapter, being 'othered' in this way and placed on the margins of criminology of war is nowhere more evident than when gender is centred as a salient variable. This is not to say that researchers within the discipline have not concerned themselves with the gendered consequences of war in all its forms, in particular, its associated sexual violence(s). The work of Mullins (cited) above is exemplary in this regard to name but one. However, it is to suggest that if gender were centred as part of an agenda for a criminology or zemiology of war, it would involve starting in a different place (see also Jamieson 2014). In what follows, this chapter explores one place in which to begin.

Putting the Violence(s) of War and Everyday Violence(s) in the Same Critical Plane

Recently, Crawford and Hutchinson (2016) have made a case for the reorientation of criminological concerns with security (either national or human) towards 'everyday security'. In so doing, they proffer some acknowledgement of feminist interventions that arguably have been long concerned with the question of security in women's everyday lives.

This is particularly the case if that everyday security is understood in part as freedom from violence/freedom from harm. As Crawford and Hutchinson (2016) acknowledge, it is well recognised that the study of security has, to date, been dominated by those concerned with international relations: a preoccupation with security as a big noun, as it were. In this domain 'critical security studies' and its associated schools of thought (Copenhagen, Aberystwyth and Paris), has been significant in framing how security and/or the processes of securitisation are understood. Such dominance notwithstanding the space for other disciplinary and cross-disciplinary input is evident (see Bourbeau 2015) and the capacity for an offering from criminology on this issue is the focal concern for Crawford and Hutchinson (2016). In a similar fashion, it is possible to discern a parallel imbalance in respect of the study of war and its violence(s). This has been long dominated by international relations and other more specific areas like peace studies and holocaust studies. At the same time, criminology and feminist informed work especially, has much to say about the question of violence: from violence on the street to violence behind closed doors to more recently the violence(s) associated with terrorism. Much of this violence is routine, ordinary and every day (particularly in the context of domestic violence), as Genn (1988) observed: 'just part of life'. It is 'folded into everyday life' (Das 2007, 14), silenced (Jordan 2011), smoothed out (Machado et al. 2010), with the evidence being routinely denied (Walby et al. 2016). So, following on from the implications of the question raised by Mooney (2007) concerning why violence against women was public anathema but a private commonplace all at the same time, the provocation posed in this chapter is: what are the implications for criminology when the violence(s) of war and the violence(s) against women are put into the same critical plane? Or perhaps expressed slightly differently, whose harm counts, when and why?

In some respects, it could be argued that this provocation is not so profound. For example, feminist researchers and campaigners have long used the language of war to capture the nature of women's everyday lives. Frances Power-Cobbe (1878) talked of 'wife torture in England', Robin Morgan (1989) talked of women's fears as everyday terrorism, and more recently Pain (2014) has analysed her findings on violence against women in the same vein. If this body of knowledge is placed side by side with that work documenting the experience of war as gendered, then the simplicity of this provocation becomes transparent. From the sexual violence(s) documented by Mullins and Visargatnam (2015) (see also Davies and True 2015); to the disruption of war, conflict and violence associated with sexual trafficking and labour exploitation (True 2012), to the gendered nature of migration prompted by fleeing from conflicts (Hudson 2016); all of these are everyday violence(s) for those affected by them. Taken together they constitute powerful evidence for placing these experiences within the same critical plane as violence against women as more conventionally understood. There is, however, a conceptual framework that enables criminology (or even zemiology) to do this derived from feminist-informed work.

One place to start might be with the work of Kelly (1988). She introduced the concept of a 'continuum of sexual violence'. This concept was rooted in listening to women's voices and experiences of sexual violence and its impact. She put those experiences, from 'flashing' to murder, whether in public or private, whether single or multiple offences, from single to multiple offenders, all in the same conceptual plane. This was violence as experienced by women over and through time. This intervention fundamentally challenged conventional thinking preoccupied as it was by considering these 'offences' as separate and separable. In a parallel vein, Cockburn (2013, 2) offers a further challenge. Her development of a continuum of violence runs as follow:

> For instance, a continuum of scale of force: so many pounds per square inch when a fist hits a jaw; so many more when a bomb hits a military target. A continuum on a social scale: violence in a couple, in a street riot, violence between nations. And place: a bedroom, a street, a police cell, a continent. Time: during a long peace, pre-war, in armed conflict, in periods we call 'postconflict'. And then type of weapon: hand, boot, machete, gun, missile.

Again Cockburn (2013) challenges the assumption, in all the examples she cites, that such behaviours are separate and separable. Yet once they are put within the same conceptual frame of a continuum of violence (qua Bourke 2015) the utility of such thinking is called into question.

So placing war, its genesis and consequences, within the conceptual frame of a continuum, as suggested above, poses a challenge for criminology: are such violence(s) separate and separable? Moreover, this is a challenge interestingly resulting in asking very conventional criminological questions; like, for example, who is violent, who are they violent against, whose violence counts and under what conditions, how is this violence counted, what renders such violence visible and/or invisible within the discipline, and finally, having made it count, what conceptual tools does criminology have to make sense of violence? (These questions and the answers to them are developed more fully by McGarry and Walklate 2016). In whatever shape and form such questions as these are asked the answer, for the most part, is that men, on all fronts are the perpetrators of violence; and that violence is perpetrated mostly on women and sometimes on other men frequently endorsed by states peopled by men (Connell 2016). Once these 'different' violence(s) are placed side by side in this way the gendered nature of violence is stark. Sometimes perpetrated in contexts in which, as Ruggiero (2015, 29) observes, 'torture becomes a patriotic act while rape may become an act of heroism' and sometimes perpetrated in the safe haven of the home (see also Carrington 2015). Despite the apparent simplicity associated with placing the violence(s) of war and the violence(s) against women in the same critical plane, the problems generated for criminology in so doing are almost palpable. This becomes particularly pertinent when reflecting on the silences within the discipline concerning these interconnections in the aftermath of the events in Cologne (and elsewhere) during 2016.

Making Sense of Cologne, 2016

In January 2015, newspaper headlines carried messages such as 'Migrant rape fears across Europe as women are told not to go out at night alone' (*Daily Mail Online*, 9 January 2016). Such headlines featured in the aftermath of reported sexual attacks by migrants on women in cities in Switzerland, Finland, Sweden, Austria and Germany. The most telling of these, and the most widely reported, appeared to be those reputedly occurring in Cologne on New Year's Eve. Hutton (2016) reports:

In Cologne up to 1,000 men, many described as of North African or Arab appearance, and aged between 18 and 35, gathered in the huge square between Cologne cathedral and the main railway station. They let off fireworks and robbed passers-by. Of the complaints, 117 involved sexual assault, including two allegations of rape.

Of course, in the aftermath of a peak in migration to Europe consequent to the ongoing conflict in Syria, in particular, such events were always going to provoke comment. During the summer of 2015 media coverage of the migration, crisis had been equally prescient in excavating public feelings about the plight of Syrian refugees with the widely promoted picture of Aylan Kurdi whose young, dead body was washed ashore on the Turkish coast having drowned in the process of fleeing the war in Syria. It was not a surprise that right wing politicians and activist groups were quick to seize the opportunity presented by the events in Cologne in support of their case for not admitting any more refugees to Germany (Hutton 2016). In the midst of the political furore generated, the events in Cologne nonetheless put to the fore some important issues. In Germany, the slowness of the police response on New Year's Eve has been subjected to critical scrutiny (followed by the Chief of Police being relieved of his duties) as was the slowness of the media to take the reports being made on board. The speed at which women were blamed for what had happened was also equally remarkable. The political pressure put on Angela Merkel's open policy towards refugees was only to be expected. In addition, some commentators began to ask quite fundamental questions about the problems and possibilities of cultural coexistence (see inter alia, Hutton 2016). However, in the commentary and debate which followed these events, few of them, with the possible exception of Klein (2016), placed these events in the overall context of Western engagement in war in the Middle East more generally, and even fewer placed them within the context of criminological or zemiological debates, with the exception of Hudson (2016), who is in fact not a criminologist or zemiologist. This criminological and zemiological lacuna is the point of what follows.

Hudson (2016), a political scientist with interests in gender and security, comments on what she calls, 'Europe's man problem'. Focusing, in particular, on the migration policy dilemmas being faced by Sweden, she goes on to point out the wider issues of concern for a number of countries in Europe in which the changing balance of the sex ratio has largely gone, if not unnoticed, at least not commented on. According to the International Organisation of Migration during 2015, 66.26% of adult migrants registered through Italy and Greece were male. A figure that becomes particularly problematic when disaggregated by age: a high proportion of these registered are unaccompanied minors (particularly males under 18) and with that status come entitlements. Moreover, it is important to remember that these constitute only those *officially* registered as migrants. Nonetheless, Hudson (2016, 5) goes on to point out:

> Numerous empirical studies have shown that sex ratios correlate significantly with violence and property crime—the higher the sex ratio, the worse the crime rate. Our research also found a link between sex ratios and the emergence of both violent criminal gangs and anti-government movements. It makes sense: When young adult males fail to make the transition to starting a household—particularly those young males who are already at risk for sociopathic behavior due to marginalization, common concern among immigrants—their grievances are aggravated. There are also clearly negative effects for women in male-dominated populations. Crimes such as rape and sexual harassment become more common in highly masculinized societies, and women's ability to move about freely and without fear within society is curtailed.

Hudson's point is that few governments (perhaps with the exception of Canada) appear to be taking these potential consequences seriously. My point is criminologists who also write about these issues appear not to be taking these particular consequences on board either. The criminological canon is replete with evidence in support of her observations not least of which is the often cited work of Braithwaite (1989). His first rule of criminological explanation is that crime is for the most part committed by young men.

However, a German forensic psychologist, Dr. Rudolf Egg, was appointed to investigate the cause and consequences of these events. His report, issued in October 2016, draws on the 'broken windows' thesis and suggests the majority of those who went to Cologne on that evening did not go to commit sexual offenses but '[i]t was only after the men realized that police were not intervening, that the attackers felt encouraged to carry out the sexual assaults' (Brady, 5 October 2016). Žižek (2016) offers a different analysis of these events. He situates these events within an historical appreciation of the carnival. Thus,

> During carnival the common people suspended the normal rules of behavior and ceremoniously reversed the social order or turned it upside down in riotous procession. Carnival was high season for hilarity, sexuality, and youth run riot, and the crowd often incorporated cat torture into its rough music. While mocking a cuckold or some other victim, the youths passed around a cat, tearing its fur to make it howl. Faire le chat, they called it. The Germans called it Katzenmusik, a term that may have been derived from the howls of tortured cats. The torture of animals, especially cats, was a popular amusement throughout early modern Europe. The power of cats was concentrated on the most intimate aspect of domestic life: sex. Le chat, la chatte, le minet mean the same thing in French slang as "pussy" does in English, and they have served as obscenities for centuries.

Whilst there may well be historical continuities to be drawn out here in gendered understandings of carnival, in both accounts above the wider criminological/victimological and zemiological context is lost.

To press this point a little further, in the first newsletter sent out to all members of the European Society of Criminology in 2016, the agenda that the issue of migration might pose for criminology featured in some detail. Guia and Skilbrei (2016) offer the following list of concerns: the relationship between the decision to migrate and migration policies, media coverage of migration issues, the role of migration brokers, the relationship between migration and trafficking, hate crimes, integration and discrimination, and the relationship between migration and crime. In respect of this last item, they make the following observation:

> For example, the incidents that took place on Cologne on New Year's Eve, and, not least, the question of whether police there and other places intentionally have been undercommunicating the level of crime committed by migrants from their populations, have particularly highlighted the link between migration and crime. As a result of this, media

commentaries raised the question of how crime statistics should be registered. (Guia and Skilbrei 2016, p. 8)

In some ways, the presences and the absences in this statement speak for themselves. It is important to note that this observation does not imply that the list of concerns for criminology produced by Guia and Skilbrei (2016) is not important or should not be subjected to further scrutiny. Indeed the discipline has been proactively engaged in issues related to borders and border control, trafficking and organised crime, hate crime and so on for several decades (see inter alia, Pickering and Ham 2014; Aas and Grundhus 2015). That work in these areas could be developed and more nuanced is, without doubt, the case. Moreover, Guia and Skilbrei (2016) are, by implication, pointing to an important mechanism of silencing (in the nature of the available evidence) in contributing to when and how events become recognised as problems of harm. However, in this particular instance (remembering that Cologne was only one city in which complaints of sexual assault and sexual harassment occurred) the absence of the wider context of the underlying causal mechanisms prompting the contemporary migration to Europe (war and conflict in the Middle East), particularly its gendered characteristics and its potential consequences, is telling. In some respects, it speaks volumes about the historical capacity for the discipline to proceed as if the violence(s) of war and violence(s) against women are separate and separable.

Nonetheless, at the level of policy and practice, some countries have begun to grasp this knotty problem. Hudson (2016) references Canada. Norway has adopted a slightly different approach by requiring all new migrants to attend courses on gender equality and what this means for how women are treated. However, much of criminology and zemiology remain silent on these issues. Herein lies the implicit denial of the gendered nature of violence(s) and its consequences. It is a denial of connections long recognised by the kind of feminist interventions outlined earlier. How might a disciplinary lacuna such as this be understood? The answer can be found in two interrelated issues: criminology's intimate relationship with a concept of crime as the uniform and unifying signifier for the existence of the discipline and the dominance within the discipline of a particular version of criminology.

Conclusion: Crime, Harm and (Liberal) Criminology

The harms generated by conflicts and their associated violence(s) whether those conflicts be interpersonal, institutional, structural, regional or global, are well documented in the academic literature and in our everyday collective exposure to wide-ranging media reportage. Indeed they are also well documented in the criminological literature (as alluded to above) and the victimological literature. In the case of the latter, the connections between the emergence of victimology as a (sub)-discipline of criminology is intimately connected to the aftermath of the Holocaust with Mendelsohn (considered as one of the Founding Fathers of this area of investigation and attributed with assigning the label victimology to it) profoundly concerned that victimology took the harms of war as one of its focal concerns (Victimology has a less happy relationship with feminism which is also well documented). That many of the harms drawn together here are also criminal is self-evident. Nonetheless, disputes remain concerning the way in which crime, taken to be that which is defined as criminal in law, takes precedence over harm in setting an agenda for criminology.

However, it is the contention of this chapter that, in some respects, this crime/harm and criminology/zemiology debate is set up as if these two exist in binary opposition to each other in terms of framing the concerns of the discipline, and as a result is not helpful. Increasingly, as the presence of victim-focused studies (both individual and collective, see McGarry and Walklate 2015) have gained momentum, embracing the impact of all kinds of harms generated by offences recognised and responded to as criminal, alongside those not so labelled, has arguably become a less problematic feature of both the discipline and criminal justice policy. The latter illustrated, for example, by the preoccupations with 'emotionally sensitive justice' (Sherman 2003). Moreover, it should be noted that the problems of recognition (what and who is recognised, understood and responded to in terms of harm), pose equally difficult questions for the zemiologist as for the criminologist. As Quinney (1972) observed quite some time ago, such processes are in many ways arbitrary and can result in different hierarchies whether that be a hierarchy of victimhood (Carrabine et al. 2004) or a hierarchy of harm

(Featherstone and Kaladelfos 2014). In some respects, it can be argued that this harm/crime debate deflects attention from a much more fundamental problematic for the discipline, epitomised in the separation of war's violence(s) from other violence(s) (focused on here in terms of violence(s) against women). This lies in the dominance of what Young (2011) has called the 'nomothetic impulse'.

Young (2011) offers a compelling argument that if criminology is to make sense of issues prescient across the globe it needs to loosen the conceptual and methodological hold that, what he calls the bogus of positivism, has over the discipline. For Young (2011), the bogus of positivism embeds a fundamental contradiction within the discipline. This contradiction projects American (liberal) values particularly those centring individualism, on criminology across the globe. This projection of values is developed in Morrison's (2014) elucidation of criminology's nomos and the imperialistic processes inherent in this. As Young (2011) argues, this liberal vision of knowledge and the knowledge production process facilitates liberal analyses of othering, demonization and denial. All of which are prescient in treating violence(s) against women and the violence(s) of war as separate and separable as discussed here. The harm done by this version of (liberal) criminology, takes its toll on the discipline across the globe. One way out of the conundrum that this presents for the discipline is to begin to think differently about the gendered interconnections with which this chapter has been concerned and to challenge the silences that pervade about them.

References

Aas, Katja F., and Helene O.I. Gundhus. 2015. Policing Humanitarian Borderlands: Frontex, Human Rights and the Precariousness of Life. *British Journal of Criminology* 55: 1–18.

Bonger, Willem A. 1916. *Criminality and Economic Conditions*. Boston: Little, Brown and Company.

Bourbeau, Philippe (ed.). 2015. *Security: Dialogue across Disciplines*. Cambridge: Cambridge University Press.

Bourke, Joanna. 2015. *Deep Violence*. Berkeley: Counterpoint Press.

Brady, Kate. 2016. Germany Floats Bonus for Rejected Asylum Seekers to Go Home. *Deutsche Welle*, Oct 5. http://www.dw.com/en/forensic-psychologist-report-sheds-new-light-on-cologne-new-years-eve-assaults/a-35962769.

Braithwaite, John. 1989. *Crime, Shame and Reintegration*. Cambridge: Cambridge University Press.

Carrabine, Eamonn, Paul Iganski, Maggy Lee, Ken Plummer, and Nigel South. 2004. *Criminology: A Sociological Introduction*. London: Routledge.

Carrington, Kerry. 2015. *Feminism and Global Justice*. London: Routledge.

Cockburn, Cynthia. 2013. Towards a Different Common Sense. www.cynthiacockburn.org.

Connell, Raewyn. 2016. 100 Million Kalashnikovs: Gendered Power on a World Scale. *Debate Feminista* 51: 3–17.

Crawford, Adam, and Steven Hutchinson. 2016. Mapping the Contours of 'Everyday Security': Time, Space, and Emotion. *British Journal of Criminology* 56: 1184–1202.

Das, Veena. 2007. *Life and Words*. California: University of California Press.

Davies, Sara E., and Jacqui True. 2015. Reframing Conflict-Related Sexual and Gender-Based Violence: Bringing Gender Analysis Back In. *Security Dialogue* 46: 495–512.

Featherstone, Lisa, and Amanda Kaladelfos. 2014. Hierarchies of Harm and Violence: Historicising Familial Sexual Violence in Australia. *Australian Feminist Studies* 29: 306–324.

Genn, Hazel. 1988. Multiple Victimisation. In *Victims of Crime: A New Deal?* ed. Mike Maguire and John Pointing, 90–100. Buckingham: Open University Press.

Guia, Maria J., and May-Len Skilbrei. 2016. How the Current 'Migration Crisis' Challenges European Criminologists. *ESC Newsletter* 1: 4–11.

Hagan, John. 2015. While Criminology Slept: A Criminal War of Aggression in Iraq. *The Criminologist: The Official Newsletter of the American Society of Criminology* 40: 2–4.

Hagan, John, and Wenona Rymond-Richmond. 2009. *Darfur and the Crime of Genocide*. Cambridge: Cambridge University Press.

Hagan, John, Joshua Kaiser, Daniel Rothenberg, Anna Hanson, and Patricia Parker. 2012. Atrocity Victimisation and the Costs of Economic Conflict Crimes in the Battle for Baghdad and Iraq. *European Journal of Criminology* 9: 481–498.

Hudson, Valerie. 2016. Europe's Man Problem. *Politico*, January 11.

Hutton, Will. 2016. After Cologne, the Uneasy Question: Is Cultural Coexistence Still Possible? *The Guardian*, January 10.

Jamieson, Ruth. 1998. Towards a Criminology of War in Europe. In *The New European Criminology: Crime and Social Order in Europe*, ed. Vincenzo Ruggiero, Nigel South, and Ian Taylor, 480–506. London: Routledge.
———. 1999. Councils of War. *Criminal Justice Matters* 34: 25–26.
———. 2003. Introduction. *Theoretical Criminology, Special Issue: War, Crime and Human Rights* 7: 259–263.
——— (ed.). 2014. *The Criminology of War*. London: Ashgate.
Jordan, Jan. 2011. Silencing Rape, Silencing Women. In *Handbook on Sexual Violence*, ed. Jennifer M. Brown and Sandra L. Walklate, 253–286. London: Routledge.
Kelly, Liz. 1988. *Surviving Sexual Violence*. Oxford: Polity Press.
Klein, Naomi. 2016. Let Them Drown. *London Review of Books* 38: 11–14.
Machado, Carla, Ana R. Dias, and Claudia Coelho. 2010. Culture and Wife Abuse. In *International Handbook of Victimology*, ed. Shlomo G. Shoham, Paul Knepper, and Martin Kett, 639–668. Boca Raton, FL: CRC Press.
Mannheim, Hermann. 1941. *War and Crime*. London: Watts & Co.
McGarry, Ross, and Sandra Walklate. 2015. *Victims: Trauma, Testimony and Justice*. London: Routledge.
——— (eds.). 2016. *The Palgrave Handbook of Criminology and War*. London: Palgrave.
Mooney, Jayne. 2007. Shadow Values, Shadow Figures: Real Violence. *Critical Criminology* 15: 159–170.
Morgan, Robin. 1989. *The Demon Lover: On the Sexuality of Terrorism*. New York: Norton Books.
Morrison, Wayne. 2006. *Criminology, Civilization and the New World Order*. Oxon: Routledge.
———. 2014. War and Normative Visibility: Interactions in the Nomos. In *Invisible Crimes and Social Harms*, ed. Pamela Davies, Peter Francis, and Tanya Wyatt, 178–198. London: Palgrave-Macmillan.
Mullins, Christopher W. 2009. 'He Would Kill Me with His Penis': Genocidal Rape in Rwanda as a State Crime. *Critical Criminology* 17: 15–33.
———. 2011. War Crimes in the 2008 Georgia–Russia Conflict. *The British Journal of Criminology* 51: 918–936.
Mullins, Christopher W., and Nishanth Visagaratnam. 2015. Sexual and Sexualised Violence in Armed Conflict. In *Criminology and War: Transgressing the Borders*, ed. Sandra Walklate and Ross McGarry, 139–157. London: Routledge.
Pain, Rachel. 2014. Everyday Terrorism: Connecting Domestic Violence and Global Terrorism. *Progress in Human Geography* 38: 531–550.

Park, Robert E. 1941. The Social Function of War Observations and Notes. *American Journal of Sociology* 46: 551–570.
Pickering, Sharon, and Julie Ham. 2014. Hot Pants at the Border: Sorting Sex Work from Trafficking. *British Journal of Criminology* 54: 2–19.
Power-Cobbe, Frances. 1878. Wife Torture in England. *The Contemporary Review* 32: 55–87.
Quinney, Richard. 1972. Who is the Victim? *Criminology* 10: 314–323.
Ruggiero, Vincenzo. 2015. War and the Death of Achilles. In *Criminology and War: Transgressing the Borders*, ed. Sandra Walklate and Ross McGarry, 21–37. London: Routledge.
Sherman, Lawrence W. 2003. Reason for Emotion: Reinventing Justice with Theories, Innovations, and Research. *Criminology* 41: 1–38.
Steinert, Heinz. 2003. The Indispensable Metaphor of War: On Populist Politics and the Contradictions of the State's Monopoly of Force. *Theoretical Criminology, Special Issue: War, Crime and Human Rights* 7: 265–291.
Sutherland, Edwin H. 1949. *White Collar Crime*. New York: Holt, Rinehart and Winston.
True, Jacqui. 2012. *The Political Economy of Violence Against Women*. Oxford: Oxford University Press.
Walby, Sylvia, Jude Towers, and Brian Francis. 2016. Is Violent Crime Increasing or Decreasing? *British Journal of Criminology* 56: 1203–1234.
Walklate, Sandra, and Ross McGarry (eds.). 2015. *Criminology and War: Transgressing the Borders*. London: Routledge.
Whyte, Dave. 2007. The Crimes of Neo-Liberal Rule in Occupied Iraq. *British Journal of Criminology* 47: 177–195.
Young, Jock. 2011. *The Criminological Imagination*. London: Polity Press.
Žižek, Slavoj. 2016. The Cologne Attacks Were an Obscene Version of Carnival. *The New Statesman*, January 13.

Author Biography

Sandra Walklate is Eleanor Rathbone Chair of Sociology at the University of Liverpool conjoint Chair of Criminology at Monash University, Melbourne. She was awarded the British Society of Criminology's outstanding achievement award for contribution to the discipline in 2014 and is currently Editor in Chief of the British Journal of Criminology.

Gender Murder: Anti-Trans Rhetoric, Zemia, and Telemorphosis

Avi Boukli and Flora Renz

Introduction

In her seminal book 'Sex/Gender: Biology in a Social World', Anne Fausto-Sterling (2012, 119) asserts '[t]he development of sex and gender in humans is layered'. From chromosomal to foetal hormonal and anatomical, there are several layers of sexes/genders that develop in utero. This multiplicity results in 'the multi-layered phyllo dough … pastry we call sex-gender' (Fausto-Sterling 2012, 4). Therefore, it is difficult, if not impossible, to determine whether behavioural differences between men and women, often referred to as 'sex', do actually have a biological basis or are 'merely' the consequence of social conditioning, recurrently typified as 'gender' (Fausto-Sterling 2012, 42). It is further impossible to pin down the specific biological and environmental

---

A. Boukli (✉)
The Open University, Milton Keynes, UK
e-mail: avi.boukli@open.ac.uk

F. Renz
Kent Law School, University of Kent, Canterbury, UK

factors that contribute to the development of gender and sexuality. Particularly in the field of genetic contribution to gender non-conformity, if genes and environment interact then the effect of a gene might be great in one environment and small or non-existent in another. But we currently 'really don't know what the relevant environments are' (Fausto-Sterling 2012, 93) in order to study them. Similarly, current research suggests that sexuality is perhaps better understood as dynamic and multidimensional, rather than as a concept that follows causally from the sex and gender identity of a person (Fausto-Sterling 2012, 98). As such there seems to be a move towards more fluid and diverse understandings of sex, gender, and sexuality. Extending this line of reasoning, Claire Colebrook (2012) suggests that sexual difference and a binary understanding of sex as ordering principles of society *must* ultimately become extinct for humanity to develop and survive in a changing environment.

Moreover, in the Global North, over the last ten years trans activists and scholars have campaigned extensively and often successfully to amend the ways in which states record sex and gender to allow for the inclusion of trans, intersex, and non-binary people (see, e.g., Currah and Moore 2009; House of Commons 01 December 2016; Press Association 2 January 2016). These efforts have led to the creation of mechanisms that allow for a change of legal gender (for the UK see, e.g., Renz 2015), the introduction of new gender 'options' on passports and birth certificates (Australian Government July 2013), and the removal of gender as an identity marker on some official documents. At the same time, trans characters are increasingly included in mainstream television programmes such as *Hollyoaks* (Kilkelly 15 May 2014), *Orange is the New Black* (Steinmetz 29 May 2014), and *Transparent* (Hughes 23 January 2015), suggesting a growing social and cultural awareness of trans issues. This is also evident in the inclusion of trans voices in national newspapers. The US-based *Time* magazine has argued that society has reached the 'Transgender Tipping Point' with trans rights becoming the new civil rights frontier (Steinmetz 29 May 2014).

Against this backdrop of fluidity, in many contexts trans people are still treated by both academics and laypeople as marginal or outliers in terms of their specific social and legal concerns. Queer criminologists have been much concerned with gaining acceptance in the field of criminology for the study of gender, sexuality, crime, and harm—and the related implications for future societies, the criminal justice system, and the legal system as a whole. By focusing on both macro-level harms and offenders, queer criminologists have been considering issues such as interpersonal hate crimes and state discriminatory laws (Ball 2014, 2016; Dwyer et al. 2016). More recently, Boukli and Dymock (2017) suggest, by drawing together queer criminology and queer victimology, that queer criminology has focused on individual-level 'hate crime' offenders, while structural harms have been left unaddressed. The sum of these trends may suggest that we are moving (albeit slowly) towards a future in which the relevance of gender, as a legal category, becomes increasingly contested (Cooper and Renz 2016; Katyal 2017).

Before considering a genderless future, however, it is vital to recognise that trans people, particularly trans women of colour, are still disproportionally affected by structural bias and harm. As such trans people are frequently economically marginalised (Hill et al. 2017; Spade 2015) and at much greater risk of harm and death than the general population (Fitzgerald 2017; Bettcher 2014; Stotzer 2009). Further, the increasing visibility of trans issues seems to go hand in hand with the proliferation of visual representations of gender-based harms and violence. Against the grain of normative thinking, we are proposing a zemiology that has at its core a conception of sexual *in*difference. We will now turn to a brief consideration of harm, and subsequently of telemorphosis as a lens to analyse and interpret visual representations of interpersonal and structural harms.

Harms Against Trans

Liberal positivist and administrative paradigms have tended to focus on the causal factors that contribute to crime. Drawing on pathologisation and situational and opportunity-driven causal explanations of 'street-crime' and interpersonal violence, these perspectives have tended to focus on the criminal (positivist criminology), the victim (positivist victimology), or the crime (administrative criminology) (see, e.g., McLaughlin and Muncie 2001, 6–7). The classical criminological concern with creating more effective criminal justice systems to deter offending can indeed be useful to explain harmful acts and omissions against trans communities. This in its current form is what we might refer to as the *hate crime* framework. The hate crime approach has been particularly prominent in the extension of existing types of 'aggravated' offences that are motivated by hatred or hostility towards specific groups. For instance, in the UK hate crime laws have now been extended to include gender identity as a protected category (see the amended s.146 Criminal Justice Act 2003). This hate crime framework has a certain degree of appeal because it can help strengthen wide-ranging, normative applications of criminal sanctions against perpetrators of hate crime, as well as assist criminologists (queer or otherwise) who deploy administrative and positivist methods to understand why people engage in actions that harm specific communities. This framework, however, carries two key limitations.

1. Most importantly, zemiology has challenged this framework (see Brisman and South in this volume; Tombs in this volume) in relation to criminal law definitions of related injurious and harmful acts and omissions (Pemberton 2004). This line of reasoning suggests that sanctioning individuals increases prison rates and reinforces imaginary penalities (Carlen 2008)—the idea that punishment works, without actually addressing or solving any of the underpinning social 'problems'. Following this our call for greater attention to various actors who become accessories to harm against trans people is not suggesting any expansion of criminalisation measures, nor of the prison industrial complex (Davis and Barsamian 1999). Rather, we suggest that both structural and interpersonal harms should be taken into account, and we seek to highlight the interconnections between these harms. Particularly, we note the importance of holding corporations accountable, in spite of their insistence that they offer 'apolitical'—neutral platforms and necessary fluidity in communications. To further exemplify this point, in the 'beyond criminology' (Hillyard et al. 2004) project, Lois Bibbings (2004, 217) addresses hegemonic heterosexuality that can be harmful due to processes of normalisation, discrimination, marginalisation, exclusion, and punishment

that are attached to the 'heterosexual imperative'. By no means, does this advocate the criminalisation of heterosexuality. Rather, it highlights the harmful consequences of its frequent portrayal as a global heterosexist norm.
2. Further, we follow Christina Pantazis (2004) to recalibrate the focus of investigation towards an approach that is attuned to social and cultural attitudes. The harms that are discussed in this chapter can ultimately contribute to death or serious injuries, but have so far been ignored by both criminal justice mechanisms and criminology. Statistics offered by the Human Rights Campaign (2017), the International Transgender Day of Remembrance (2012), the US Transgender Survey (2016), and Transgender Europe (2016) suggest that at least 2264 killings of trans and gender-variant people occurred between 1st January 2008 and 30th September 2016 worldwide. In addition to this many different layers of gender identity-based harms take place at different stages of people's lives, such as discrimination in employment and housing, lack of health care, and verbal abuse. As a result, our focus on harms affecting trans people serves a dual purpose:

Firstly, we wish to problematise assumptions that can be found in relation to identity in all its forms, by highlighting the importance of social and cultural divisions at play in the experience and enactment of one's identity. Secondly, by highlighting the importance of audio-visual representations of harm, we draw on the tradition of Alison Young's approach in which images of crime and justice are understood to constitute as well as represent the social world through the power of affect (Carrabine 2012; Young 2005). To this, we add one more layer comprised of the corporate machinery that operates the engines, which create and transmit the images of harm that we shall explore.

Telemorphosis in Mediated Gender Harms

A useful concept to help reconsider the importance of media representations of harmful acts is the concept of 'telemorphosis'. The term telemorphosis is a compound word comprised of the word 'tele-' meaning 'distant', especially 'transmission over distance', and the word 'morphosis' indicating the sequence or manner of development or change in an organism or any of its parts. Morphosis derives from the ancient Greek word 'morfoo' (verb, μορφόω) = to morph, which indicates that someone gives shape to something or someone. Some of the derivatives of the verb morfoo are *mórfosi* (noun, μόρφωσις) = the act of giving shape or education, and *morphono* (verb, μορφώνω) = give shape or educate. In this sense, a familiar use of telemorphosis is associated with the expanding variety of media both online and offline and the potential for education associated with this proliferation of media. For instance, if I say that your position is based on telemorphosis, what I am generally suggesting is that your position is reached through the unreflective and layperson views on a topic. This kind of usage has a potential polemical value as it also connects to the ongoing commercialisation of education and the restructuring of educating powers as they move away from schools and academic institutions to the media. But this is by no means the only way in which the term telemorphosis has been and is used, whether in everyday language or in academic writing.

The association of telemorphosis with the legitimation of ruling power goes back to Jean Baudrillard. Writing at the beginning of the twenty-first century one of Baudrillard's last texts, *Telemorphosis* (2011), takes on the task of prophetically reflecting upon the proliferation of digital media and its social media underpinnings. Unravelling the screenification of a techno-social community, collective reality has entered the realm of telemorphosis: the actual storyline of reality or of unscripted videos (transmitted through TV, YouTube, Vimeo, and relevant online distribution platforms) is non-existent and even uninteresting. Contradictorily, however, the lack of intentional spectacle exerts immense fascination, it can even go 'viral'. Spectators either immerse themselves within the void of the spectacle or they compare themselves to it, feeling less idiotic and superior to the spectacle. In unscripted reality TV and in vlogging there is no equivalence between merit and fame. For Baudrillard (2011, 26) 'it is everything in exchange for nothing. A complete principle of inequivalence … the maximal exaltation for a minimal qualification'. Drawing connections between telemorphosis and this disequilibrium between merit and public recognition,

Baudrillard (2011, 28) took telemorphosis to refer to 'the disaster of an entire society caught up in the race towards meaninglessness and swooning in front of its own banality'. His most celebrated illustration of this relates to consensus building. With tongue in cheek, he explains that television succeeded in kidnapping society towards an integral telemorphosis—a *re*morphing of society—through which

> [w]e've become individuated beings: non-divisible with others or ourselves. This individuation, which we are so proud of, has nothing to do with personal liberty; on the contrary, it is a general promiscuity. It is not necessarily a promiscuity of bodies in space – but of screens from one end of the world to the other ... There will soon be nothing more than self-communicating zombies .... (Baudrillard 2011, 30)

Even if this does not fully capture the nuances of a real world of mediated social relations, the point for Baudrillard is the way that telemorphosis imagines, projects, and perpetuates the illusion of the social, where the social is taking shape through the compulsion of confinement. Spaces of confinement and the process of submitting groups to sensory deprivation experiments become the ultimate consensus-building project. From the *Big Brother* house, to the *Survivor* island, from a luxury gated community to a gay village, or to any experimental nest or privileged zone, the key incentive is not to protect a symbolic territory but to close oneself off with one's own self-image. Telemorphosis, in other words, both masks social conditions and provides a context in which we may begin to transform these conditions. As such, the mediated images of most scripted reality shows are based on 'on-line' interaction and quasi fabricated events that are nevertheless presented as real: 'The gestures, the speeches, and actors already respond to the conditions of prefabrication, of programmed representation' (Baudrillard 2011, 32). For instance, the video from the show *Survivor*, which we discuss below, features frequent references by the participants to the format of the show and the type of behaviour that is expected of contestants within the rules of the show (YouTube 12 April 2017, 01:20–01:23). Cynically, while the roles are pre-fabricated and while it is precisely at a point in time when we are trying to technologically eliminate harm, for Baudrillard, harm enters onto the stage as an experimental event in these virtual-actions. To this end, Baudrillard (2011, 36) suggests that soon we will have 'snuff films and televised bodily torture'. In our current socially mediated universe, social reengineering through reality television, YouTube videos, and networking sites may lead us to integrate harm within this theatricality and fascination with mundane, every-day events. There is no point in disconnecting the dots between individuation, self-surveillance, confinement, deprivation, and harm; the circuit is switched on.

More recently, authors like Tom Cohen (2012) have used the concept of telemorphosis to reclaim certain harms that have been naturalised or 'a certain violence that has seemed occluded or anaesthetized'. This has been characterised as an 'unfolding eco-eco disaster', an event at once economic and ecological. For Cohen, in the context of eco-catastrophes (see also Brisman and South in this volume), the figure of an ecology that is ours and that must be saved precludes us from confronting the displacement and dispossession, which conditions all production, including the production of homelands. While the construct of a homeland that needs to be secured has been insistently defended, these systems of security have in fact accelerated the vortices of eco-catastrophic imaginaries. This, for Cohen, leads to the zone of telemorphosis: the intricacy by which referential regimes, memory and reading, participate in, or even accelerate, the twenty-first century mutations that extend from financial systems to the biosphere. In other words, telemorphosis exceeds any political, economic, or conceptual model and focuses on the impasse of an emerging era of climate change and eco-catastrophic acceleration. The social, therefore, is created not by human labour but by disasters.

The conception of telemorphosis used in this chapter takes up the Baudrillardian idea of individuation, confinement, deprivation, and harm but extends it to class, gender, and ethnicity-based domination to encompass all kinds of power relations that are systematically asymmetrical and harmful. Instead of hovering over the topics of disaster and mega-catastrophe, ultimately Gender Murder focuses on the scene of social transformation against the backdrop of screenified representations of gender harm. In analysing images of anti-trans harm, the analysis draws on the concept of telemorphosis to capture the fathoms of the basic ontological uncertainty that our age of accelerating electronic images has imposed. This is vital in thinking how the political, social, and digital body pass through the screen in a telegenetically modified sociality. Here, it is anti-trans harms that are added to the televisual universe as one more televised and recorded detail of global reality. With this televised harm, the screen is the scene of harm itself. This is no longer a case of rendering things visible to the external eye, but it is a case of forced participation in a spectacle of harm. The public, while participating in ongoing gender transformations, is itself mobilised as a judge. With previous analyses suggesting that dominant modes of gender and sexual expression reproduce harmful situations (Bibbings 2004; Pantazis 2004), the remainder of this chapter considers how cisnormativity and heteronormativity become televised via a perfusion of harms.

Methodology

We will now briefly outline how we selected and analysed the three videos we will turn to in the following section. Starting with the pioneering study by social psychologist Siegfried Kracauer (1947) of German cinema from 1918 to 1933, scholars have argued that the films produced for and consumed by a nation allow privileged insight into the 'deep psychological dispositions' of a society. Similarly, Martin Bauer (2000, 133) suggests that recorded images, sounds, and texts are records of events that occurred, but also of prevailing rules and norms, as well as debates and arguments circulating at a given time. Furthermore, Carrabine (2012, 467) suggests that all visual records of events inherently relate to politics of 'testimony and memory'. Following this reasoning, we chose three videos engaging with the topic of gender identity in various ways, in differing audio-visual contexts, and in dispersed geographic areas. We chose one clip from a US-based unscripted reality television competition, one clip from a UK-based daytime television chat show, and one YouTube clip from a recording of a University lecture in Greece. For the purposes of this book chapter, it would not have been feasible to review the entirety of available and relevant programmes in one national context. We have therefore chosen these clips as illustrations of wider issues, rather than as comprehensive representations of available material.

In this sense we are taking an oral content analysis approach to highlight prevailing 'public opinion', discursive positions, and certain worldviews that continue to affect trans people across the Western world in harmful ways. We therefore read these videos as a 'medium of appeal' (Bauer 2000, 134); they are intended to influence the audience's attitudes, opinions, and even emotions in specific ways. It is important to note that 'audiovisual media are a complex amalgam of meanings, images, techniques, shot framing, shot sequence and much more' (Rose 2000, 246). We have therefore tried to take this complexity into account in our analysis. As audio-visual media is too complex to be translated into text, our analysis necessarily includes an element of simplification (Rose 2000, 247). The focus is primarily on the oral content, the words being said and discursive positions occupied, rather than the type of staging or filming techniques being used. In the next section, we highlight three research findings that stand in contradiction to the dominant idea that harm can simply extend or replace our understanding of crime, a notion which gave support to various attempts to ground an ontological approach (Pemberton 2016; Yar 2012).

Harm Videos

The first video we analyse is from the 2017 season of the American reality TV show Survivor, in which contestants compete against each other on a 'deserted' island for a cash prize of US$1,000,000. This video, from the 6th episode of this season, features one contestant, Jeff Varner, outing a fellow contestant, Zeke Smith, as a trans man. Varner and Smith had initially bonded over their shared identity as 'gay men' (Parsons 2017, 05:55–06:00). Yet, this short video clip illustrates two different understandings of harm in relation to trans people. On the one hand, as argued by Varner, Smith is supposedly causing harm to fellow contestants, by relying on 'deception' regarding his trans identity, which had apparently been unknown to other contestants until that point. This construction of harm deriving from someone being trans has echoes of the figure of the 'deceptive transsexual', a figure common across both literature and litigation prominent during the twentieth and beginning of the twenty-first century (Sharpe 2010), which was often used to justify legal restrictions and discrimination against trans people. It also shows many similarities to official understandings of trans identities as being inherently harmful to others (Renz 2015). Varner argues that Smith's 'deception' regarding his gender identity supposedly shows his wider 'ability to deceive' (YouTube 12 April 2017, 01:20–01:23). In a later interview Varner directly acknowledges that this reasoning plays into a common, harmful stereotype about trans people (Dalton 13 April 2017).

In contrast to this, other contestants as well as the show's host Jeff Probst highlight the harm deriving from Varner outing Smith publicly on national television. Fellow contestants argue strongly that 'nobody has the right to out anybody' (YouTube 12 April 2017, 00:50–00:55). Even Varner acknowledges that his actions could be seen as controversial, stating that he does not want to be seen as 'this evil, hateful person' (YouTube 12 April 2017, 01:07–01:12). Varner is subsequently voted off the show by his fellow contestants and apologises tearfully for his actions in the credit sequence of the episode (YouTube 12 April 2017, 03:05–03:15) and in his later interview describes his outing of Smith as 'assault' (Dalton 13 April 2017) by drawing explicitly on the language of criminal law. The act of outing someone therefore is understood, both explicitly by Varner, and more implicitly by other contestants, as equivalent to the type of physical harm normally prohibited by criminal law. Based on the editing of the episode, it is evident that both Varner's and Smith's fellow contestants, as well as the show's producers are closely aligned with the interpretation of outing as harm. Varner's actions are portrayed in a strongly negative light and the other contestants and the show's host explicitly condemn his actions. The end credit sequence ultimately focuses solely on his very emotional apology and regret over his actions.

The second video challenges the idea that we always automatically know *who* the person is that is being harmed. For instance, the ITV breakfast show 'Good Morning Britain', broadcast on 17 May 2017, featured the presenters Piers Morgan and Susanna Reid discussing non-binary gender identities with guests Fox Fisher and Owl. The segment begins with a compilation of clips from previous discussions about gender neutrality, most of which feature the host Piers Morgan making mocking and derogatory comments about gender-neutral language and accommodations made for non-binary people (YouTube 17 May 2017, 00:36–01:26). Morgan's co-host describes the topic as 'exercising Piers with great vigour and passion and one that many of our viewers feel confused about' (YouTube 17 May 2017, 02:00–02:07). While confusion about non-binary identities is here portrayed as a common and seemingly relatable issue for the audience, what is not addressed is the interpersonal and structural harms non-binary people actually face. Throughout the interview, which at times feels more like an interrogation, Morgan positions himself as hostile to the identity claims of Fisher, Owl, and other non-binary people and describes different gender terminology as 'gobbledidook' (YouTube 17 May 2017, 03:39–07:03). He goes on to argue that the transgression of the gender binary ultimately destabilises society itself. He does this by providing an anecdote about a friend whose daughter allegedly has eight classmates that identify as non-binary and argues that this is a 'contagion' and that schools 'are now running-riot' (YouTube 17 May 2017, 08:58–09:15). By drawing on the language of disease and social disorder he explicitly characterises non-binary identities as harmful. He goes on to make a link between the transgression of gender norms and the breaking of laws by challenging Fisher and Owl about whether they 'abide by the laws of the land' and that if they do, they should also adhere to the gender binary (YouTube 17 May 2017, 14:25–14:30).

In contrast to Morgan's understanding of non-binary identities as harmful to society, Fisher and Owl argue that misrecognition and lack of accommodations for non-binary and trans people are inherently connected to harm in the form of high rates of attempted suicides among trans youth. However, Morgan contests this understanding and equates accommodation for trans and non-binary people with changing 'the gender of the planet'. Thereby returning to his earlier argument and implicitly suggesting that even minor accommodations would be evidently ridiculous and burdensome for the majority of the population

(YouTube 17 May 2017, 12:10–12:43). As a result, the actual documented harms suffered by trans people are seemingly equated, if not subjugated, to the primarily hypothetical harm to society of abandoning gender, which is not something actually demanded by Fisher and Owl.

Finally, the concept of telemorphosis becomes most relevant in its literary form in the YouTube Video titled 'Transphobic Rhetoric by Professor D.P.' (a Professor at the University of Crete, whose full name is disclosed in the video), uploaded by 'Polyhromo Sholeio'/'Rainbow School' a non-profit and volunteering group of scientists. When dealing with Internet archives such as YouTube, one can assume that the videos 'found are produced by users with the intention of public use and distribution' (Vergani and Zuev 2011, 215). The group members that uploaded the video are involved with LGBTQ issues in education, mental health, and social sciences (Rainbowschool 2017). The video is an extract from the 4th lecture out of 10 classes under the title '10 Classes of Simple Contemporary Radical Theory: Classical Marxism and the Materialist Conception of History' delivered at the National Technical University of Athens. Leaving aside the various questions around the purpose of the video—is it to disseminate the lecture or to capture the transphobic remarks—the fact that the video was uploaded on YouTube with a title explicitly referring to it as 'transphobic', suggests that uploading it may be interpreted as an act of resistance and conflict with the content of the video.

In his lecture Professor D.P. makes an explicit link between gender 'transition', racism, and Western imperialism (YouTube 27 November 2015, 00:12–01:00). He argues that the increasing acceptance of LGBTQ identities 'is water to the mill of manipulation' and part of a wider imposition of capitalism (YouTube 27 November 2015, 00:56–02:02), aided by global corporations such as Microsoft and IBM (YouTube 27 November 2015, 04:54–07:12). For D.P., corporations act as 'systematic sponsors' of LGBTQ rights through the funding of NGOs and the supposed creation of special financial incentives, such as 'credit cards for LGBTQ people'. While some of the evidence mentioned by D.P. aims to portray an exaggerated intimacy between LGBTQ communities and capitalist financial institutions, D.P. fails to tease out how wider socio-economic disadvantage disproportionally affects LGBTQ people (see, e.g., Ray and Berger 2007). Instead, by largely quoting biological positivist evidence, D.P. suggests that 'LGBTQI technologies' present a form of capitalist expansion, through the creation of artificial needs (YouTube 27 November 2015, 00:56–02:02). Furthermore, D.P. blames the influence of parents or teachers who, he claims, may fundamentally 'deconstruct' and damage the personality of a child by educating them about gender transitioning and sexual identities (YouTube 27 November 2015, 04:03–04:53). Allowing young people to transition and accommodating their gender identity, D.P. claims, is ultimately a form of 'biological degeneration of the human race' and therefore a form of 'genocide' (YouTube 27 November 2015, 04:54–07:12). This leads to what he terms 'reversed refraction' where society is not just refracted through the biological, but where 'the biological core of human personality' is under attack by what he considers 'sex and gender capitalist propaganda'. For him trans people, and LGBTQ communities more widely, are the ideal capitalist subjects, since their supposedly narrow focus on LGBTQ issues makes them easily acquiesce to capitalist demands (YouTube 27 November 2015, 08:39–11:55). To complicate matters further, D.P.'s analysis suggests that these 'imposed techno-needs' extend to all gender identity and sexuality related social and policy issues (from same-sex marriage and adoption to gender affirming practices), as they all have the same aim: 'to alienate the human biological core' (YouTube 27 November 2015, 02:38–04:02).

The video gained particular attention upon its circulation on YouTube in November 2015 due to an emotive blog riposte by the President of the Greek Transgender Support Association, Marina Galanou (29 November 2015), in which she highlights a discernible clash between biological determinism and a Marxist class-based analysis. The video's striking high rate of viewings is particularly notable against the viewing figures of the remaining nine lectures by D.P., which are automatically activated once you have watched this video. This specific lecture has been viewed over a hundred thousand times, while the other ones have three to four thousand views. The disparity in viewing figures highlights the capacity for online audio-visual portrayals of gender harms and the discourses around them to be transmitted to a potentially unlimited audience.

Epilogue: A Harmless Telemorphosis?

It has become a truism to remark that in the Global North research on harm and crime affecting trans people has gained momentum, while at the same time crucial problems persist in identifying and dealing with such harms (see, e.g., Lombardi 2009). Clearly in some states effort has been put into documenting the extent of violence against trans people and in exploring more appropriate methods to handle the relevant offences, as well as the associated social harms and their consequences. Yet discourses around anti-trans crime and structural harms remain highly contested. The above exploration focuses on the processes whereby speech is registered as harmful contact, not so much by following principles of criminal law, but regardless of how criminal law defines the said contact. Following Carol Smart (1999), our analysis challenges the idea that 'harm' is a transcendental notion, which is automatically knowable and recognisable at any moment in history by any member of a culture. Instead, processes of redefinition take place over time, and hence what is seen as harmful changes over time. It is, therefore, for criminology and zemiology to map these processes of redefinition.

From outing a transman on reality TV to a YouTube video of a university lecture equating trans identities with genocide, we observe that a good deal of public discourse does not engage with strictly legal definitions of harm in the context of gender identity. Paradoxically, the videos present some of the 'ordinary' attempts that are made to defy, resist, or scorn these definitions and instil instead a sense of 'lawfully' ordered human life. For instance, video 1 suggests that being shamed on national television may be the most efficient form of punishment for the self-assessed and confessed 'assault' committed by outing someone, in order to restore the humanity of the perpetrator. Video 2 criticises non-binary identities on the basis of the supposedly impending extinction of sexual difference and the social harm this may cause. It does so not by directly inciting violence or threats against non-binary people, but by referencing the supposed stability the maintenance of normative sex-gender categories brings to society. In doing so it also links non-binary gender identities to illegal and law-breaking behaviour. Lastly, video 3 describes LGBT communities, and specifically trans people, as accessories of neoliberal 'genocidal' technologies and in doing so it aligns with a moralising anti-capitalism, which links the structural harm of capitalism to the perceived harm caused by the existence of LGBT identities. At the same time, the group that posted this video turns the message on its head, as it uses this public platform to highlight that the content of it is harmful to trans people. Essentially, the videos may be seen as indicative of still prevailing discourses, prejudices, and structural harms, as in all three videos the speakers frame trans people as the source of harm. Conversely, in all three videos there are also attempts to oppose those harms. It is however the force of public speech, rather than the force of law, or the force of censorship that has been applied in these instances to tackle and highlight harms.

In this sense, the offensive call, or the call perceived as offensive, inaugurates a subject in speech who comes to use language to counter the offensive call (Butler 1999, 2). The fact that this linguistic battle about harm is captured in video form ultimately creates effects that are not the same as the battle itself, as can be seen by the fact that all three videos led to further responses, either by the parties involved or by other commentators. The televised battle is extended beyond prior and future invocations, through telemorphosis, to mould these two opposing sides—the injurious speech, and the one it injures. This can also be seen in the fairly significant viewing figures all three videos reached after their publication and the wider debates they triggered. While unpleasant or even harmful, none of the examples used here can be defined as criminal. Further, the harmful speech in the videos is not defined by a single name that one is called, but by the identification of one's capacity to disrupt the current order of things, a capacity to turn the mill of sexual difference to *in*-difference. Returning to Colebrook (2012) sexual *in*difference has always been warded off as evil and unthinkable, usually associated with a 'monstrous inhumanity'—a theme that is picked up implicitly in videos 2 and 3. Hence, the fear of sexual indifference is precisely that which has imprisoned thinking within its logic of self-enclosing sameness and ongoing repetition of sex-gender norms. Instead, we are proposing a zemiology that has at its core a conception of sexual *in*difference akin to the forces of life, mutation, generation, and exchange without any sense of ongoing identity circulation, bounded normative forms of gender, and dyadic reasoning.

References

Australian Government. July 2013. *Australian Government Guidelines on the Recognition of Sex and Gender*. Commonwealth of Australia.

Ball, Matthew. 2014. Queer Criminology, Critique, and the "Art of Not Being Governed". *Critical Criminology* 22 (1): 21–34.

Ball, Matthew. 2016. *Criminology and Queer Theory: Dangerous Bedfellows?* Basingstoke: Palgrave.

Baudrillard, Jean. 2011. *Telemorphosis*, trans. Drew S. Burk. Minneapolis: Univocal.

Bauer, Martin W. 2000. Classical Content Analysis: A Review. In *Qualitative Researching with Text, Image and Sound*, ed. Martin W Bauer and Georg Gaskell, 131–151. London: Sage.

Bettcher, Talia Mae. 2014. Transphobia. *TSQ: Transgender Studies Quarterly* 1 (1–2): 249–251.

Bibbings, Lois. 2004. Heterosexuality as Harm: Fitting in. In *Beyond Criminology: Taking Harm Seriously*, ed. Paddy Hillyard, Christina Pantazis, Steve Tombs, and Dave Gordon, 217–234. London: Pluto Press.

Boukli, Avi, and Alex Dymock. 2017. Queering Victimology: Victim Services and Queer Precarities. Law and Society Association Mexico City.

Butler, Judith. 1999. *Gender Trouble: Feminism and the Subversion of Identity*. London and New York: Routledge.

Carlen, Pat (ed.). 2008. *Imaginary Penalities*. Devon and Oregon: Willan Publishing.

Carrabine, Eamonn. 2012. Just Images Aesthetics, Ethics and Visual Criminology. *British Journal of Criminology* 52 (3): 463–489.

Cohen, Tom (ed.). 2012. *Telemorphosis: Theory in the Era of Climate Change*, vol. 1. London: Open Humanities Press.

Colebrook, Claire. 2012. Sexual Indifference. In *Telemorphosis: Theory in the Era of Climate Change*, vol. 1, ed. Tom Cohen. London: Open Humanities Press.

Cooper, Davina, and Flora Renz. 2016. If the State Decertified Gender, What Might Happen to Its Meaning and Value? *Journal of Law & Society* 43 (4): 483–505.

Currah, Paisley, and Lisa Jean Moore. 2009. "We Won't Know Who You Are": Contesting Sex Designations in New York City Birth Certificates. *Hypatia* 24 (3): 113–135.

Dalton, Ross. 13 April 2017. Survivor: Jeff Varner Says 'I am Absolutely Devastated' Over Outing Zeke as Transgender. http://ew.com/tv/2017/04/13/survivor-jeff-varner-zeke-transgender-game-changer/. Accessed 1 May 2017.

Davis, Angela Yvonne, and David Barsamian. 1999. *The Prison Industrial Complex*. Oakland, CA: AK Press.

Dwyer, Angela, Matthew Ball, and Thomas Crofts. 2016. *Queering Criminology*. Basingstoke: Palgrave.

Fausto-Sterling, Anne. 2012. *Sex/Gender: Biology in a Social World*. New York and London: Routledge.

Fitzgerald, Kathleen J. 2017. Understanding Racialized Homophobic and Transphobic Violence. In *Violence Against Black Bodies: An Intersectional Analysis of How Black Lives Continue to Matter*, ed. Sandra E. Weissinger, Dwayne A. Mack, and Elwood Watson, 53–70. New York and London: Routledge.

Galanou, Marina. 29 November 2015. Η επαναστατική τρανσφοβία. http://amagi.gr/content/i-epanastatiki-transfovia. Accessed 1 Oct 2017.

Hill, Brandon J., Kris Rosentel, Trevor Bak, Michael Silverman, Richard Crosby, Laura Salazar, and Michele Kipke. 2017. Exploring Individual and Structural Factors Associated with Employment Among Young Transgender Women of Color Using a No-Cost Transgender Legal Resource Center. *Transgender Health* 2 (1): 29–34.

Hillyard, Paddy, Christina Pantazis, Steve Tombs, and Dave Gordon (eds.). 2004. *Beyond Criminology: Taking Harm Seriously*. London: Pluto Press.

House of Commons. 01 December 2016. Transgender Equality. 617 (390).

Hughes, Sarah. 23 January 2015. Transparent Season One Is Free for a Day—Here's Why You Should Watch It. *The Guardian*. http://www.theguardian.com/tv-and-radio/2015/jan/23/transparent-season-one-free-on-amazon-for-a-day. Accessed 20 April 2015.

Human Rights Campaign. 2017. Violence Against the Transgender Community in 2017. https://www.hrc.org/resources/violence-against-the-transgender-community-in-2017. Accessed 10 June 2017.

International Transgender Day of Remembrance. 2012. Statistics and Other Info. https://tdor.info/statistics/. Accessed 10 June 2017.

Katyal, Sonia K. 2017. The Numerus Clausus of Sex. *University of Chicago Law Review* 84: 389–495.

Kilkelly, Daniel. 15 May 2014. Exclusive: Hollyoaks Writer Jonathan Larkin Talks Blessing Transgender Story. *Digital Spy*.

Kracauer, Siegfried. 1947. *From Caligari to Hitler*. Princeton: Princeton University Press.

Lombardi, Emilia. 2009. Varieties of Transgender/Transsexual lives and Their Relationship with Transphobia. *Journal of Homosexuality* 56 (8): 977–992.
McLaughlin, Eugene, and John Muncie. 2001. *The SAGE Dictionary of Criminology*. London: Sage.
Pantazis, Christina. 2004. Gendering Harm From a Life Course Perspective. In *Beyond Criminology: Taking Harm Seriously*, ed. Paddy Hillyard, Christina Pantazis, Steve Tombs, and Dave Gordon, 192–216. London: Pluto Press.
Parsons, Charlie. 2017. Episode 5. In *Survivor*, ed. Charlie Parsons. USA: CBS.
Pemberton, Simon A. 2004. A Theory of Moral Indifference: Understanding the Production of Harm by Capitalist Society. In *Beyond Criminology: Taking Harm Seriously*, ed. Paddy Hillyard, Christina Pantazis, Steve Tombs, and Dave Gordon, 67–83. London: Pluto Press.
Pemberton, Simon A. 2016. *Harmful Societies: Understanding Social Harm*. Bristol: Policy Press.
Press Association. 2 January 2016. Call to Remove Gender From UK Passports and Driving Licences. *The Guardian*. http://www.theguardian.com/world/2016/jan/02/call-to-remove-gender-from-uk-passports-and-driving-licences.
Rainbowschool. 2017. Ποιες/-οι Είμαστε. http://rainbowschool.gr/. Accessed 1 May 2017.
Ray, Nicholas, and Colby Berger. 2007. Lesbian, Gay, Bisexual and Transgender Youth: An Epidemic of Homelessness. National Gay and Lesbian Task Force Policy Institute.
Renz, Flora. 2015. Consenting to Gender? Trans Spouses After Same-Sex Marriage. In *From Civil Partnership to Same-Sex Marriage: Interdisciplinary Reflections*, ed. Nicola Barker and Daniel Monk, 79–94. London and New York: Routledge.
Rose, Diana. 2000. Analysis of Moving Images. In *Qualitative Researching with Text, Image and Sound*, ed. Martin W Bauer and Gregor Gaskell, 246–262. London: Sage.
Sharpe, Alex. 2010. *Foucault's Monsters and the Challenge of Law*. London: Routledge.
Smart, Carol. 1999. A History of Ambivalence and Conflict in the Discursive Construction of the "Child Victim" of Sexual Abuse. *Social & Legal Studies* 8 (3): 391–409.
Spade, Dean. 2015. *Normal Life: Administrative Violence, Critical Trans Politics and the Limits of Law Revised and Expanded Edition*. Durham and London: Duke University Press.
Steinmetz, Katy. 2014. The Transgender Tipping Point. *Time Magazine*, May 29.

Stotzer, Rebecca L. 2009. Violence Against Transgender People: A Review of United States Data. *Aggression and Violent Behavior* 14 (3): 170–179.

Transgender Europe. 2016. TDoR 2016 Press Release. https://tgeu.org/tdor-2016-press-release/. Accessed 1 June 2017.

US Trans Survey. 2016. 2015 U.S. Transgender Survey Report. http://www.ustranssurvey.org/report. Accessed 10 June 2017.

Vergani, Matteo, and Dennis Zuev. 2011. Analysis of YouTube Videos Used by Activists in the Uyghur Nationalist Movement: Combining Quantitative and Qualitative Methods. *Journal of Contemporary China* 20 (69): 205–229.

Yar, Majid. 2012. Critical Criminology, Critical Theory, and Social Harm. In *New Directions in Criminological Theory*, ed. Steve Hall, and Simon Winlow, 52–65. Abingdon: Routledge.

Young, Alison. 2005. *Judging the Image: Art, Value, Law*. London: Routledge.

YouTube. 12 April 2017. Survivor—Jeff Varner OUTS Zeke Smith as TRANSGENDER!!

YouTube. 17 May 2017. Non Binary Trans Debate: Piers Morgan vs. Fox & Owl.

YouTube. 27 November 2015. Τρανσφοβική ρητορική στο Μετσόβιο Πολυτεχνείο Δ. Π.

Authors' Biography

Avi Boukli is a lecturer in criminology at The Open University. Avi joined The Open University in 2016, after previously having held lectureships at the London School of Economics, Teesside University, and Birkbeck College. Their activist and academic work bring insights from queer theory and Marxism to victimology and zemiology.

Flora Renz is a lecturer in law at Kent Law School, University of Kent. Flora's research is concerned with the legal regulation of (trans)gender identities and sexuality in society and broader questions focusing on the interface between structural inequalities, law, gender, sexuality, and emotion.

A Doubling of the Offence? 'Extreme' Pornography and Cultural Harm

Alex Dymock

Introduction: Pornography and Harm

In the second half of the twentieth century, there have been two seismic shifts in discussions about how pornography should be regulated. One major change—predominantly as a result of the impossibility of vetting international content online—has been a move to regulate not the distributor or producer of pornography, but to criminalise the possessor: anyone who downloads, streams or perhaps even accidentally clicks on a link to certain categories of pornography. This is illustrated by Section 63 of the Criminal Justice and Immigration Act 2008, which outlaws possession of 'extreme' pornographic images in England and Wales. A second major paradigm shift in research on how the criminal law can be utilised to curb pornography is the turn from questions of obscenity to questions of harm. Pornography regulation has historically been treated as a kind of 'hygienic censoring' (Hunt 1993, 12), aiming

A. Dymock (✉)
Royal Holloway, University of London, London, UK
e-mail: alex.dymock@rhul.ac.uk

to keep the sexual interests and appetites of the general population 'clean'. The Obscene Publications Act 1959 sets out the requirement in Section 1 that for an article to be found obscene, a jury must put themselves in the shoes of the likely audience and come to a decision as to whether the material has the effect, 'if taken as a whole, such as to tend to deprave and corrupt persons who are likely, having regard to all relevant circumstances, to read, see or hear the matter contained or embodied in it'. Thus, the test for a jury is to decide whether the intended or, indeed, unintended viewer is likely to be morally corrupted by pornographic imagery or texts.

Much of the recent commentary on the harms of pornography links harm to the industry itself, and the supposed amplification of violence and 'extremity' within pornographic material (see, e.g., Dines 2010; Jensen 2007). However, there is a much longer standing debate on the effects of pornography on users, and the harmful outcomes to which use of pornography may lead. The production of evidence concerning the potential harms of pornography is notoriously contradictory and positivist, focusing either on how pornography affects attitudes towards sexuality and consent, or behavioural studies that attempt to establish a causal link between exposure to pornography and the risk of violent and sexual offending, has become a veritable industry. Much of this research took place in university laboratories in the 1980s with voluntary student participants and was predicated on social learning theory (Bandura 1973). For example, Check and Malamuth (1983) claimed that exposure to violent pornography may aid the acceptance of rape myths; others (Malamuth and Ceniti 1986) suggest that—measured by wiring participants up to an 'aggression machine'—there is a link between sexual arousal and increased aggression stimulated by repetitive viewing of pornography. Still other studies (Linz et al. 1988) deal with attitudinal change in the wake of long-term exposure. However, despite an increasing diversity of research methods and tools, none of these researchers are willing to suggest that there is any conclusive link between exposure to pornography and violent behaviour, nor that their findings should be used to justify legislative constraints on pornography (Donnerstein et al. 1987). Indeed, in a recent meta-analysis of a broad base of research findings on the possible link between pornography and sex crime

(Fisher et al. 2013, 362), it was concluded that neither experimental, observational nor confluence models permitted researchers to 'decide whether a causal direction of pornography effects is justified'.

Notwithstanding increased interest in attempting to establish a causal relationship between pornography and sexual violence over the past 40 odd years, the evidence base for this assertion is no more conclusive than it was when these studies first proliferated in the early 1980s. It has also been subjected to vociferous critique. The effects model, as Karen Boyle (2005, 17) points out, 'conceives of the audience as passive and uncritical and, further, assumes that all audience groups will respond to the same material in the same way'. Surette (2014, 122) has argued that the artificiality of the lab settings in many such studies fatally compromises them. In addition, Toynbee (2008, 267) suggests that it is impossible to isolate pornography use from 'among a complex of putative causes of violent behaviour among research subjects'. Thus, even those studies which attempt to assemble a correlation between the very immediate effects of pornography on physiognomy fail to fully convince.

The lack of evidential basis, however, has failed to stall attempts to find ways of legislating against the possible harms of pornography. In recent years, the emergence of the idea of 'cultural harm' (McGlynn and Rackley 2009) has changed the tenor of the debate for the criminalisation of possession of pornography, suggesting that although evidence of causal harm has not conclusively been found, the meaning of harm is to be considered less oblivious to structural considerations. Indeed, cultural harm has been considered a 'radical departure' (Easton 2011, 391) from approaches to the evaluation of pornography that came before it. In this purview, pornography is to be considered a major contributing factor to the normalisation of the institutional denial of sexual violence against women, as well as contributing to 'pro rape attitudes'. Further, the argument goes, it contributes to attitudes which may minimise the harms of sexual violence, removing the stigma feminists have striven to attach to it.

In this chapter, I suggest that although the concept of cultural harm appears at first to borrow from zemiology's concern with structural harms, there are two departing points for the way in which the cultural harm argument has been used with respect to pornography.

Firstly, while zemiological perspectives identify the harms of continual reliance on criminalisation as a solution to social problems (see, e.g., Muncie 2000), the cultural harm argument emerged in the wake of an insufficient body of empirical evidence to argue *for* the criminalisation of possession of 'extreme' pornography, resulting in 1000 prosecutions within a one-year period (Fae 2012). Secondly, zemiology often takes a victim-centred approach to harm, suggesting that 'victims are apt to call harmful what perpetrators and bystanders do not' (Presser 2013, 4). However, the offence of possessing 'extreme' pornography does not have a clear victim, so it is difficult to assuage precisely what the harms attached to this might be, and whom it affects. Drawing on Foucault's work on the 'doubling of the offence', I contextualise the emergence of the cultural harm argument by examining how a single case of homicide led to the production of a new criminal offence, and provide a critique of the way in which cultural harm in the arena of pornography is continually wielded as evidence of the potential for *dangerousness*.

Cultural Harm and 'Extreme' Pornography

On 14 March 2004, a 31-year-old special needs teacher named Jane Longhurst was reported missing in West Sussex. Five weeks later her naked body was found burning at a local beauty spot, a pair of tights wrapped around her neck. Once the body had been located, police quickly traced her death back to a man named Graham Coutts, whose girlfriend had been a friend of Longhurst. Upon entering his home and seizing his computer's hard-drive, police found hundreds of pornographic images depicting erotic asphyxiation and sexual interference with a corpse. In court Coutts pleaded not-guilty to murder, stating that the death of Longhurst was a tragic accident, the result of a consensual sex game gone wrong. Much attention during the trial was given over to evidence of Coutts' history of 'macabre'[1] sexual deviance, in particular his keen interest in asphyxiation, which he had

---

[1] *R v. Coutts* [2005] EWCA Crim 52.

practiced consensually on a woman with whom he spent seven years in a relationship previously. She subsequently appeared as a defence witness. While the defence's rationale might have been that claiming a prior, verifiable interest in consensual erotic asphyxiation long before Longhurst's death would give weight to a manslaughter verdict, providing evidence of Coutts' perversion merely aided the prosecution's case that this was an exceptional, dangerous individual who had committed an exceptional crime. Mr. Kelsey-Fry QC, prosecuting, said: 'On 14 March, Graham Coutts murdered Jane Longhurst by strangling her to death, taking an opportunity that arose to act out in reality his bizarre and macabre fantasies fostered on his computer' (BBC 2007).

Believing the internet sites presented in court as evidence fed into the fantasies of Coutts and 'had a direct bearing on her daughter's death', Liz Longhurst, the victim's mother, started a petition to call for legislative change to block these 'vile and monstrous' sites. Her campaign attracted the attention of the MP for Reading West, Martin Salter, who secured a first debate in the Commons on the subject on 18th May 2004. 'As Members of Parliament', he opened, 'we have a responsibility to take action that will be a lasting memorial to Jane Longhurst.'[2] Rather than adding an additional clause to the Obscene Publications Act 1959, this lasting memorial took the form of a new criminal offence, Section 63 of the Criminal Justice and Immigration Act 2008. Section 63 creates the offence of 'possessing an extreme pornographic image' and came into force in January 2009. An image in England and Wales is categorised as 'extreme' if it 'is grossly offensive, disgusting or otherwise of an obscene character' and portrays in a realistic or explicit way the following:

(a) an act which threatens a person's life,
(b) an act which results, or is likely to result, in serious injury to a person's anus, breasts or genitals,
(c) an act which involves sexual interference with a human corpse, or
(d) a person performing an act of intercourse or oral sex with an animal (whether dead or alive);

---

[2]David Lepper MP, HC Deb 3 May 2004, vol. 421, col. 173.

The penalties were set out as follows:
Where (a) or (b) apply, the maximum sentence is 3 years; otherwise the maximum is 2 years. Those sentenced to at least two years will be placed on the Violent and Sex Offender Register.

Significantly, two UK-based feminist legal scholars, Clare McGlynn and Erika Rackley, have written extensively on the legislative process for pornography regulation. Their initial response was that the Consultation undertaken to assuage the views of the public and special interests groups signalled a satisfactory balance between acknowledging the cultural harm and possibility of actual harm done to women through the normalisation of sexual violence, and a reliance on legal precedents for obscenity set by the OPA (McGlynn and Rackley 2007). McGlynn and Rackley, at first sight, appear to borrow from critical criminological and zemiological accounts of social harm to make their case for 'cultural harm' caused by pornography, suggesting that cultural harm is predicated on the idea that there may be 'strong *experiential* evidence of the adverse effects on women of pornography' (McGlynn and Rackley 2007, 3). In other words, like zemiological accounts of harm (see, e.g., Hillyard and Tombs 2004; Lasslett 2010; Presser 2013), in their view, pornography's cultural harms can be adjudicated on the basis of those who experience them. This experiential account of harm is different from previous moralist accounts of the harms of pornography, which describe the contamination of public morality as pornography's most harmful facet. Feminist accounts, by contrast, taking stock of the problematic effects such an argument has had historically on the repression and criminalisation of homosexuality, specifically refer to the degradation and subjugation of women. Pornography, these feminists argue, is culturally harmful because it perpetuates gender inequalities and educates those watching to view female sexuality as passive and solely mobilised in the service of male pleasure (see, e.g., Dines 2010; Jensen 2007; Long 2012; McGlynn and Rackley 2014). In the case of violent pornography, the argument for cultural harm is that it normalises sexual violence against women, removing the social stigma feminists have striven over the last thirty years to attach to it. As McGlynn and Rackley (2014, 2) put it, 'the proliferation and tolerance of such websites and images, and the messages they convey, contributes to a climate in which sexual violence is condoned, and seen as a form of entertainment'. A further link to zemiology here might be that pornography shores up heteropatriarchal assumptions about feminine sexuality which, as Bibbings (2004, 218) has argued, construct a 'hegemonic heterosexuality', in which women's pleasure is consistently sidelined and depreciated.

While I would have some sympathy with a zemiological account of the potential harms of pornography, and find current feminist approaches the most convincing of any for some form of pornography regulation, my critique of the approach taken by McGlynn and Rackley to cultural harm is threefold. Firstly, by advocating for the criminalisation of possession on the grounds of a 'category based approach' to 'extreme' images (McGlynn and Rackley 2007), the focus is displaced from the corporate interests which profit from pornography, and the harms those interests may perpetuate to those working in the industry. This might form the basis of a truly collegial zemiological and criminological account of pornography, aiming to investigate the interaction between the structural harms of capitalist interest in instrumentalising performers' bodies in the service of profit, and interpersonal violence, in particular the violation of consent on set. Instead, the recent move towards criminalising possession on the basis of cultural harm merely individualises and exceptionalises the cultural problem with pornography, which feminists have convincingly argued is a systemic one, by attaching the full weight of responsibility for the harms it may cause to the individual viewer rather than paying attention to corporate and workplace-based harms. Furthermore, by mobilising zemiological arguments in service of pro-criminalisation efforts, what the cultural harm argument really does is suggest that the viewer of 'extreme' pornography is not only a willing accessory to cultural harm, but already has the propensity to carry out sexual violence. It shores up the shift in criminal law in the late twentieth and early twenty-first century from penalising clear guilt (the infliction of harm) to assessing and punishing dangerousness (the risk that harm will be committed). This 'betokens a movement to merge the criminal law with the administrative process of civil commitment' (Fletcher 2000, xix) and expands the reach of the carceral state, itself a perpetrator of harm.

Secondly, if we follow Bibbings' argument about the harms of heterosexuality, it could be argued that although violent pornography in McGlynn and Rackley's account is said to perpetuate the harm of normalising sexual deviance, category-based approaches to the regulation of pornography themselves cause harm. For example, in the case of Simon Walsh, a gay barrister found to be in possession of private images of himself and another, which depicted sexual acts such as fisting and urethral sounding (Roberts 2012), the message of the Crown Prosecution Service seems to be that no matter the context, the acts *themselves* on display have the potential to harm. Although Walsh was found not-guilty on all counts, and McGlynn and Rackley argued subsequent to his acquittal that the law in his case had been 'misused and misunderstood' (Rackley and McGlynn 2013), the very assumption that sexual acts that lie close to the reproductive ideal of sexuality in pornography are harmless, while those that appear 'extreme' are harmful, perpetuates myths about the 'charmed circle of sexuality' (Rubin 1984), outside of which Walsh found himself.

Lastly, there is another significant difficulty with this argument, and that is that the language mobilised in the media, Parliament, and the law to discuss pornography itself betrays a pornographic sensibility. It is no coincidence that the term 'pornography' has been repurposed to describe an increasing number of media productions that are not explicitly sexual. For example, it is now readily applied to a horror film genre ('torture porn') and reality TV 'documentaries' whose sole purpose appears to be to perpetuate hatred against the poor ('poverty porn'). Of course, if we follow Rackley and McGlynn's argument vis-a-vis pornography to its logical ends, it could be argued that the cultural harms such programmes do to viewers, in normalising the vilification and hatred of the most vulnerable people in society, are not only more egregious, but much more wide-spread than those 'extreme' pornography could ever achieve, and therefore the viewers of those programmes should also be criminalised.

As a result of the expanding range of media representations associated with the grammar and logic of the pornographic, it has become increasingly difficult to draw a line between the often lurid terms in which pornography is talked about, and the potential social harms it may really cause. As Hester has argued, the ever-expanding cultural repository of 'porn' has begun to displace sex in the way in which we think about pornography altogether (Hester 2014), and I have suggested subsequently that the same is true of criminologists, who weaponise the term 'pornography' to describe the general viewing public of crime-centred television programming (Dymock 2017) as harbouring a prurient 'demonic curiosity' (Friday 2000) towards its content. Equally, Atkinson and Rodgers (2015, 1293) call for the need to include the 'sado-voyeurism' of media cultures within the remit of criminology, although do not go as far as to advocate explicitly for its criminalisation. In such accounts, prurience is positioned centre-stage at the expense of more careful consideration of broader questions of social and cultural harm and the ethics of sexual representation. Prurience, in this instance, is taken to refer both to the frenzy of extreme affective responses pornography elicits, whether in media and public discourse, or the affects viewing itself provokes; and secondly, the simultaneous condemnation of pornography. In this instance, we might go so far as to say that the kinds of descriptions of pornography used in the parliamentary process, and even in the academic literature pushing for its criminalisation, display a similar degree of, if qualitatively different, prurience that they suggest those who view pornography exhibit.

The Doubling of the Offence

If porn can be construed as 'culturally harmful', what role might it have played in Jane Longhurst's death, to the extent that it was determined by Parliament that the material Coutts watched should have been illegal to view? The move from a single case of murder to the criminalisation of extreme pornography betokens what Foucault described as a 'doubling of the offence', first revealed in a collection of his lectures given at the College de France between 1974 and 1975, shortly after the publication of *Discipline and Punish*. While criminologists have drawn on other materials from this period of Foucault's work, collectively entitled *Abnormal* (2016) (see, e.g., O'Malley and Valverde 2014), less attention has been paid to his insights in the earlier lectures in this series on the 'doubling of the offence'. For the purposes of this chapter, what is intriguing about Foucault's claims in these earlier lectures is the way in which 'deviant' legal conduct below the threshold of criminal law, and the offence for which a party is being tried, are brought into conversation, and his suggestion that it is usually not the incident of crime itself that seems to be the main concern of the courts, but the *legal* conduct and its potential harms.

Foucault traces this shift in penal thinking to the seventeenth and eighteenth century courts, and suggests that it is at this point in history that the 'doubling of the offence' becomes a common feature of criminal trials. By this, he means that an offence as defined by the criminal law is doubled with:

> a whole series of other things that are not the offence itself but a series of forms of conduct, of ways of being that are, of course, presented in the discourse of the psychiatric expert as the cause, origin, motivation, and starting point of the offense. In fact, in the reality of judicial practice they constitute the substance, the very material to be punished. (2016, 15)

While Foucault's concern was principally with the application of the Napoleonic Code of 1810, in which criminality referred to absolute or strict liability, the questions he asks about the politics of expert opinion in the courts, and the way it is often used to render legal conduct as the 'double of an offence' are of universal and cross-jurisdictional importance. For Foucault (2016, 16), pronouncements of experts on the criminal subject's 'serious emotional disturbance' or 'poor grasp of reality', 'function […] to repeat the offence tautologically in order to register it and constitute it as an individual trait'.

There is, of course, no law in England and Wales that specifically criminalises 'serious emotional disturbance'. But what psychiatric opinion of this kind allows a court to do is prove that the subject formed the necessary mens rea on the basis of a psychologico-ethical double of the offence itself. As Foucault remarks, a psychiatric pronouncement of an individual's state of mind makes space for not 'exactly an offense in the legal sense of the term, but an irregularity in relation to certain rules, which may be physiological, psychological, or moral' (2016, 16).

The mens rea of an offence in England and Wales is legally distinct from a motive or explanation for crime. But what Foucault explicates is how the shift from the eighteenth century—in which culpability was articulated, as Lacey (2008, 17) tells us, on the offender having acted "maliciously', 'wickedly', 'feloniously' or 'animus furandi"—to present-day notions of responsibility became formulated within psychological and capacity-based requirements of mens rea. What the contemporary judge can punish, suggests Foucault (2016, 17), 'is precisely these irregular forms of conduct that were put forward as the crime's cause and point of origin and the site at which it took shape, and which were only its psychological and moral double'. In other words, what is at stake in constructing the 'double' of an individual's offence is the extent to which this is used to suggest the defendant does not measure up to some arbitrary notion of human development.

The second important pronouncement of Foucault in these lectures is the *surplus* provided by expert psychiatric opinion establishing the 'antecedents below the threshold, as it were, of the crime', and how this can be translated into the substance of new offences. In the case of Graham Coutts, the way in which psychiatric evidence produced over the course of his trial was used encapsulates well the phenomenon of the 'doubling of the offence'. Indeed, the justices seemed far more pruriently interested in his sexual fetishes than the immediate circumstances surrounding Longhurst's death. Evidence was presented which exhaustively detailed his fetish for women's necks, described by Lord Woolf in the following terms:

> The appellant claimed that he had held a fascination for women's necks for approximately 20 years. He described how his fetish had evolved from initial curiosity, into something that was a matter of some concern to him for a while, but eventually into something that he was comfortable with. When he was younger he had thought he was the only person who had had such thoughts and was worried that they might lead to something going wrong, and that someone might die. However, these fears had subsided by the time he was older as he had discovered that his fetish was not connected with violence. He had no interest in violence to women and his fetish for necks had generally remained the same since it started.

His fetish did not extend to women being strangled to death for sexual purposes. (*R v Coutts* [2005] EWCA Crim 52 [28])

Although not precisely constituted as an illness, nor, legally as an offence, the evidence nonetheless demonstrated to the jury that the accused already resembled the facts which led to Longhurst's death by strangulation, and that Coutts had watched pornography that contained the very act that led to her death served to corroborate his guilt in the eyes of the court. The aim is, therefore, to demonstrate that the defendant resembled the crime for which he was on trial *before* he had committed it. Legal behaviour construed as harmful, and illegal behaviour are inextricably interwoven as the substance of the same problem.

The move to criminalise 'extreme' pornography, then, read through Foucault, is the perfect accomplishment of 'doubling', in that the traces or misdeeds of Coutts that were not, at the time of his crime, illegal in themselves, were swiftly incorporated into the system of the criminal-legal. What Foucault achieves here is conveying how 'abnormal' traits and desires that themselves would previously have been deemed criminal before the modern period instead become the property of psychiatry, reconstituted in criminal evidence as traces or 'irregularities' that would otherwise have been invisible to the modern criminal law, and thus must be made visible to it by means of the creation of new offences.

The question we are left with, however, is whether it can be argued that Coutts himself can be considered 'culturally harmed' by pornography, as surely by the logic of McGlynn and Rackley, he would himself constitute a victim of a culture of the normalisation of violent pornography. The judgment in his case provides no such support, since Coutts' fascination with women's neck and his decision to visit a psychiatrist for this purpose well predated his use of 'extreme' pornography. In fact, the Lords pause far longer on his sexual history than his pornographic interests. The only viable argument would be that perhaps the pornography he viewed normalised erotic asphyxiation to the point of treating it carelessly, or else to buy into the 'slippery slope' argument (Dines 2010, 68), in which pornography 'users need to eventually seek out more extreme acts as a way to keep them interested and stimulated'.

Indeed, the conclusion of the rapid evidence assessment (Itzin et al. 2007) eventually carried out in order to provide empirical support for the legislation, citing one of the authors' own work, states:

> The problem of pornography is that it corrupts not morals, but desire. It is the fusion of sexual arousal and orgasm with physical and/or sexual violence against women, and their objectification, commoditisation, dehumanisation, degradation and subordination which is both intrinsically and instrumentally the harm of pornography. (Itzin 2002, 23)

Nevertheless, if it is once again the individual viewer who appears to be at risk of being harmed by pornography itself, their responsibilisation seems misplaced. Even if one accepts that extreme pornography is monotonal in its message, that it is both the literal demonstration and inevitable product of a culture of misogyny, criminalisation of possession simply atomises and individualises the problem of pornography. It sends out the message that pornography may have the effect of normalising the degradation and objectification of women *only* in these few specific individuals, rather than addressing the problem that we live in a culture that reaffirms the paucity of women's 'imaginary domain' (Cornell 1995) when it comes to sexuality.

The eventual shape of the offence and its focus on the individual in possession of the image also gestures towards a much broader problem with the use of approaches, such as McGlynn and Rackley's (2007), that seek to address structural harms through criminalisation efforts. Bumiller's (2008) survey of the relationship between neoliberal political economy and feminism has cautioned that once feminism became sutured with the markers of social control, it functioned as an *enabling* force for broader programmes of criminalisation. The hope was, and still is, that enlisting further state prosecutorial powers will improve the lives of individual women and change social norms surrounding female sexual agency, male dominance and violence against women. The criminalisation of 'extreme' pornography might be described as one of these efforts but, as McGlynn and Rackley (2009) admitted, unfortunately attempts to find a harm-based argument were in the end eclipsed by the language of traditional morality-driven debates about obscenity.

As a consequence, the potential effects of pornography on normalising damaging attitudes towards women and sexuality were eclipsed. In fact, a clause designed to demonstrate 'extreme' pornography's obscenity was *added* to the statute. When the Bill reached the House of Lords, Lord Hunt made society's *moral* rather than ethical obligation to regulate very clear:

> I actually felt very sick [seeing the images], because they were pretty disgusting images, and I frankly find it horrific that they are available and that people can see them. I am sorry, but I do not take this very liberal approach of 'if it does no harm to the people taking part, why should we worry about it?' I do worry about it, and about the access that people have to that kind of disgusting material… We are targeting that material not on account of offences which may or may not have been committed in the production of the material, but because the material itself… is to be deplored.[3]

The clause (Section 63(6)(b)) which was eventually inserted harks back to the OPA 1959, asking a jury to adjudicate on the level of disgust the material arouses, stipulating that the material must be 'grossly offensive, disgusting, or otherwise of an obscene character'. Thus, despite best efforts on the part of feminists to campaign for recognition of the structural harms pornography may cause, in the hands of legislators the regulation of pornography turned back the clock to the 1950s and obscenity-based measures of potential corruption of morals.

Conclusion

This short chapter enters the debate surrounding the connection between crime and harm by demonstrating how 'signal crimes' (Innes 2004) such as Coutts' function to introduce new forms of criminalisation, where previously unnoticed forms of harm enter the popular

---

[3]Lord Hunt HOL Deb 21 April 2008, vol. 700, cols. 1357–8.

imagination, and tap into public fear of 'the levels and distribution of criminogenic risks' (2004, 17). Attempts to locate sufficient evidence in the wake of a single crime to demonstrate such risks in practice are thus always likely to be both retrospective and highly speculative, and the argument for the cultural harms of pornography suffers in this respect.

While Atkinson and Rodgers (2015) attend to the need to incorporate non-criminalised harm in the remit of criminology, should the object of those of us concerned with structural harms be to use the rhetoric of zemiology to argue for further opportunities for criminalisation to deal with these harms? As is clear from this chapter, even when the impetus behind such campaigns is predicated on attempts to deal with structural inequalities and violence, there is ever the distinct possibility that efforts to send out feminist messages about gendered harms are continually drowned out by the thundering din of criminal justice's declaration of the war on crime.

References

Atkinson, Rowland, and Thomas Rodgers. 2015. Pleasure Zones and Murder Boxes: Online Pornography and Violent Video Games as Cultural Zones of Exception. *British Journal of Criminology* 56: 1291–1307.
Bandura, Albert. 1973. *Aggression: A Social Learning Analysis*. Upper Saddle River, NJ: Prentice Hall.
BBC. 2007. Teacher's Death Was No Accident. *BBC News* (Southern Counties), Jan 29. http://news.bbc.co.uk/1/hi/england/southern_counties/3442095.stm. Accessed 20 Jan 2011.
Bibbings, Lois. 2004. Heterosexuality as Harm: Fitting in. In *Beyond Criminology: Taking Harm Seriously*, ed. Paddy Hillyard, Christina Pantazis, Steve Tombs, and Dave Gordon, 217–235. London: Pluto.
Boyle, Karen. 2005. *Media and Violence: Gendering the Debates*. London: Sage.
Bumiller, Kristin. 2008. *In an Abusive State: How Neoliberalism Appropriated the Feminist Movement Against Sexual Violence*. Durham, NC: Duke University Press.
Check, James V., and Neil M. Malamuth. 1983. Sex Role Stereotyping and Reactions to Depictions of Stranger Versus Acquaintance Rape. *Journal of Personality and Social Psychology* 45: 344–356.

Cornell, Drucilla. 1995. *The Imaginary Domain: Abortion, Pornography and Sexual Harassment*. London: Routledge.

Dines, Gail. 2010. *Pornland: How Pornography Has Hijacked Our Sexuality*. Boston, MA: Beacon Press.

Donnerstein, Edward, Daniel Linz, and Steven Penrod. 1987. *The Question of Pornography: Research Findings and Policy Implications*. New York: Free Press.

Dymock, Alex. 2017. Prurience, Punishment and the Image: Reading 'Law-and-Order Pornography'. *Theoretical Criminology* 21: 209–224.

Easton, Susan. 2011. Criminalising the Possession of Extreme Pornography: Sword or Shield? *The Journal of Criminal Law* 75: 391–413.

Fae, Jane. 2012. Are We Seeing the Death of Obscenity? *Politics.co.uk*, Jan 6.

Fisher, William A., Taylor Kohut, Lisha A. Di Gioacchino, and Paul Fedoroff. 2013. Pornography, Sex Crime, and Paraphilia. *Current Psychiatry Reports* 15: 1–8.

Fletcher, George P. 2000. *Rethinking Criminal Law*. Oxford: Oxford University Press.

Foucault, Michel. 2016. *Abnormal: Lectures at the College de France 1974–1975*, trans. Graham Burchell. London: Verso.

Friday, Jonathan. 2000. Demonic Curiosity and the Aesthetics of Documentary Photography. *British Journal of Aesthetics* 40: 356–375.

Hester, Helen. 2014. *Beyond Explicit: Pornography and the Displacement of Sex*. Albany: State University of New York Press.

Hillyard, Paddy, and Steve Tombs. 2004. Beyond Criminology? In *Beyond Criminology: Taking Harm Seriously*, ed. Paddy Hillyard, Christina Pantazis, Steve Tombs, and Dave Gordon, 10–29. London: Pluto.

Hunt, Lynn (ed.). 1993. *The Invention of Pornography: Obscenity and the Origins of Modernity, 1500–1800*. New York: Zone Books.

Innes, Martin. 2004. Signal Crimes and Signal Disorders: Notes on Deviance as Communicative Action. *The British Journal of Sociology* 55: 335–355.

Itzin, Catherine. 2002. Pornography and the Construction of Misogyny. *Journal of Sexual Aggression* 8: 4–42.

Itzin, Catherine, Ann Taket, and Liz Kelly. 2007. The Evidence of Harm to Adults Relating to Exposure to Extreme Pornographic Material: A Rapid Evidence Assessment (REA). In *Ministry of Justice Research Series* 11/07. London: Ministry of Justice.

Jensen, Robert. 2007. *Getting Off: Pornography and the End of Masculinity*. Cambridge, MA: South End Press.

Lacey, Nicola. 2008. *Women, Crime and Character: From Moll Flanders to Tess of the D'Urbervilles*. Oxford: Oxford University Press.

Lasslett, Kristian. 2010. Crime or Social Harm? A Dialectical Perspective. *Crime, Law and Social Change* 54: 1–19.

Linz, Daniel G., Edward Donnerstein, and Steven Penrod. 1988. Effects of Long-Term Exposure to Violent and Sexually Degrading Depictions of Women. *Journal of Personality and Social Psychology* 55: 758–768.

Long, Julia. 2012. *Anti-porn: The Resurgence of Anti-pornography Feminism*. London: Zed Books.

Malamuth, Neil, and Joseph Ceniti. 1986. Repeated Exposure to Violence and Nonviolent Pornography: Likelihood of Raping Ratings and Laboratory Aggression Against Women. *Aggressive Behavior* 12: 129–137.

McGlynn, Clare, and Erika Rackley. 2007. Striking a Balance: Arguments for the Criminal Regulation of Extreme Pornography. *Criminal Law Review* September: 677–690.

———. 2009. Criminalising Extreme Pornography: A Lost Opportunity. *Criminal Law Review* (4): 245–260.

———. 2014. *Why Criminalise the Possession of Rape Pornography?* Durham Law School Briefing Document. Durham: Durham University.

Muncie, John. 2000. Decriminalizing Criminology. *British Criminology Conference: Selected Proceedings* 3. http://britsoccrim.org/volume3/010.pdf. Accessed 30 Jan 2017.

O'Malley, Pat, and Mariana Valverde. 2014. Foucault, Criminal Law and the Governmentalisation of the State. In *Foundational Texts in Modern Criminal Law*, ed. Markus D. Dubber, 317–334. Oxford: Oxford University Press.

Presser, Lois. 2013. *Why We Harm*. New Brunswick, NJ: Rutgers University Press.

Rackley, Erika, and Clare McGlynn. 2013. Prosecuting the Possession of Extreme Pornography: A Misunderstood and Misused Law. *Criminal Law Review* (4): 400–405.

Roberts, Alison. 2012. Simon Walsh: How Bodged Arrest and 'Profoundly Damaging' False Charges Have Ruined My City Hall Career. *The Evening Standard*, August 14.

Rubin, Gayle. 1984. Thinking Sex: Notes for a Radical Theory of the Politics of Sexuality. In *Social Perspectives in Lesbian and Gay Studies: A Reader*, ed. Peter M. Nardi and Beth E. Schneider, 100–133. London: Routledge.

Surette, Ray. 2014. *Media, Crime, and Criminal Justice*. Stamford: Cengage Learning.

Toynbee, Jason. 2008. Media Making and Social Reality. In *The Media and Social Theory*, ed. David Hesmondhalgh and Jason Toynbee, 265–279. Oxon: Routledge.

Author Biography

Alex Dymock is a lecturer in Criminology and Law at Royal Holloway, University of London. She completed her PhD in 2015 at the School of Law, University of Reading, where her thesis examined the interaction between the genealogy of discourses of sexual perversion and the criminal law. She has published articles on pornography and the normalisation of sexual 'deviance' in journals such as *Theoretical Criminology* and *Sexualities*.

Zemiology at the Border

Victoria Canning

Introduction

The study of migration has long encompassed the input of variable disciplines and subject areas: refugee studies, sociology, law, psychology and human geography. The list goes on. However, as the global experience of mobility continues to transform—where more people from the global North become ever more able to transgress borders at a time when more people than ever from the global South are increasingly legally restricted—so too does the list of disciplines interested in the study of borders. This has particularly been the case within criminology, a transdisciplinary subject area which has often otherwise failed to address the significance of borders and in particular their impact on people entangled in them, figuratively and literally. As such, the fairly recent upsurge in studies around border policing, crimmigration, deportation and the incarceration of foreign prisoners, has made

V. Canning (✉)
The Open University, Milton Keynes, UK
e-mail: Victoria.Canning@open.ac.uk

for an interesting addition to criminology. Indeed, the ever-expanding landscape of criminology at the border (Aas and Bosworth 2013; Melossi 2003; Pickering and Ham 2015; Weber and Pickering 2011) is iterative of the current climate in global mobility, exposing the paradox of the increasing militarisation of controls at a time when more people than ever require sanctuary.

This chapter reflects on the prominence of border studies in contemporary criminology and asks whether the discipline itself can offer enough to our understanding of state and state/corporate responses to refugees. As Hillyard and Tombs have argued (2004, 2008), criminology is historically administrative, focussing predominantly on elitist interpretations and implementations of so-called[1] criminal justice practices. The harms or violences in everyday processes or experiences can become obfuscated by legal analyses, state-centric perspectives and in adhering to normative definitions of crime and crime control. As such, the question arises as to whether criminology itself is the best home for the study of borders. Since the language of criminology remains bound to the concept of crime, it arguably cannot be shifted away from state-centric discourses and definitions. Terms I use myself: 'the criminalisation of migrants', 'crimmigration' (Stumpf 2006), 'criminal justice responses', all embed the inherent web of criminality which has become ever more affiliated with the transgression of borders. Life seeking asylum, and life with precarious immigration status more broadly, is multilateral in experience, and much more complex than the boundaries of criminal law or so-called criminal justice.

The central focus of this chapter is thus to consider the contentions between zemiological and criminological analyses of border controls, and specifically the structurally violent implementation of punitive legal and social policies and their micro-level consequences. In using a social

---

[1] The term 'so-called' is used in conjunction with 'criminal justice' throughout this chapter. This is to emphasise my disapproval of combining the concept of justice with criminal. Much of the 'criminal justice system' embeds practices which allow for the infliction of pain on some of the poorest and most powerless members of society, and in my experience continues to fail on affecting systematic changes which may mitigate harm infliction on victims (particularly women), or by states or corporations. It could be argued that the term 'subjugation system' may be more appropriate (a conclusion drawn from conversations with Paddy Hillyard in 2016).

harm perspective, we are arguably able to move beyond the confines of criminality and 'criminal justice'. Drawing from empirical research and reflecting on activist participation with women seeking asylum, this chapter argues for the addition of a zemiology at the border to centralise the concerns of migrants themselves, and to document the harms of asylum so that they might be mitigated or ultimately eradicated.

A Landscape of Control

By all accounts, the process of seeking asylum (and the social institutions affiliated with asylum) is deeply entrenched in criminalisation. As Ana Aliverti has shown, whilst 70 immigration offences were passed in the UK from 1905 to 1996, 84 new immigration offences were created from 1997 to 2010 (quoted in Zedner 2013, 410). Although not all of these relate solely to asylum, opportunities to enter Britain or indeed the UK have reduced for non-European Union citizens and, as the reality of a Brexit Britain looms, it is becoming clearer that restrictions will likely extend to EU nationals.

As in other parts of Europe, Australasia and North America, law and social policy in the UK have become increasingly punitive towards immigrants (Fekete 2008; Webber 2012). This has been particularly noticeable since the 1980s, with escalations from the late 1990s onward. For example, the 1987 Immigration (Carriers Liability) Act introduced civil penalties to airlines carrying passengers without a visa; the Immigration and Asylum Act (1996) made it a criminal offence to employ a person without a legal permit to work; and the Immigration and Asylum Act (1999) introduced 35 new offences. Thus, whilst those who seek the right to sanctuary are placed in the precarious position of being a border transgressor, those who work and live *within* civil society are simultaneously placed in the precarious position of law transgression. At the same time, civil life has long been increasingly restrictive for people seeking asylum who are now subject to geographical dispersal without being able to choose where to live, and where those awaiting the outcome of asylum appeals are forced to depend on a restrictive

'Azure' card[2] instead of cash. By the mid-2000s, the increase in outsourced border checks had effectively shifted responsibility to some third party countries, so those without valid visas to travel to the UK were not liable to do so.[3]

More recently, the Immigration Act (2014) turned its attention to absorbing more aspects of everyday life into the criminal justice system by introducing provisions requiring landlords to check the immigration status of tenants, whilst simultaneously reducing the possibilities for asylum seekers to appeal asylum decisions from 17 reasons to four. By 2016, the latest Immigration Act facilitates criminal sanctions for employers of illegal immigrants, and has introduced a five-year possible prison term for landlords who rent to an illegal immigrant. Moreover, the act brought in a 'deport first, appeal later' approach, allowing for the deportation of any immigrant who was awaiting the outcome of an appeal, instead requiring them to appeal from their country of origin. As we move further into the twenty-first century, the creeping claws of border controls have shifted beyond the physical border to the everyday. Private citizens who rent property to illegalised migrants can be fined or imprisoned; lorry drivers and cargo carriers are likewise held accountable if illegalised migrants are found in or on their vehicle, i.e. they fail to act as border guards; academic staff are required to monitor the attendance of students who rely on student visas to study in the UK. Stanley Cohen's vision of the dispersal of social control across all sectors of society has arguably been met in the truest sense (1985).

The implosion of immigration-related offences certainly provides justification to Liz Fekete's claims in 2007 that, 'refugees are being criminalised twice over: first, as illegal immigrants and secondly, as an army of preying destitutes, scrounging off the welfare state' (Fekete 2008, 105). Sanctions against those seeking asylum can be criminal *but are always*

---

[2]The Azure card is operated by the French catering corporation Sodexo, and is used in some supermarkets but cannot be exchanged for cash or used to buy cigarettes, alcohol or fuel. A single person in 2016 receives £35.39 per week to cover all toiletries, food, clothes, travel and use of phones.

[3]Needless to say, this has specific implications for people seeking asylum who may be avoiding authorities or who are mobilising with falsified or no documents during conflict or unrest.

implicitly social, entrenched in criminalisation as well as discourses of Othering. By facilitating the entanglement of criminal with migrant, crime control industries justify expansion (Christie 1993) and absorption (Mathiesen 2004, 32–33). In reiterating a predominantly criminological discourse, broader aspects of social control, and the harms embedded therein, can be side-lined.

Sitting in Limbo

As we can see then, the absorption of control agendas into criminal law and social policy means that aspects of seeking asylum which had previously been relatively unregulated or indeed even legal, such as paid work or gaining access to private housing whilst seeking asylum, have all but diminished. Moreover, the conflation of criminalisation with immigration, or *crimmigration* (Stumpf 2006), and its extension to social policies facilitate a Cohenesque vision of net-widening into the criminal justice system (Cohen 1985). Some of the fruits of this have resulted in the increased detention and imprisonment of irregular and illegalised immigrants. In the UK, just over 14% of the prison population are foreign nationals, 95% of whom are male and 42% of whom are from the EU (House of Commons 2017). Although significant, this remains less than some other European countries: according to Aas and Bosworth (2013, vii), 'rapidly growing foreign populations represent on average 20% of prison inmates, reaching extraordinary highs in countries such as Switzerland (71.4%), Luxembourg (68.8%), Cyprus (58.9%), Greece (57.1%) and Belgium (44.2%)'. Importantly, many of those are imprisoned based on immigration policy or legislation violations rather than for violent crimes or other offences.

Seeing that Britain has the largest prison population in Western Europe (n: 95, 248 as of March 2016, Travis 2016), the fact that it lags behind on the incarceration of foreign nationals is surprising. The first point to make here relates to the fact that fewer people seeking asylum have been able to actually make it to the UK since the implementation of carrier sanctions outlined above. Therefore, fewer people are able to be criminalised under the umbrella of immigration legislation.

In 2002, the UK saw over 84,000 applications for asylum, its greatest number thus far. By 2014, this had slowed to 32,344 and by 2015, a year that saw unparalleled migration into Europe since the Second World War 38,878 applications were made: a rise of only 20% (Blinder and McNeil 2016). Rather than recognising this as a serious gap in response, and one which enables further deaths at borders whilst people try to flee persecution,[4] 'reductions in asylum applications are seen as signs of governments' success, asylum seekers thus becoming populations one needs to be protected *from*, rather than people who need our protection' (Aas 2007, 80). The outcome of this agenda has arguably met the intention, since applications for asylum have decreased significantly, even as the need for sanctuary relating to the Refugee Convention has increased in light of the so-called[5] 'Refugee Crisis'.

The second point is that Britain's foreign national population held in prisons does not account for the over 30,000 migrants who pass through Britain's Immigration Removal Centres (IRCs) each year. Indeed, the capacity for holding migrants in IRCs at any given time surged from 250 in 1993 to 3275 in 2014 (Girma et al. 2014). These spaces, which form the heart of many criminological studies, are perhaps where most fractures lie where the focus on crime is concerned, for it is such spaces that emphasis can lie on control rather than criminalisation. As Bosworth has pointed out, IRCs *are not prisons* (2014). They are built *like* prisons, some *in* and *on* former prison sites. They mirror the physical restrictions set in the temporal and physical boundaries

---

[4]In 2011, Weber and Pickering had already drawn correlations between increases in border controls with increases in border-related deaths, deeming this structural violence since it is avoidable but no actions are taken to adequately prevent so many needless deaths (Weber and Pickering 2011). By the end of August 2016, the recorded number of refugee deaths in the Mediterranean alone had reached 3, 164 (International Organisation for Migration 2016).

[5]I say 'so-called Refugee Crisis' here because I contest the use of the term 'crisis' in this context. A crisis is unforeseeable or unpredictable. The events unfolding at Europe's borders have been wholly predictable: conflict, country occupation and economic dismantlement of any given region creates influxes in migration, and Greece and Turkey had already been experiencing significant increases in refugee populations since the 1990s. We also know that when legal routes are closed, refugees will find more dangerous routes through which to move, leading to increased deaths at borders (Weber and Pickering 2011). As such, the Refugee Crisis is arguably more aligned to militarised neoliberal border mismanagement than an unforeseeable crisis (see Canning 2018).

embedded in locked cell doors and prison gates. However, whilst some people awaiting deportation may have been convicted of criminal offences beyond immigration legislation, those forced to reside in them are not all products of criminalisation per se, but also complex identities affected by civil law and border bureaucracy. Thus, whilst criminal law indeed reflects and encompasses more aspects of immigration than ever (Stumpf 2006), the spectre of the IRC is not confined to criminalisation. It sprawls across civil society and the consciousness of those threatened by arbitrary detention within them, thus becoming part of the everyday for some rather than the criminal Other.

The Value and Limitations of Criminology at the Border

Considering these points, it is perhaps unsurprising that the related literature is increasingly placed within or on the periphery of criminology, even if the discipline itself had initially been slow on the uptake (Aas and Bosworth 2013). A fairly recent proliferation of studies has encouraged the growth of 'border criminologies' (at the University of Oxford) as well as further establishing 'the criminology of mobility' (Pickering et al. 2015, 382–395). Contributions have opened doors to discussion and critique on state-implemented controls such as the policing of mobility, deaths at global borders, border militarisation, immigration detention and the practice of deportation (Bhatia 2015; Bosworth and Turnbull 2015; Bowling and Sheptycki 2015; Fekete 2005; Melossi 2003; Weber 2015; Wilson 2015). Although significant proportions of research are concerned with legislation and statistical analysis, there has been a refreshing amount of criticism levelled at such practices, specifically arbitrary and unlimited detention and the increasing use of law as a weapon of control.

With all this said, there are a number of explicit problems in the over-dependence of criminology in the study of borders and the impacts thereof. Firstly, the upsurge in a criminological gaze towards borders can include descriptive or uncritical discussions of bordering. In particular, as the number of people entering or trying to enter Europe has surged so too, it seems, has the number of academics suddenly interested in studying borders. The easy conflation between prison and immigration detention, discussed above, arguably draws attention from those working within fields related to criminal justice and yet, as Mary Bosworth has argued, although similarities exist, they are categorically different (Bosworth 2014). Likewise, the criminalisation of asylum and other aspects of immigration open doors to researchers who have limited experience or perhaps even interest in the rights of refugees.

Secondly, and a pressing issue here is precisely reflective of Hillyard and Tombs (2004) and Hillyard's (2013) main concern: that for as long as studies are based in criminology, particularly administrative criminology, the objectives of the state and the use of state-centric language can never be eroded or moved away from. Indeed, in such a setting, it may be that criminology 'can never escape the dictatorial definitions of crime and criminality set by the State' (Hillyard 2013, 227). This is evident in the reproduction of a focus on 'crime' in studying borders from a criminological lens. Even if and when border 'crimes' are recognisably socially constructed, in that they are the product of the expansion of legal restrictions aimed at border transgressors, the focus cannot avoid people making the connection between 'migrant' and 'crime'—despite there being no ontological connection between these concepts.

This leads neatly to the third point. As argued by Bhatia and Canning (2016), criminological interests in border-related issues can reiterate problematic discourses which may seek to criticise state actions, but can instead play to reformist agendas. Taking the use of IRCs as an example, sporadic investigations and reviews often advocate surface level changes or recommendations for improvement at centre or managerial level. Indeed, reviews such as those undertaken in IRCs and published in 2016,[6] offered timely recommendations including influencing

---

[6]The Review into the Welfare in Detention of Vulnerable Persons (by Stephen Shaw) and the *Independent Investigation into Concerns about Yarl's Wood Immigration Removal Centre (by Kate Lampard and Ed Marsden)*. Shaw's review contained 64 recommendations for improvement, including banning the detention of pregnant women and suggesting there should be a 'presumption against detention' of sexual violence victims, victims of FGM, people with learning difficulties, those with Post Traumatic Stress Disorder and transgender people. Likewise, Lampard and Marsden's review has led to SERCO agreeing 35 changes at Yarl's Wood. A fuller analysis is available from Mary Bosworth (2016).

a change in legislation that limits the immigration of pregnant women to 72 hours (Immigration Act 2016; Shaw 2016). Widely praised amongst refugee advocacy groups, these were no doubt helpful recommendations for those working at the coalface of detention, or indeed those living through it. However, what this now risks is entering a phase of reform agendas and 'bad apple' politics (see Sim 2009) which will serve only to justify the existence of the immigration detention estate in the same way that it has the prison industrial complex. These wholly deflect from the key issue at hand: that confinement is harmful and inflicts pain on those held in detention. The likelihood is that working within or alongside state agendas will not lower the use of detention, but instead facilitate its increase through managerialism, absorption (Mathiesen 2004) and low-level 'improvements' such as accessing education or health care. This is damage limitation, but none of these things have the capacity to replace freedom of person.

Lastly, and perhaps most pertaining to wider concerns around the diminishing of civil liberties has been administrative criminology's adherence to discourses around 'national security' in pursuit of restricting borders. Counter-insurgency 'experts', counter-terrorism 'experts' and border police 'experts' regularly have their voices heard on how best to 'tackle' extremism. In our current political climate, this specifically means violent forms of Islamic fundamentalism, and increased border policing is regularly pointed to as part of the solution (Pantazis and Pemberton 2009). What they seldom do is look to the harms that are inflicted by state and its corporate allies to control immigrants, or consider how these impact on individuals at a micro level, including those seeking asylum (Canning 2017).

Inflicting and Enabling Harm: The Significance of Zemiology in the Study of Borders

What we can see then is a disciplinary discourse which potentially reflects and reproduces a similar trajectory to other historical aspects of criminal justice, albeit sometimes from much more critical perspectives in the mainstream. Many criminological advances have allowed for the documentation of problems in immigration controls, and work created has formed a solid critical base from which other disciplines can draw or indeed contribute to. However, two aspects remain. The first is that, as argued earlier, criminological constructions of borders cannot move away from the inherently state-centric language of 'criminal justice', and thus crime and migration become interlocked. The second is that from a feminist perspective, criminology overall continues by and large to overlook the gendered experiences of borders, and indeed intersectional interpretations of the impacts thereof. Whilst this field is developing in that sense (see Canning 2011, 2014a, b, 2017; Gerard and Pickering 2014; Milivojevic 2014; Pickering et al. 2014), it remains peripheral overall: perhaps, a reflection of the circular trajectories criminology seems to work within, despite sustained critiques over a half-century period.

Likewise, the issue of 'the everyday', one which is developed in social sciences (Gabb 2009; Neal and Murji 2015; Scheper-Hughes 1992) and well established in feminist discourses (Herman 1992; Kelly 1988; Smith 1987; Yuval-Davis 2006) has been central to zemiology where harm is concerned (if not necessarily from a feminist perspective). Hillyard and Tombs (2004, 2008) were always clear that the fundamental flaw with law is that it is elitist, and that crime has no ontological reality. Instead, discourses of justice and criminality are often regurgitated from a state-centric perspective. Considering that capitalistic interests are intrinsic to these, and that law and criminal justice agencies work to primarily control and punish some of the poorest and most powerless in society, then studies of crime cannot fully comprehend harms inflicted on those who are either most criminalised, or who are most afflicted by state and corporate harms (Tombs 2016; Tombs and Whyte 2015). As Hillyard argues, 'we need to analyse systematically the many harms which restrict and damage our lives from the cradle to the grave on a daily basis and bring this work within the boundary of zemiology' (Hillyard 2013, 232).

Since Hillyard et al. (2004) first set out to document cradle to grave harms, the field of zemiology has seen contributions on multiple forms of harm: corporate and workplace harms (Tombs 2016), gendered harms (Cain and Howe 2008) and socio-economic harms (Pemberton 2015). Theoretical contributions (see Copson 2016; Pantazis and Pemberton 2009) have been complemented by empirical research (Pantazis 2004; Canning 2017; Pemberton 2015), although the study of social harm historically depended heavily on critical statistical analysis. As will now be discussed, however, recent developments have facilitated a disciplinary direction which can allow for the study of harm to be more empirically—indeed qualitatively—focussed. This, I will argue, diverges from criminology in seeing and addressing the micro-level aspects of harm inflicted by the structural level decisions at Britain's borders: some perhaps related to aspects of criminalisation, but *all* inherently reflective of the dispersal of social controls.

Structural Decisions, Micro-Level Impacts

As we can see above, the insatiable efforts of the British state to reduce access to sanctuary creates infinite opportunities for criminalisation or treatment amounting to criminalisation. Political decisions have also facilitated further harms—outside of the mirroring of punitive aspects of criminal justice—which are arguably just as harmful but made less visible. From a decade of undertaking research with women seeking asylum in Merseyside, England, the true impacts of legislation have been visible through two lenses: qualitative research and activist participation.

The first of these has been discussed at length elsewhere (see Canning 2011, 2014a, 2016). Interviews, focus groups and oral history with women seeking asylum showed serious implications for accessing welfare and maternity care, gaining sexual or domestic violence support, having adequate or nutritious food and have living conditions which are often substandard. These issues have the capacity to inflict varying harms: physical, emotional and social, all of which are serious and damaging. However, it has been activist participation which has allowed for an even less sanitised view of asylum. The daily worry of not being able to afford enough food for herself or her children, the everyday terror experienced when women are forced to stay with abusive partners because they fear deportation or have no recourse to public funds to facilitate self-removal, the grinding irritation of pest infestations or constant coughs due to damp in temporary housing. These issues, supplemented with lengthy waits for asylum, help develop the kind of insights which concern

Hillyard (2013) in the everyday. Three further harms thus become recognisable: autonomy harm, relational harm and temporal harm.

Autonomy harms affect a person's self-worth or esteem, and can result from role deprivation and the absence of available opportunities to engage in productive activities. For people seeking asylum, this includes deciding where to live, as well as accessing learning activities, work and leisure, all of which are directly determined by legislation, including the removal of the right to work and limitations on welfare allowance and spending. Women, men and children are effectively forced into an infantilised state of dependency, with limited autonomy over what they can do or where they can go. This is grinding, but it also holds a clear element of degradation.

Relational harms include enforced exclusion from social relationships. Although seemingly less serious at the surface, the implications of relational harm are highly significant and, as argued elsewhere (Canning 2017), often compound emotional and even physical harms. The lack of funds available for travel impedes people's capacity to visit family or communicate with friends, or even to engage in support services which are outside of walking distances, since bus and train travel are seldom affordable on the meagre amounts people are forced to depend upon. Perhaps more insidiously, the sprawling net of social control has reached such lengths that even buses can be subject to immigration checks in a form of 'stop and search'. Women tell of electronic fingerprinting and even document searches on coaches and buses between Liverpool and London or Manchester, as well as within the city itself (unsurprisingly, in poorer areas with high percentages of dispersed asylum seekers). What is clear from activist participation with women is that this form of surveillance is inherently controlling: even those whose cases are under review or who are awaiting the outcome of appeals—i.e. whose stay has not been illegalised—are reluctant to face immigration controls. Women often dread interactions with the Home Office, feeling fearful of detention, refusal and deportation, or even simply being patronised or made to feel subhuman (see Canning 2017, Chapter 4).

Lastly, temporal harms link to the arduous journey of seeking asylum. As Bosworth reflected during her time studying detention, 'Their lives felt frozen, as if time had stopped' (2014, 125). This is a common experience for anyone who is held in confinement with no knowing when their time there will be complete. And yet the whole process of seeking asylum: the decision to move away from ones' country of origin, experiences during migration, the unclear and often confusing application process; are all time suspended. Add to that the unknowing of one's long term or even immediate future; the potential for dispersal; the threat of detention or deportation; bimonthly Home Office interviews; and the uncertainty of where you or your family might be in a month or a years' time. For women subjected to ongoing domestic violence or who have survived or are surviving sexual violence, this unknowing impacts not only on her present, but if she is unable to move away from violent circumstances due to a lack of support, then also her future. For men who work illegally to avoid the pains of destitution, criminalisation looms whilst poor conditions and exploitative hours impact on his physical and mental well-being (Bhatia 2015; Burnett and Whyte 2010). For women, such work can be sexualised, another example of state-facilitated vulnerability due to enforced welfare dependency and destitution.

In short, many people feel that time has stopped (Turnbull 2016). Although criminological concerns are significant and are embedded at many points in the process of seeking asylum, it is often the banality of harm in the everyday which is recognised by people awaiting the outcome of their claim or appeal. This is not always linked to aspects of crimmigration of so-called criminal justice but, as argued earlier, based on civil law, social policy and the dispersal of control. As Pemberton points out, 'criminologists have traditionally focused on harms resulting from intentional acts. This distinction appears to be difficult to sustain, if it results in partial analyses of harm that exclude the more serious structural harms' (2015, 8). What is evident here is that all such harms are directly attributable to political decision making and political action or, indeed, inaction. The everyday experiences of women, men and indeed children are marred by structural decisions which are political as well as social, and autonomous life is suspended as a result. These are *structurally violent*. As discussed elsewhere (Canning 2017), resistance and collegiality run deep amongst refugee communities and asylum activists. But the fact is, the daily harms inflicted through punitive sanctions and inadequate welfare or support are grinding: they cannot necessarily be reflected in statistical or political analysis, but in the seeing of the micro-level impacts of such insidious harms. This requires not *only* empirical research and the centralisation of the voices of the powerless but also to grasp what is being seen and call it for what it is: inherently harmful.

Conclusion

The objective of this chapter has been to question the value of criminology in the face of the criminalisation of asylum, and to ask how or if the realities of the lived experiences of harm can truly be communicated within this domain. The short answer is no. For those seeking asylum, such experiences might be bound with practices that mirror those within 'criminal justice'—particularly in relation to the infliction of autonomy harms in detention through the disintegration of rights. However, a zemiological lens facilitates the potential for us to see harm infliction from *beyond* criminology. Criminalisation and punitive legislation are embedded in the British asylum system, but the process itself is also harmful and limiting. The suspension of time whilst awaiting lengthy asylum decisions, the loss of a past and uncertainty for the future, the limitations set in gaining support beyond basic welfare: all of these are experiential and none can be challenged adequately by criminology alone.

However, whether it would be more prudential to wholly reject criminology in this regard is more complex. As Hillyard and Tombs (2004, 2008) and Hillyard (2013) indicate, criminology (in particular, administrative criminology) can still fail to engage with systematic analyses of the lived experiences of harm at a micro level and at the same time inherently conflate 'migrant' with 'criminal' by placing a key focus on border crimes and policing, even such focus comes from critical perspectives. This leads me to advocate for a zemiology at the border which might draw from critical analyses of problematic state and corporate practices, but which focuses empirically on the experiences of micro-level harms. It is ever more crucial that harms are documented, recognised and *actively opposed* so that they might be mitigated and ultimately eradicated. For this, two things must be central: a strong empirical base which centralises the voices and agendas of refugee communities, including challenging gendered harms, and to actively advocate against the proliferation of state actions which inflict or enable harm. The time has passed to rely on critical analysis alone, or to make surface-level recommendations for change. Dominant political approaches to asylum—as in the UK, Australia, New Zealand, North America and other parts of Europe—can be utterly toxic, and it is up to us to say so rather than to continuously engage state actors and agencies intent on inducing further harms. This is a danger that contemporary criminology would do well to avoid, lest we end up mirroring criminology's precarious administrative history with the so-called criminal justice system.

References

Aas, Katja Franko. 2007. *Globalisation and Crime*. London: Sage.
Aas, Katja Franko, and Mary Bosworth. 2013. *The Borders of Punishment: Migration, Citizenship and Social Exclusion*. Oxford: Oxford University Press.
Asylum and Immigration Act. 1996. http://www.legislation.gov.uk/ukpga/1996/49/section/8. Accessed 16 Sept 2017.
Bhatia, Monish. 2015. Turning Asylum Seekers into 'Dangerous Criminals': Experiences of the Criminal Justice System of Those Seeking Sanctuary. *International Journal for Crime, Justice and Social Democracy* 4: 97–111.
Bhatia, Monish, and Victoria Canning. 2016. *Immigration Detention: A Tale of Two Reviews*. The Institute of Race Relations, May 5. http://www.irr.org.uk/news/immigration-detention-a-tale-of-two-reviews/. Accessed 16 Sept 2017.
Blinder, Scott, and Rob McNeil. 2016. *Migration to the UK: Asylum*. The Migration Observatory at the University of Oxford, July 20. http://migrationobservatory.ox.ac.uk/briefings/migration-uk-asylum. Accessed 16 Sept 2017.
Bosworth, Mary. 2014. *Inside Immigration Detention*. Oxford: Oxford University Press.
Bosworth, Mary. 2016. Immigration Detention in the UK Under Review (Again), Border Criminologies. Available at https://www.law.ox.ac.uk/research-subject-groups/centre-criminology/centrebordercriminologies/blog/2016/01/immigration. Accessed 16 Jan 2018.
Bosworth, Mary, and Sarah Turnbull. 2015. Immigration Detention, Punishment and the Criminalisation of Migration. In *The Routledge Handbook on Crime and International Migration*, ed. Sharon Pickering and Julie Ham, 91–107. Oxon: Routledge.

Bowling, Ben, and James Sheptycki. 2015. Global Policing, Mobility and Social Control. In *The Routledge Handbook on Crime and International Migration*, ed. Sharon Pickering and Julie Ham, 91–107. Oxon: Routledge.

Burnett, Jon, and David Whyte. 2010. *The Wages of Fear: Risk, Safety and Undocumented Work*. Leeds: PAFRAS.

Cain, Maureen, and Adrian Howe (eds.). 2008. *Women, Crime and Social Harm: Towards a Criminology for the Global Era*. Portland: Hart Publishing.

Canning, Victoria. 2011. Women Seeking Sanctuary: Questioning State Responses to Violence Against Women in the Asylum System. *Criminal Justice Matters* 85 (September): 28–30.

———. 2014a. International Conflict, Sexual Violence and Asylum Policy: Merseyside as a Case Study. *Critical Social Policy* 34: 23–45.

———. 2014b. Women, Asylum and the Harms of Detention. *Criminal Justice Matters* 98 (December): 10–11.

———. 2016. Unsilencing Sexual Torture: Responses to Refugees and Asylum Seekers in Denmark. *British Journal of Criminology* 56: 438–456.

———. 2017. *Gendered Harm and Structural Violence in the British Asylum System*. Oxon: Routledge.

———. 2018. Border (Mis)Management, Ignorance and Denial. In *Agnotology, Power and Harm: The Study of Ignorance and the Criminological Imagination*, ed. Alana Barton and Howard Davis. Basingstoke: Palgrave Macmillan.

Christie, Nils. 1993. *Crime Control as Industry: Towards Gulags, Western Style*. London: Routledge.

Cohen, Stanley. 1985. *Visions of Social Control*. Cambridge: Polity Press.

Copson, Lynne. 2016. Realistic Utopianism and Alternatives to Imprisonment: The Ideology of Crime and the Utopia of Harm. *Justice, Power and Resistance* 1: 73–97.

Fekete, Liz. 2005. The Deportation Machine: Europe, Asylum and Human Rights. *Race and Class* 47: 64–78.

———. 2008. Xeno-Racism and the Demonisation of Refugees: A Gendered Perspective. In *Women, Crime and Social Harm: Towards a Criminology for the Global Era*, ed. Maureen Cain and Adrian Howe, 95–107. Portland: Hart Publishing.

Gabb, Jacqui. 2009. Researching Family Relationships: A Qualitative Mixed Methods Approach. *Methodological Innovations Online* 4: 37–52.

Gerard, Alison, and Sharon Pickering. 2014. Gender, Securitization and Transit: Refugee Women and the Journey to the EU. *Journal of Refugee Studies* 27: 338–359.

Girma, Marchu, Sophie Radice, Natasha Tsangarides, and Natasha Walter. 2014. *Detained: Women Asylum Seekers Locked Up in the UK*. London: Women for Refugee Women.
Herman, Judith. 1992. *Trauma and Recovery: From Domestic Abuse to Political Terror*. London: Pandora.
Hillyard, Paddy. 2013. Zemiology Revisited: Fifteen Years On. In *Critique and Dissent*, ed. Joanna Gilmore, John Moore, and David Scott, 219–237. Ottawa: Red Quill Books.
Hillyard, Paddy, Christina Pantazis, Steve Tombs, and Dave Gordon (eds.). 2004. *Beyond Criminology: Taking Harm Seriously*. London: Pluto Press.
Hillyard, Paddy, and Steve Tombs. 2004. Introduction. In *Beyond Criminology: Taking Harm Seriously*, ed. Paddy Hillyard, Christina Pantazis, Steve Tombs, and Dave Gordon, 7–25. London: Pluto Press.
———. 2008. Beyond Criminology? In *Criminal Obsessions: Why Harm Matters More Than Crime*, ed. Danny Dorling, Dave Gordon, Paddy Hillyard, Christina Pantazis, Simon Pemberton, and Steve Tombs, 7–25. London: Centre for Crime and Justice Studies.
House of Commons. 2017. *UK Prison Population Statistics*. Available at http://researchbriefings.parliament.uk/ResearchBriefing/Summary/SN04334#fullreport. Accessed 10 Nov 2017.
Immigration and Asylum Act. 1999. http://www.legislation.gov.uk/ukpga/1999/33/contents. Accessed 16 Sept 2017.
Immigration (Carriers Liability) Act. 1987. https://www.gov.uk/government/publications/chapter-33-immigration-carriers-liability-act-1987. Accessed 16 Sept 2017.
Immigration Act. 2014. http://www.legislation.gov.uk/ukpga/2014/22/contents/enacted. Accessed 16 Sept 2017.
Immigration Act. 2016. http://www.legislation.gov.uk/ukpga/2016/19/contents/enacted. Accessed 16 Sept 2017.
International Organisation for Migration. 2016. Recorded Deaths in the Mediterranean by Month, 2014–2016. *Missing Migrants Project*. https://missingmigrants.iom.int/mediterranean.
Kelly, Liz. 1988. *Surviving Sexual Violence*. Minneapolis: University of Minnesota Press.
Lampard, Kate, and Ed Marsden. 2016. Independent Investigation into Concerns About Yarl's Wood Immigration Removal Centre. Verita, available at http://www.verita.net/wp-content/uploads/2016/04/Independent-investigation-into-concerns-about-Yarls-Wood-immigration-removal-centre-Serco-plc-Kate-Lampard-Ed-Marsden-January-2016-1.pdf. Accessed 19 Feb 2018.

Mathiesen, Thomas. 2004. *Silently Silenced: Essays on the Creation of Acquiescence in Modern Society*. Winchester: Waterside Press.

Melossi, Dario. 2003. "In a Peaceful Life": Migration and the Crime of Modernity in Europe/Italy. *Punishment and Society* 5: 371–397.

Miles, Nathanael. 2010. No Going Back: Lesbian and Gay People in the Asylum System. *Stonewall*. https://www.stonewall.org.uk/sites/default/files/No_Going_Back__2010_.pdf. Accessed 17 Sept 2017.

Milivojevic, Sanja. 2014. Stopped in the Traffic, Not Stopping the Traffik: Gender, Asylum and Anti-trafficking Interventions in Serbia. In *Routledge Handbook on Crime and International Migration*, ed. Sharon Pickering and Julie Ham, 287–230. Oxon: Routledge.

Neal, Sarah, and Karim Murji. 2015. Sociologies of Everyday Life: Editors Introduction to the Special Issue. *Sociology* 49: 811–819.

Pantazis, Christina. 2004. Gendering Harm Through a Life Course Perspective. In *Beyond Criminology: Taking Harm Seriously*, ed. Paddy Hillyard, Christina Pantazis, Steve Tombs, and Dave Gordon, 192–217. London: Pluto Press.

Pantazis, Christina, and Simon Pemberton. 2009. Policy Transfer and the UK's "War on Terror": A Political Economy Approach. *Policy & Politics* 37: 363–387.

Pemberton, Simon. 2015. *Harmful Societies*. Bristol: Policy Press.

Pickering, Sharon, and Julie Ham. 2015. *The Routledge Handbook on Crime and International Migration*. Oxon: Routledge.

Pickering, Sharon, Mary Bosworth, and Marie Segrave. 2014. Introduction for Special Issue on Borders, Gender and Punishment. *Punishment & Society* 16: 131–134.

Pickering, Sharon, Mary Bosworth, and Katja Franko Aas. 2015. The Criminology of Mobility. In *The Routledge Handbook on Crime and International Migration*, ed. Sharon Pickering and Julie Ham, 382–395. Oxon: Routledge.

Scheper-Hughes, Nancy. 1992. *Death Without Weeping: The Violence of Everyday Life in Brazil*. California: University of California Press.

Shaw, Stephen. 2016. Review into the Welfare in Detention of Vulnerable Persons. *Home Office*, January 2016. https://www.gov.uk/government/uploads/system/uploads/attachment_data/file/490782/52532_Shaw_Review_Accessible.pdf.

Sim, Joe. 2009. *Punishment and Prisons*. London: Sage.

Smith, Dorothy. 1987. *The Everyday World as Problematic: A Feminist Sociology*. Boston: Northeastern University Press.

Stumpf, Juliet. 2006. The Crimmigration Crisis: Immigrants, Crime and Sovereign Power. *American University Law Review* 52: 367–419.

Tombs, Steve. 2016. *Social Protection After the Crisis: Regulation Without Enforcement*. Bristol: Policy Press.
Tombs, Steve, and David Whyte. 2015. *The Corporate Criminal: Why Corporations Must Be Abolished*. Oxon: Routledge.
Travis, Alan. 2016. UK Prison Population is Biggest in Western Europe. *The Guardian*, March 8.
Turnbull, Sarah. 2016. "Stuck in the Middle": Waiting and Uncertainty in Immigration Detention. *Time & Society* 25: 65–79.
Webber, Frances. 2012. *Borderline Justice: The Fight for Refugee and Migrant Rights*. London: Pluto Press.
———. 2014. Justice Blindfolded? The Case of Jimmy Mubenga. *Institute for Race Relations*, December 16. http://www.irr.org.uk/news/justice-blindfolded-the-case-of-jimmy-mubenga/.
Weber, Leanne. 2005. The Detention of Asylum Seekers as a Crime of Obedience. *Critical Criminology* 13: 89–109.
———. 2015. Deciphering Deportation Practices Across the Global North. In *The Routledge Handbook on Crime and International Migration*, ed. Sharon Pickering and Julie Ham, 155–179. Oxon: Routledge.
Weber, Leanne, and Sharon Pickering. 2011. *Globalisation and Borders: Death at the Global Frontier*. Basingstoke: Palgrave Macmillan.
Wilson, Dean. 2015. Border Militarisation, Technology and Crime Control. In *The Routledge Handbook on Crime and International Migration*, ed. Sharon Pickering and Julie Ham, 141–155. Oxon: Routledge.
Yuval-Davis, Nira. 2006. Intersectionality and Feminist Politics. *European Journal of Women's Studies* 13: 193–209.
Zedner, Lucia. 2013. Is the Criminal Law Only for Citizens? A Problem at the Borders of Punishment. In *The Borders of Punishment: Migration, Citizenship and Social Exclusion*, ed. Katja Franko Aas and Mary Bosworth, 40–58. Oxford: Oxford University Press.

Author Biography

Victoria Canning is a feminist and asylum rights activist, and a lecturer in Criminology at the Open University. Her research interests include sexual violence, torture and state responses to women seeking asylum. From 2016 to 2018, she is undertaking an ESRC-funded project researching trajectories of harm in asylum systems in Britain, Denmark and Sweden.

Green Criminology, Zemiology, and Comparative and Inter-Relational Justice in the Anthropocene Era

Avi Brisman and Nigel South

Introduction

In his seminal paper, 'Against "Green" Criminology', Halsey (2004, 836), asserts 'one of the greatest perpetrators of ecological damage is the *(post-)modern state* (see Goff and Geis 1993; Williams 1996; Halsey 1997)' (emphasis added). At the time of his writing, criminologists had been very much concerned with simply trying to gain acceptance within the field of criminology for the study of environmental crime and harm—and their related implications for human and non-human

---

A. Brisman (✉)
Eastern Kentucky University, Richmond, KY, USA
e-mail: Avi.Brisman@eku.edu

N. South
University of Essex, Colchester, Essex, UK
e-mail: n.south@essex.ac.uk

© The Author(s) 2018
A. Boukli and J. Kotzé (eds.), *Zemiology*, Critical Criminological Perspectives,
https://doi.org/10.1007/978-3-319-76312-5_11

animals, their ecosystems and the biosphere as a whole.[1] 'Green criminologists', as they came to be known, focused these initial efforts on macro-level harms and offenders, such as corporate and organized crime's control and manipulation of waste disposal processes (see Rodríguez and South 2017 for a discussion).

More recently, Ruggiero and South (2010a), in their paper drawing together green criminology and studies of organized and corporate crime, admit that green criminology has focused on *institutional-level* offenders, rather than *individual-level* offenders. Reasons for this vary, but include both 'the ambiguous nature of environmental harm, which is difficult to capture in a criminological framework as definitions of harm and definitions of crime do not always overlap', as well as 'the high status of those causing the most harm who (like other powerful offenders) frequently reject the proposition that criminal definitions should apply to them while constantly striving to persuade legislators that the imposition of norms of conduct on them would be detrimental to all' (Ruggiero and South 2010b, 246). This is unfortunate but reflects the reality of the latitude given to state agents and corporate elites responsible for numerous crimes of the powerful. That said, this line of argument can also be applied to the privileged consumer classes (particularly of northern/western nations but globally as well) that are responsible for an enormously disproportionate amount of consumption-related environmental harm. For example, Ockwell and colleagues (2009, 306) note that, '[w]ith over one third of many nations' carbon emissions coming from private travel and domestic energy use (DEFRA 2005; ONS 2004), governments across the globe recognize the urgent need to encourage individuals to adopt low carbon lifestyles'. Thus, without exonerating state- and corporate-level actors, we would like to suggest that green criminology has not adequately addressed *individual-level* environmental harms and crimes.

We begin by identifying some of the ways in which green criminology has discussed or might approach individual-level environmental

---

[1] See, e.g., various papers reprinted in sections 2 and 3 of South and Beirne (2006).

harm-doing. As with other individual-level theories, this also raises some potential concerns, particularly in this case where apparent 'offenders' e.g., excessive consumers, can also be seen as 'victims,' encouraged and manipulated within consumption-dependent economies by advertising, availability and credit. We then contemplate some ways of thinking about social harm in terms of the idea of inter-relational justice, which is based on human responsibility for, and interdependence with, the environment.

Ordinary Acts and Omissions that Contribute to Ecocide

Mainstream criminology has tended to focus on the causes, consequences and possible ways to respond to—i.e., prevent and punish—so-called 'street-level' crimes, such as assault, larceny, robbery and illegal drug use and trade. Drawing on existing social-psychological theories of crime that have been developed to explain street crimes, Agnew (2013, 58) turns his attention to 'ordinary acts' or 'ordinary harms' that contribute to 'ecocide', which he defines as 'the contamination and destruction of the natural environment in ways that reduce its ability to support life (South 2009, 41)'. These quotidian behaviours possess several characteristics: 'they are widely and regularly performed by individuals as part of their routine activities; they are generally viewed as acceptable, even desirable; and they collectively have a substantial impact on environmental problems' (Agnew 2013, 58). Agnew's examples include discarding and replacing still functional technological goods that have fallen out of favour or been advertised as 'obsolete', driving automobiles with poor fuel efficiency in lieu of using public transportation, living in a large, suburban home heated or cooled to comfortable levels, and regularly eating meat—livestock grazing that supports meat consumption is a major source of deforestation, water pollution and greenhouse gas emissions contributing to climate change. To this, we might add various 'ordinary omissions' that can degrade the environment—such as neglecting to turn off the lights or turn down the thermostat when leaving one's home and failing to separate compostable and recyclable items from rubbish destined for landfills—although the distinction between an ordinary 'act' and an ordinary 'omission' may become blurred when it comes to environmental harm. As Cooper (2017, 5) writes:

> When we consider all of the silly ways that Americans waste electricity, some examples probably come quickly to . . . mind: unnecessary household appliances like the 20-year-old refrigerator out in the garage being used to keep cases of soda pop; antiquated incandescent light bulbs (still widely used and sold throughout [parts of the United States]); garish outdoor advertising like lighted billboards....

Keeping/refusing to discard or recycle a 20-year-old refrigerator would probably constitute an *omission*; stocking it would amount to an *act*; turning lights *on* is obviously an *act*; insisting on keeping them on is probably also an *act*; failing to use more energy-efficient light bulbs would likely fall into the category of *omission*.

While the above-mentioned ordinary acts and omissions are environmentally harmful—and thus 'ecologically deviant' (Brisman 2015)—they are generally socially *acceptable* among people such that *not* engaging in them 'may subject one to informal sanction, jeopardize one's stake in conformity, and challenge one's beliefs' (Agnew 2013, 69). Herein, we see Agnew's attempt to apply general strain theory to the aetiology of ordinary harms, and we can readily envision how other mainstream criminological theories could be employed to explain daily, harmful acts and omissions: *control theory* might be employed to examine how a lack of a significant relationship with nature can lead to environmental insensitivity or environmentally malevolent behaviour; *social learning theory* could help unpack how an individual's behaviour with respect to the environment can and often is affected by the behaviour of others (e.g., parents, teachers, peers, other adults)[2]; *routine activities*

---

[2]As Herbig (2010, 117–118) has suggested in the context of the illegal reptile trade,
Such actions not only rape the natural environment, but serve to instil [sic] criminal tendencies and antisocial behaviour among the youth that are exposed to these actions and who look to their parents and other community role models for guidance, readily emulating and normalizing deviant behaviour perceived to be the norm (Herbig 2003). This state of affairs, essential

theory could illuminate the extent to which environmentally degrading behaviour is a function of both disposition and opportunity (see Gibbs et al. 2009, 128); and *techniques of neutralization* could highlight denial of injury (e.g., 'nature can recover'), denial of victim (e.g., 'trees and plants do not feel'), denial of responsibility (e.g., 'others contribute to air pollution, climate change, loss of biodiversity'), condemning the condemners (e.g., 'environmentalists are hypocrites'), and appeal to higher loyalties (e.g., 'God made this Earth for human use').[3]

Employing mainstream criminological theories to explain individual- and group-level environmental harm has a certain degree of appeal because it can help to strengthen their wide-ranging, normative application, as well as assist green criminologists in understanding why people behave in ways that despoil ecosystems, destroy biodiversity and degrade the biosphere (see Brisman 2014; Brisman and South 2013). Doing so is not without its concerns, however.

One concern relates to a major strand of critique directed at the explanation of crime and harm solely in terms of the individual. This argues that categorization and sanctioning of the individual follow, accompanied by net-widening and system specialization, increasing the momentum of social control developments without actually solving any social 'problems' (see, e.g., Austin and Krisberg 1981; Cohen 1979, 1985; McMahon 1990; see generally Brisman 2016). By contrast, our call for greater attention to individual-level environmental offenders/

---

social learning, undoubtedly serves to weaken social control and results in the manifestation of poor self-control mechanisms, in essence predisposing the youth to crime (Van der Hoven and Joubert 1997), and in this manner escalating the illegal reptile exploitation dilemma. In a more candid criminological context, social learning, as suggested above, typically entails the imitation of observed (criminal) behaviour performed by venerated role models (as well as the (enriching) consequences of the behaviour), which has been reinforced and defined as desirable, facilitating, as it were, the transition to criminal behaviour.

[3]It bears mention that the concept of 'techniques of neutralization' has been suggested or explored to varying degrees, albeit in the context of state- and corporate-level actions (or inactions). For example, Du Rées (2001) applies techniques of neutralization in her analysis of Swedish supervisory agencies' praxis of not always reporting suspicions of environmental offenses, while White (2002, 486) asserts that 'environmental issues call forth a range of neutralization techniques on the part of nation-states and corporations that ultimately legitimate and justify certain types of environmentally unfriendly activities'. See also analysis of 'denial' in relation to climate change (Brisman 2012; Brisman and South 2015b; Wyatt and Brisman 2016), and to arguments for unrestrained economic growth (South 2016).

offending, is not suggesting an expansion of the criminal justice system so as to draw more subjects into its remit. We are certainly not advocating the *criminalization* of the 'ordinary' acts and omissions that contribute to ecocide. Rather, following Mares (2010), we would suggest that we emphasize both collective *and* individual responsibility for our actions and that we underline their negative impact by employing a shaming approach (Braithwaite 1989; Edelman and Harris 2017; see Barragan 2015; and Takepart.com 2015 for a discussion of 'drought-shaming'; Brisman and South 2018 for a discussion of approaching environmental harm, more generally, through shaming). Mares (2010, 290) asserts—and we would agree (although we also wish this were not so)—that 'sustained shaming efforts are needed to instil a greater degree of ecological self-restraint in the *habitus* of people'. Thus, our interest in individual- and group-level environmental harm—and in the application of mainstream criminological theory to explain the causes of such harm—is based on a desire to understand the aetiology of environmental harm-doing and to seek means of expressing disapproval of an act or omission that despoils the environment, rather than enlarging the scope and ambit of the criminal justice system.

A second concern is what we might refer to as the challenge of *zemiology*. In their article, 'State Crime, Human Rights, and the Limits of Criminology', Green and Ward (2000) cautioned that broadening the definition of 'crime' too widely would destroy what coherence criminology has as a distinct field of study. More specifically, they argued against stretching the term 'crime' to cover all social harms and turning criminology into zemiology—the study of social harms (Hillyard et al. 2004; Presser 2017). Green and Ward also reminded readers that '[t]he core subject matter of criminology is behaviour that not only is, or is perceived to be, socially harmful, but is also *deviant*' (2000, 104). So, while green criminology has long been a harm-based discourse (Beirne and South 2007, xiv) and has broadened the criminological gaze beyond legal terrain to include discourses on risk, rights and regulation (South 1998; see also Walters 2007, 187–188), many of us recognize that: (1) the 'ordinary acts' are instances of *conformity*, rather than *deviance*; and (2) 'many of the most serious forms of environmental harm in fact constitute "normal social practice"' (Halsey and White 1998, 346).

Assuming *arguendo* that green criminology does not want to become green *zemiology*—and thus lose its moorings[4] in the criminological enterprise—our response to the 'zemiological charge' is twofold:

1. Given the transboundary nature of many environmental harms, what might be 'normal social practice' in the country/state of origin could be *deviant*—and even *criminal*—behaviour in the nation-state or region that is the recipient of the environmental harm—the environmental victim.
2. The ordinary acts and omissions—what may be 'normal social practice'—are *ecologically* deviant. That is to say, only if one adopts an *anthropocentric* perspective of deviancy—a perspective that considers just the impact of acts and omissions on *humans* (rather than on flora and fauna)—could one contend that the ordinary acts and omissions are *not* deviant (see Brisman 2015). Thus, the ordinary acts and omissions are deviant in the context of 'ecotopia', as conceived of by Benton (2007, 5). According to Benton, such a 'green society' would be one in which, among other things, humans would live in ways which minimally disrupt the rest of nature.

This last idea—this concept of 'ecotopia'—is, perhaps, the more problematic of the two. For we need to avoid the perception that a 'green vision'—*any* green vision—is a sort of 'elite pursuit of environmental preservation', to quote again from Benton (2007, 27). As Benton maintains, working to protect the environment 'at the expense of social justice is counterproductive. If struggles for social justice are experienced as struggles against the privileges of the defense of the environment, then the environmental case is delegitimated. ….' (2007, 27). And thus, what we wish to do next is sketch out some of the parameters and list some of the considerations that provide guidance and direction for the evaluation of ordinary acts and omissions that contribute to ecocide.

---

[4]'Moorings' is a deliberately chosen and appropriately suggestive term for we would also emphasize that the concerns of a 'green criminology' are also frequently of a broad sociological nature and, indeed, often of inter-disciplinary relevance.

Responsibility, Interdependence and the Environment: Inter-Relational Justice

As a starting point, we note the need to situate environmental harm in its social, economic, political and institutional context. This entails recognizing and respecting different (environmental) values—as products of different histories and different circumstances. As Benton (2007, 25) explains '[g]ardeners, hunters, anglers, farmers, landscape painters, ecologists, naturalists, ramblers, astronomers, ornithologists, climbers and others come to their different understandings and valuations of the world they engage with through activity and reflection upon it'. Similarly, in the context of climate change, Hulme (2009, 112) writes, 'Individuals and societies ascribe value to activities, assets, constructs and resources in many different ways. One of the reasons we disagree about climate change is because we ascribe these values differently'. This, in turn, requires acknowledging and accepting not only different cultural attitudes towards environment, nature, and risk, but structural constraints that may affect everything from food choice to transportation options.

Again, Hulme's observations on climate change are instructive and these connect us back to our earlier point about the disproportionate impact of privileged individual consumers of the global north/west. Thus, says Hulme (2009, 159),

> All individuals should not be held equally morally culpable for the emissions for which they are responsible. This was the argument of Indian social scientists Anil Agarwal and Sunita Narain in their powerful pamphlet *Global Warming in an Unequal World* published in 1991. They drew the distinction between 'luxury emissions' and 'survival emissions' in order to argue that one unit of carbon dioxide emitted by an Indian peasant farmer, essential for subsistence, carried a different moral weight to a unit of carbon dioxide emitted by an American tourist flying to the Bahamas. The level of blame is massively different in the two cases. This line of moral reasoning leads quickly into considerations of the economic, social and political structures within which individuals live their lives. [internal footnote omitted]

What we therefore propose is that we consider ordinary acts and omissions in both *relational* or (*comparative*) and *inter-relational* terms. By *relational*, we mean *based on the specific circumstances of (the) harm*; by *inter-relational*, we wish to accentuate that our interactions with our environment are fundamentally mutual and reciprocal—even if humans do not engage fairly, generously or responsibly in this relationship. Thus, for example, instead of *absolutist* positions, such as 'the taking of wild animals is bad and should be illegal' or 'the taking of wild animals is bad *because* it is illegal', we might consider the poor person who poaches for food to feed his family *in relation to*—or *in comparison to*—the wealthy person who poaches for sport and trophy. Our *inter-relationship* with nature then needs to be conceptualized *in relation to* our *means* and *capacity* to act. Thus, to offer another example, someone who drives a private vehicle because he/she finds subways to be crowded and smelly would, under our proposed orientation, be viewed differently from someone who drives a private vehicle because he/she lives in an area without (reliable) public transportation.

Our orientation, then, is really one based on two questions:

- What is the *inter-relationship* between an individual and the environment *in comparison to* other individuals' relationship(s) to the environment?
- What *might* or *could be* the *inter-relationship* between the individual and the environment (based on factors such as geography and economic or material means)?

Such an approach offers the possibility of maintaining green criminology's commitment to a harm-based discourse without rendering it a purely zemiological endeavour by abandoning entirely the notions of *crime* or *deviance* or *security*. This seems a usefully intellectually flexible and justifiably 'open' stance because competing claims about the merits or otherwise of different positions (i.e., limiting criminology to legalistic definitions of 'crime', replacing criminology's focus on 'crime' with a concern for 'deviance', supplanting 'criminology' with 'securitology') are not always entirely convincing. As Hillyard and colleagues

(2004, 64)—and many others—have pointed out, criminology certainly has its limitations, in part because it 'entails some privileging of law and criminal justice' which may impose some narrowing of thought and concerns. Equally, though, there are epistemological and semantic uncertainties inherent in sole reliance on the concept of 'deviance,' which over the course of the last sixty years, has been pronounced as the alternative to criminology, out of date, dead and buried, and then resurrected (Taylor et al. 1973; Sumner 1994, 2012; Horsley 2014). Furthermore, although some writing from a social harm perspective suggests that the idea of 'human security' is worth adopting and developing (Roberts 2009; see also Cao and Wyatt 2016), others—from disciplines like political science where this concept has had longer currency—would question employing 'security'—or 'securitology' (Shearing 2015, 264)—in place of 'criminology,' not least because 'the age of the Anthropocene gives renewed relevance to crime and criminalization' (Floyd 2015, 277).

So, to come full-circle here, as Floyd (2015, 281) continues, '[w]ith regards to bio-diversity loss, for example, great advances have been made by criminalizing transnational environmental crime, including poaching, illegal logging, fishing and trade of animal parts'. The 'discipline of criminology' could also contribute to the work needed to bring together 'greater and more systematic cooperation between countries and across legislative treaties (UNEP 2012)' (Floyd 2015, 281). The Anthropocene and environmental challenges should prompt a reconsideration of what 'crime' (and indeed criminology) might mean in this context (see Floyd 2015, 281; South 2015, 270–276) but this does not mean these terms—crime and criminology—are redundant.

To illustrate, Roberts' (2009, 3–4) contribution includes an important analysis of the social and global harms that are consequences of scarcity, control and privatization of water. This is a discussion concerning one of the most precious resources on the planet, largely overlooked by criminology until recently (Johnson et al. 2016; see also Brisman and South 2016; Brisman et al. 2016; Brisman et al. 2018; McClanahan et al. 2015). Roberts adopts what he terms a 'human security' approach to outline a bottom-up, local development and social enterprise approach to water supply as an alternative to the 'top-down approach run by the World Bank and multi-national corporations'. This is a stimulating argument that is underpinned by a helpful and constructive approach of the kind we would endorse—one that aims to take 'broad harms' as seriously as 'narrow crimes'. As Roberts (2009, 2) says, we should not forget the violence of so many crimes that injure and kill but nor should we overlook the 'socio-economic impact of neo-liberalism on a great number of people'.

But there is a danger here that we simply talk to ourselves in a circular argument about classifications and categories. To cut through the definitional conflicts perhaps we can draw upon Hall (2015, 17) by pointing out that were we to arrive at any overly rigid definitions of crime, harm and similar terms we might well end up defeating 'the purpose of the critical exercise, which is to be inclusive rather than exclusive'. Hall elaborates by referring to White's (2008) view that 'it is important for commentators, especially those concerned with green issues, to move beyond *defining* harm and onto *debating* harm, because only the latter can lead to real-life, operational developments' (Hall 2015, 17). We would take this yet one step further—beyond *defining and* beyond *debating*—to *asking questions*, such as those above, about the nature of harm and the range of possibilities to reduce or eliminate such harm, given an individual's particular circumstances (e.g., geographical location, economic or material means). Existing law might be a consideration, but it need not be the only one; *deviance* might be a factor—either because of statute or custom—but it need not be dispositive; issues of *security* might have bearing, but only insofar as they raise further questions regarding the 'recipients' of such security (Brisman and South 2017b; South 2012). In essence, then, in order to contemplate how to assess *individual-level* environmental harm/offenses to the environment, we may need an approach based on questions, aspirations and possibilities rather than one limited to (or by) criminology, zemiology or securitology.

This may not lead to comforting conclusions at the present juncture. Clearly the individual ways in which people make sense of the world mean that (inevitably) there are significant differences of opinion about how we would like the world to be; different people will view evidence of environmentally-related issues or 'problems' in various ways. In doing so, they will take account of what they perceive their own interests to be. In some cases, this will have a very tight time horizon; in others, some sense of responsibility for the planet that will be inherited by future generations (Brisman and South 2015a, 2017a).

Conclusion

The incidence of *individual-level* environmental harm/offenses to the environment can certainly be understood in terms of the theories described earlier but we have set out a broader set of questions to address. These concern the *inter-relationship* between an individual and the environment (What is the *inter-relationship* between an individual and the environment *in comparison to* other individuals' relationship(s) to the environment?) and an element of aspiration and hope (What *might* or *could be* the *inter-relationship* between the individual and the environment (based on factors such as geography and economic or material means?).

From birth we sense, and grow to understand, that we—as individual humans—have a relationship with nature based on both dominance and dependence. For many there is a precarious basis to the relationship—and the abuse of nature—along with other factors (see, e.g., Louv 2006)—is making this worse. Naomi Klein (2014) suggests that humans are currently engaging in cognitive dissonance on a planetary scale, ignoring evidence of our own culpability in damaging and degrading the natural world and the resources of the planet that all our relationships are dependent upon. We need to aspire to re-build relationships with each other, with other species and with nature. At present, as Fuchs (2007, 385) argues:

> Society reflects not only narcissistic but also, to a certain degree, borderline pathology. Acceleration of momentary events, mobility of work life, futility of communication, fragility of relationships, receding loyalty and commitment—these are the symptoms of a growing fragmentation of society as a whole. … Simultaneously or successively, [individuals] live in very different worlds that are not related to one another.

And yet, we all share one real, physical, material world—and, like it or not, we are all 'connected' to it.

In relation to understanding and agreeing on the nature of the *endangered* status of this shared planet (Benton 1998) however, there is considerable 'disconnection' from reality, from science, and from the facts and process of change (South 2016). Appreciation of the inevitability of change, the significance of temporality and the need to take a long-term view, instead of the consumerist short-termism we are conditioned into (Brisman and South 2015b), are important features of the attempt to re-build sustainable coherence in our own fragmented lives, as well as motivate and guide us to see why we need to re-build our relationships based on justice, respect and responsibility.

This is not an ecotopian call but nor is it sufficient if it is simply an anthropocentric one. The global problems of fragmentation and disconnection do not help us to address either current dilemmas or future agendas. We have a relationship—in an inter-generational sense—with the future (Brisman and South 2015a, 2017a). Thinking temporally is relevant to the choices that are made now if we are to enable future generations to have some choices left (e.g. Shue 2014). Even in the age of the Anthropocene, it is not utopian or impossible to think in this way and to respect our planet. As Norgaard (2006, 362) observes,

> Environmentalists have described how Western societies' failure to think on a longer time scale is part of why we have created long-term environmental degradation such as nuclear waste. In contrast, the Iroquois nation is reputed to make decisions from the perspective of how they would affect people living 7 generations in the future.

There is a lesson to be learned here—one relevant not just to green criminology but to humanity as a whole.

References

Agarwal, Anil, and Sunita Narain. 1991. *Global Warming in an Unequal World*. Delhi, India: Centre for Science and the Environment.

Agnew, Robert. 2013. The Ordinary Acts That Contribute to Ecocide: A Criminological Analysis. In *Routledge International Handbook of Green Criminology*, ed. Nigel South and Avi Brisman, 58–72. London: Routledge.

Austin, James, and Barry Krisberg. 1981. Wider, Stronger and Different Nets: The Dialectics of Criminal Justice Reform. *Journal of Research in Crime and Delinquency* 18: 165–196.

Barragan, Bianca. 2015. Here Are 10 People Droughtshaming Their Neighbors on Twitter. *Curbed LA*. May 26. Accessed at: http://la.curbed.com/2015/5/26/9956866/here-are-10-people-droughtshaming-their-neighbors-on-twitter.

Beirne, Piers, and Nigel South. 2007. Introduction: Approaching Green Criminology. In *Issues in Green Criminology: Confronting Harms Against Environments, Humanity and Other Animals*, ed. Piers Beirne and Nigel South, xiii–xxii. Cullompton: Willan.

Benton, Ted. 1998. Rights and Justice on a Shared Planet: More Rights or New Relations? *Theoretical Criminology* 2: 149–175.

———. 2007. Ecology, Community and Justice: The Meaning of Green. In *Issues in Green Criminology: Confronting Harms Against Environments, Humanity and Other Animals*, ed. Piers Beirne and Nigel South, 3–31. Cullompton: Willan.

Braithwaite, John. 1989. *Crime, Shame and Reintegration*. Cambridge: Cambridge University Press.

Brisman, Avi. 2012. The Cultural Silence of Climate Change Contrarianism. In *Climate Change from a Criminological Perspective*, ed. Rob White, 41–70. New York: Springer.

———. 2014. Of Theory and Meaning in Green Criminology. *International Journal for Crime, Justice and Social Democracy* 3: 22–35.

———. 2015. Environmental Harm as Deviance and Crime. In *The Handbook of Deviance*, ed. Erich Goode, 471–487. Hoboken: Wiley.

———. 2016. *Geometries of Crime: How Young People Perceive Crime and Justice*. London: Palgrave Macmillan.

Brisman, Avi, and Nigel South. 2013. Introduction to the Handbook: Horizons, Issues and Relationships in Green Criminology. In *Routledge International Handbook of Green Criminology*, ed. Nigel South and Avi Brisman, 1–23. Oxford: Routledge.

———. 2015a. 'Life Stage Dissolution', Infantilization and Anti-Social Consumption: Implications for De-Responsibilization, Denial and Environmental Harm. *Young – Nordic Journal of Youth Research* 23: 209–221.

———. 2015b. New 'Folk Devils', Denials and Climate Change: Applying the Work of Stanley Cohen to Green Criminology and Environmental Harm, *Critical Criminology* 23: 449–460.

———. 2016. Water, Inequalities and Injustice: Social Divisions, Racism and Colonialism—Past and Present. In *Criminal Justice and Security in Central and Eastern Europe: Safety, Security, and Social Control in Local Communities: Conference Proceedings*, ed. Gorazd Meško and Branko Lobnikar, 359–366. Ljubljana, Slovenia: Faculty of Criminal Justice and Security, University of Maribor, Slovenia.

———. 2017a. Green Cultural Criminology, Intergenerational (In)Equity and "Life Stage Dissolution". In *Greening Criminology in the 21st Century*, ed. Tanya Wyatt, Nigel South, Angus Nurse, Gary Potter, and Matthew Hall, 219–232. Surrey: Ashgate.

———. 2017b. Food, Crime, Justice and Security: (Food) Security for Whom? In *Food Justice in US and Global Contexts: Bringing Theory and Practice Together*, ed. Ian Werkheiser and Zachary Piso, 185–200. New York: Springer.

———. in press/2018. Perspectives on Wildlife Crime: The Convergence of 'Green' and 'Conservation' Criminologies. In *Wildlife Crime: From Theory to Practice*, ed. William D. Moreto. Philadelphia, PA: Temple University Press.

Brisman, Avi, Bill McClanahan, and Nigel South. 2016. Water Security, Crime and Conflict. *Oxford Handbooks Online in Criminology and Criminal Justice*. https://doi.org/10.1093/oxfordhb/9780199935383.013.86.

Brisman, Avi, Bill McClanahan, Nigel South, and Reece Walters. 2018. *Water, Crime and Security in the Twenty-First Century: Too Dirty, Too Little, Too Much*. London: Palgrave Macmillan.

Cao, Anh Ngoc, and Tanya Wyatt. 2016. The Conceptual Compatibility Between Green Criminology and Human Security: A Proposed Interdisciplinary Framework for Examinations into Green Victimisation. *Critical Criminology* 24: 413–430.

Cohen, Stanley. 1979. The Punitive City: Notes on the Dispersal of Social Control. *Contemporary Crises* 3: 341–363.

———. 1985. *Visions of Social Control*. Cambridge: Polity Press.

Cooper, Dave. 2017. Watts the Problem? *The Cumberland* 51 (2) [February]: 5.

DEFRA. 2005. *Experimental Statistics on Carbon Dioxide Emissions at Local Authority and Regional Level*. London: Department for Environment, Food and Rural Affairs.

Du Rées, Helena. 2001. Can Criminal Law Protect the Environment? *Journal of Scandinavian Studies in Criminology and Crime Prevention* 2 (2): 109–126. Republished online in 2010.

Edelman, Meredith, and Nathan Harris. 2017. Reintegrative Shaming. In *The Routledge Companion to Criminological Theory and Concepts*, ed. Avi Brisman, Eamonn Carrabine, and Nigel South. London and New York: Routledge.

Floyd, Rita. 2015. Environmental Security and the Case Against Rethinking Criminology as 'Security-ology'. *Criminology and Criminal Justice* 15: 277–282.

Fuchs, Thomas. 2007. Fragmented Selves: Temporality and Identity in Borderline Personality Disorder. *Psychopathology* 40: 379–387.

Gibbs, C., M.L. Gore, E.F. McGarrell, and L. Rivers. 2009. Introducing Conservation Criminology: Towards Interdisciplinary Scholarship on Environmental Crimes and Risks. *British Journal of Criminology* 50 (1): 124–144.

Goff, C., and G. Geis (eds.). 1993. The Environment and Social Justice. *The Journal of Human Justice* 5 (1): 1–128.

Green, Penny, and Tony Ward. 2000. State Crime, Human Rights, and the Limits of Criminology. *Social Justice* 27: 101–115.

Hall, Matthew. 2015. *Exploring Green Crime: Introducing the Legal, Social and Criminological Contexts of Environmental Harm*. London: Palgrave Macmillan.

Halsey, Mark. 1997. The Wood for the Paper: Old-Growth Forest, Hemp and Environmental Harm. *Australian and New Zealand Journal of Criminology* 30 (2): 121–148.

———. 2004. Against 'Green' Criminology. *British Journal of Criminology* 44: 833–853.

Halsey, Mark, and Rob White. 1998. Crime, Ecophilosophy and Environmental Harm. *Theoretical Criminology* 2: 345–371.

Herbig, Friedo Johann Willem. 2003. *The Illegal Reptile Trade*. PhD Thesis. Pretoria: University of South Africa.

Herbig, Joe. 2010. The Illegal Reptile Trade as a Form of Conservation Crime: A South African Criminological Investigation. *Global Environmental Harm: Criminological Perspectives*. Devon: Willan.

Hillyard, Paddy, Christina Pantazis, Steve Tombs, and Dave Gordon (eds.). 2004. *Beyond Criminology: Taking Harm Seriously*. London: Pluto Press.

Horsley, Mark. 2014. The 'Death of Deviance' and the Stagnation of Twentieth Century Criminology. In *The Death and Resurrection of Deviance: Current Ideas and Research*, ed. Michael Dellwing, Joseph Kotarba, and Nathan Pino, 85–107. New York: Palgrave Macmillan.

Hulme, Mike. 2009. *Why We Disagree About Climate Change: Understanding Controversy, Inaction and Opportunity*. Cambridge, UK: Cambridge University Press.

Johnson, Hope, Nigel South, and Reece Walters. 2016. The Commodification and Exploitation of Fresh Water: Property, Human Rights and Green Criminology. *International Journal of Law, Crime and Justice* 44: 146–162.

Klein, Naomi. 2014. *This Changes Everything: Capitalism vs. The Climate*. New York: Simon and Schuster.
Louv, Richard. 2006. *Last Child in the Woods: Saving Our Children from Nature-Deficit Disorder*. Chapel Hill: Algonquin.
Mares, Dennis. 2010. Criminalizing Ecological Harm: Crimes Against Carrying Capacity and the Criminalization of Eco-Sinners. *Critical Criminology* 18: 279–293.
McClanahan, Bill, Avi Brisman, and Nigel South. 2015. Privatization, Pollution and Power: A Green Criminological Analysis of Present and Future Global Water Crises. In *The Routledge International Handbook of the Crimes of the Powerful*, ed. Gregg Barak, 223–234. London: Routledge.
McMahon, Maeve. 1990. Net-Widening: Vagaries in the Use of a Concept. *British Journal of Criminology* 30: 121–149.
Norgaard, Kari. 2006. "We Don't Really Want to Know": Environmental Justice and Socially Organized Denial of Global Warming in Norway. *Organization and Environment* 19: 347–370.
Ockwell, David, Lorraine Whitmarsh, and Saffron O'Neill. 2009. Reorienting Climate Change Communication for Effective Mitigation: Forcing People to Be Green or Fostering Grass-Roots Engagement? *Science Communication* 30: 305–327.
ONS. 2004. Greenhouse Gas Emissions from Transport. *Office for National Statistics News Release*. http://www.statistics.gov.uk/downloads/theme_environment/transport_report.pdf.
Presser, Lois. 2017. Social Harm/Zemiology. In *The Routledge Companion to Criminological Theory and Concepts*, ed. Avi Brisman, Eamonn Carrabine, and Nigel South. London: Routledge.
Roberts, David. 2009. *Social Harm and Crime at a Global Level*, Briefing 9, September. London: Centre for Crime and Justice Studies. Available at https://www.crimeandjustice.org.uk/sites/crimeandjustice.org.uk/files/Socialharmglobal.pdf.
Rodríguez, David G., and Nigel South. 2017. Green Criminology Before 'Green Criminology': Amnesia and Absences. *Critical Criminology* 25 (May). Special issue entitled "Researching Environmental Harm, Doing Green Criminology".
Ruggiero, Vincenzo, and Nigel South. 2010a. Green Criminology and Dirty Collar Crime. *Critical Criminology* 18: 251–262.
———. 2010b. Critical Criminology and Crimes Against the Environment. *Critical Criminology* 18: 245–250.
Shearing, Clifford. 2015. Criminology and the Anthropocene. *Criminology and Criminal Justice* 15: 255–269.

Shue, Henry. 2014. Changing Images of Climate Change: Human Rights and Future Generations. *Journal of Human Rights and the Environment* 5 (June): 50–64.

South, Nigel. 1998. A Green Field for Criminology? A Proposal for a Perspective. *Theoretical Criminology* 2: 211–233.

———. 2009. Ecocide, Conflict and Climate Change. In *Eco-Crime and Justice*, ed. Kristiina Kangaspunta and Ineke H. Marshall, 37–54. Turin, Italy: UNICRI.

———. 2012. Climate Change, Environmental (In)Security, Conflict and Crime. In *Climate Change: Legal and Criminological Implications*, ed. Stephen Farrall, Tawhida Ahmed, and Duncan French, 97–111. Oxford: Hart.

———. 2015. Anticipating the Anthropocene and Greening Criminology. *Criminology and Criminal Justice* 15: 270–276.

———. 2016. Free Trade Agreements, Private Courts and Environmental Exploitation: Disconnected Policies, Denials and Moral Disengagement. *International Journal for Crime, Justice and Social Democracy* 5: 45–59.

South, Nigel, and Piers Beirne (eds.). 2006. *Green Criminology*. Aldershot: Ashgate.

Sumner, Colin. 1994. *The Sociology of Deviance: An Obituary*. Buckingham: Open University Press.

———. 2012. Censure, Culture and Political Economy: Beyond the Death of Deviance Debate. In *New Directions in Criminological Theory*, ed. Steve Hall and Simon Winlow, 165–180. London: Routledge.

Takepart.com. 2015. 5 Ways People Are Drought Shaming Their Neighbors. *Takepart.com*. June 4. Accessed at https://www.yahoo.com/news/5-ways-people-drought-shaming-neighbors-185449003.html?ref=gs.

Taylor, Ian, Paul Walton, and Jock Young. 1973. *The New Criminology: For a Social Theory of Deviance*. London: Routledge.

UNEP. 2012. *Transnational Environmental Crime: A Common Crime in Need of Better Enforcement*. Available at https://na.unep.net/geas/getUNEPPageWithArticleIDScript.php?article_id=95. Accessed 20 Feb 2017.

Van der Hoven, A.E., and S.J. Joubert. 1997. Crime Causation and Explanation. In *Criminology. Tutorial letter 103/97 for KRM 100-5 (Crime: Causation, Explanation, Reaction and Prevention)*, ed. A.E. Van Der Hoven, S. Joubert, J.J. Neser, W.J. Jacobs and C.M.B. Naudè, 1–27. Muckleneuk, Pretoria: University of South Africa.

Walters, Reece. 2007. Crime, Regulation and Radioactive Waste in the United Kingdom. In *Issues in Green Criminology: Confronting Harms Against Environments, Humanity and Other Animals*, ed. Piers Beirne and Nigel South, 187–205. Cullompton: Willan.
White, Rob. 2002. Environmental Harm and the Political Economy of Consumption. *Social Justice* 29 (1–2): 82–102.
White, Rob. 2008. *Crimes Against Nature: Environmental Criminology and Ecological Justice*. Cullompton: Willan.
Williams, Christopher. 1996. Environmental Victims: An Introduction. *Social Justice, Special Issue on Environmental Victims* 23: 1–6.
Wyatt, Tanya, and Avi Brisman. 2016. The Role of Denial in the 'Theft of Nature': A Comparison of Biopiracy and Climate Change. *Critical Criminology* 25: 325–341.

Authors' Biography

Avi Brisman (MFA, JD, PhD) is an Associate Professor in the School of Justice Studies at Eastern Kentucky University, an Adjunct Associate Professor in the School of Justice at Queensland University of Technology, and a Conjoint Associate Professor at Newcastle Law School at the University of Newcastle.

Nigel South (BA, MA, PhD) is a Professor in the Department of Sociology and Director of the Centre for Criminology, University of Essex, and a visiting adjunct Professor at the Crime and Justice Research Centre, Queensland University of Technology. He has published widely on green criminology; drugs, use and control; and policing. In 2013 he received a Lifetime Achievement Award from the American Society of Criminology, Division on Critical Criminology, and in 2014 was elected a Fellow of the Academy of Social Sciences.

Spot the Fashion Victim(s): The Importance of Rethinking Harm Within the Context of Fashion Counterfeiting

Jo Large

Introduction

The study of counterfeiting and counterfeit markets rarely sits highly on the criminological agenda and despite some notable exceptions, remains an area which is generally under-researched and under-theorised. Yet, at the same time, counterfeiting is 'considered to be one of the largest underground industries in the world' (Sullivan et al. 2016, 1). In terms of the relationship between crime and harm, arguments against counterfeiting rely heavily on notions of harm. Harm may be particularly obvious in terms of some forms of counterfeits, notably those which can be described as 'safety critical' counterfeits (Yar 2005). These goods, such as counterfeit pharmaceuticals, airline parts and electrical products, are of concern due to their danger to the public. Consequences of these kinds of goods entering the market can be devastating to both the consumer and legitimate enterprises, with clear risks for direct and

J. Large (✉)
University of Bristol, Bristol, UK
e-mail: jo.large@bristol.ac.uk

identifiable victimisation. Thus, from an administrative perspective, it could be suggested that the dangers of counterfeits far outweigh any potential gains and there is a clear need for resources to be devoted to these counterfeit criminal markets. However, when the focus is shifted to 'non-safety critical' counterfeit goods, such as fashion products, it is suggested that these do not pose safety and public interest issues in such a clear cut manner (see Wall and Large 2010). This causes problems for justifying resources and attention to something which is suggested to be perceived as a 'victimless crime' (Anderson 1999). Victimless in the sense that it does not harm the consumer and the general public nor have any other direct and identifiable victims.

In addition to concerns about harm towards the public, business scholars and industry has for a number of years, complained that counterfeiting is detrimental to legitimate manufacturers, retailers and the wider economy. This is primarily through 'lost sales' of legitimate items and causing brand reputation damage. Notice has been afforded to other economic and social impacts of counterfeiting; such as the loss to the economy, and especially, the relationship of counterfeiting with serious and organised crimes including drug and people trafficking, extortion and money laundering (OECD 2008; UNODC n.d). This in particular has also led to law enforcement—despite local and national variations—for the large part becoming more attuned to counterfeiting as a crime problem. However, despite debates about counterfeit goods tending to centre on harm (or lack of harm in some cases), it is clear that ideals of direct and deserving victimisation play an important role in shaping responses towards the debate. Thus, despite the notional focus on harm, it can be argued that these debates fail to engage with a thorough and critical consideration of social harm, which moves properly beyond the focus on individual consumers, legitimate business and large-scale criminal activity.

It is in this sense then this chapter problematizes examining counterfeiting within a framework constrained by focusing on crime, or further by arguing that definitions of what constitutes a crime should be expanded (Hillyard and Tombs 2004; Pemberton 2016). One of the central tenets of this chapter is that it is problematic to consider the illicit market of counterfeits alone. By doing so, this constrains notions of harm and victimisation within pre-existing conceptions about crime and fails to critically consider the harms which are perpetuated by the legitimate industry (Tombs 2004, 2010; Tombs and Whyte 2007) and further, fails to contextualise how harm is embedded within the political economy of consumer capitalism (Hall et al. 2008; Raymen and Smith 2016; Smith and Raymen 2016). In addition to calls from those such as Hillyard et al. (2004) and Pemberton (2016) which argue for a focus on social harm as opposed to crime, this chapter also draws on work by those such as Smith and Raymen (2016) who, drawing upon an ultra-realist perspective (Hall and Winlow 2015), argue that a fundamental critique of consumer culture is required which shifts the focus from crime and deviance to one which considers the harms of 'socially acceptable and culturally embedded' forms of leisure. It is here that I position this analysis of the market for counterfeit fashion within a framework of fashion and consumption. Hence, this chapter will first outline the nature and 'problem' of counterfeiting before exploring the need to consider the harms of counterfeiting beyond a traditional criminological framework. Following this, I explore why counterfeiting should be considered in relation to a broader understanding of fashion, consumption and global capitalism and the need for those interested in the study of illicit markets such as counterfeits, to provide a more critical perspective of their parallel licit economy.

The Problem of Counterfeiting

The term counterfeiting has varying definitions and many other terms such as fake, imitation, copy, knock-off, replica and look-alike are often used interchangeably with counterfeit. Whilst some discuss the differing definitions of terms like counterfeit and imitation the reality is that for the large part these goods cannot be meaningfully separated in such way. In many cases, a trade mark infringing good may be infringing other intellectual property laws such as copyright. This chapter is concerned with one form of product counterfeiting, namely fashion. This is because, as a form of non-safety critical counterfeiting, the fashion industry poses a set of additional challenges for criminology (Wall and Large 2010). The focus here is on a broad notion of fashion, which encapsulates the range of fashion products counterfeited: from luxury 'high' fashion to sportswear, T-shirts and accessories such as sunglasses and bags.

Despite (limited) recent attention to counterfeiting as a criminological issue, and to the contemporary concerns about counterfeit goods, counterfeiting itself is not a new phenomenon. However, recent years have witnessed a movement away from the small-scale and relatively localised 'cottage industry' of counterfeiting (Vagg and Harris 1998, 189) to a rapidly developing complex global market, which produces, distributes and retails counterfeits. The Organisation for Economic Co-operation and Development (OECD) argued in April 2016 that the global import trade in counterfeit goods amounts to nearly half a trillion US dollars with 'much of these proceeds going to organised crime' (OECD and EUIPO 2016). Continued rapid advances in technology, most notably the growth of internet banking, online shopping and social media, have transformed the nature of the market(s) for counterfeit goods. It is easier than ever to distribute, produce and manufacture goods (Hall and Antonopoulos 2016; Heinonen et al. 2012; Treadwell 2012; Wilson and Fenoff 2014). In addition, the internet enables a heightened drive and desire for counterfeit (and legitimate) goods more generally (Lavorgna 2015; Hall and Antonopoulos 2016; Heinonen et al. 2012; Rojek 2017; Treadwell 2012; Wilson and Fenoff 2014). Alongside technological advancements, the nature of contemporary late capitalism and its resultant impact on consumer culture have all contributed to the rapidly changing nature of illegal markets (Hall et al. 2008). These kinds of concerns alone should place counterfeiting firmly on the criminological agenda and to some extent the focus on counterfeiting's relationship with organised crime has done so. However, this focus has primarily resulted in a surge of administrative focused studies which seek to inform policy, reduce the problem or highlight issues for criminal justice agencies (see Sullivan et al. 2016).

A Victimless Crime?

Given the importance placed on the consumer, and the public more generally within the context of counterfeiting (see Large 2015), deception takes on an important role when understanding fashion counterfeiting and along with quality, is considered an important factor when assessing the harms of counterfeiting. Notions of deception and quality often tend to centre on the problematic idea of the stereotypical counterfeit consumer. These ideas tend to be based on a range of assumptions, which usually relate to cheapness and the consumer looking for a 'bargain'. Underlying this is a presumption that most counterfeits are bought knowingly, or, the consumer in some way failed to spot that a product is fake (Large 2015). However, it is too simplistic to assume that all counterfeit purchasers do so knowingly and that all fashion counterfeits are sold within the same context, or indeed, are even of the same quality. Grossman and Shapiro (1988, 80) distinguished two types of counterfeit markets—'deceptive' and 'non-deceptive'. More recent work argues that it is more useful to consider a scale which runs from 'super deceptive' to 'completely non-deceptive' (Bosworth 2006, 9). However, making any distinction between deceptive and non-deceptive counterfeits relies on making assumptions about products and/or consumers of the products. If deception is assessed by reference to the seller, then at first it may seem an obvious distinction between those on the one hand, who sell counterfeits quite openly as counterfeits and on the other, those who sell counterfeits as if they are authentic products. However, whilst manufacturing and selling counterfeits in England and Wales remains an illegal activity (as for most countries), the likelihood of a seller openly advertising that they are selling counterfeits is probably quite low. Instead, when there are discussions about deception and counterfeiting, usually what is implied is that there is an onus on consumers to recognise particular cues, or indicators, about the potential likelihood of a product being a counterfeit (see Large 2015).

Closely associated with deception is quality. A poor quality product could potentially cause harm to the consumer. In the case of fashion, this would most often be with consumers being fraudulently ripped off by being duped into buying a counterfeit. However, even when focusing on fashion counterfeits alone—which typically would be categorised as non-safety critical—there may well be *safety* concerns especially with regards to consumer health. Take, for example, fashion accessories such as sunglasses with no UV protection, or jewellery coated with a skin irritant product. This problem is exacerbated when you consider a broader understanding of fashion which includes beauty products such as cosmetics, skin products and electricals such as hair straighteners and so on.

Whether counterfeiting is something that should be taken seriously by consumers, criminal justice agencies or indeed criminologists, as pointed out by Mackenzie (2010), might often depend on whether the counterfeit is purchased knowingly or unknowingly. Further, when there is a clear potential visible or direct *deserving* victim (i.e. the consumer) (Christie 1986) as is often the case with deceptive safety critical counterfeit goods—i.e. goods which will cause some kind of physical harm to the consumer (see Yar 2005)—it is possible to suggest that this will be considered the most problematic form of counterfeiting. However, such a narrow focus on victimisation and harm is really problematic and it is clear even at this stage that we need to question the boundaries administrative forms of criminology tend to place on the types of crime which are deserving of attention. Even before we get into a more critical exploration of harm, surely a consumer being ripped off or even just being complicit in the purchase of illicit goods should present dilemmas criminologists need to pay attention to?

Towards a Broader Understanding of Counterfeiting and Harm

Beyond the individual consumer (and excluding the controversial idea that counterfeits cause harm to brands and industry), increasing concern has been afforded to the social, and in particular criminal, harms of counterfeiting. Here the focus tends to be on the relationship between counterfeiting, *serious* crime, organised crime and even terrorism. This is widely cited as the primary reason why consumers should avoid buying counterfeits.

Counterfeiting is recognised as a highly profitable business, which has natural allure to criminal groups and networks. This is because its high-profit potential combines with 'pitifully low sanctions' (AIM 2005, 1)—or at the least the numerous challenges in enforcing legislation. Organisations such as the United Nations Office on Drugs and Crime (UNODC) highlight the evidence for 'organised crime groups' being involved in counterfeiting through national and international authorities' attention on counterfeit markets and supply chains. UNODC also identify the 'strategic and operational links between counterfeiting and drug trafficking,' for example (UNODC n.d). The Intellectual Property Crime Group (IPCG), based in the United Kingdom, further documents examples of the relationship between counterfeiting and criminal activities citing 'many' cases where links have been found. These 'criminal activities' include 'money laundering, people trafficking, loan sharking and the exploitation of children' (IPCG 2010, 15). Some caution must be placed here towards the uncritical usage of terms such as organised crime and organised crime groups in many of these kinds of documents (see Croall 2010; Hobbs 2002; Levi 2007), however the nature of the criminal activities and markets is of importance to wider discussions of [dis]organised crime (see Von Lampe 2016).

This leads to a need for criminologists to examine counterfeiting as there are clearly numerous issues which require investigation. However, the danger is that it becomes an administrative attempt at 'designing out crime'. A recent review of the state of the field by Sullivan et al. (2016) highlights that criminological research (published in or before 2014) on counterfeiting falls into three areas:

1. assesses the scope of counterfeiting, assessing the magnitude of the impact or awareness raising,
2. addresses the risks and opportunities structures for counterfeiting,
3. focuses on identification and prevention mechanisms for industry.

In addition, as well as larger scale criminality, counterfeiting is likely to be a key activity for smaller informal economies and illicit markets. A survey conducted by the IPCG asked authorities to comment on whether counterfeiting was linked to 'wider criminality'. The IPCG's report found that there was a range of links with 'lower level' types of criminal and antisocial behaviour, with benefit fraud being the most common (48%) (IPCG 2010, 16). Current on-going research on small-scale counterfeit markets[1] and the transnational financial flows of counterfeit goods (Antonopoulos et al. 2018) examines the differing scopes of production, distribution and

---

[1]Large, J—In The Business of Counterfeit Fashion: UK Illicit Markets (current research project).

end market supply of counterfeit goods, and the relationships between licit and illicit economies. Counterfeits are also noted for the potential to be commodities in which criminals can trade (UNODC n.d.).

It can therefore be suggested, that due to the focus on criminal activities and criminal markets, framing counterfeiting as a crime may in itself be limiting and problematic. Whilst of course this is not to dispute or take less seriously the real harms of many of the criminal acts (Hall and Winlow 2015) counterfeiting is associated with, there is a need to go beyond legal definitions of crime when examining issues such as fashion counterfeiting. Criminologists must engage critically with an understanding of why counterfeit markets exist when we know that many consumers knowingly buy counterfeit products. Thus, there is a need to consider demand for illicit goods within the context of consumer capitalism. Given the huge market for counterfeit goods, the first assumption which needs to be abandoned is the idea that counterfeit consumption can be typified demographically or as deviant. By drawing upon zemiology and advances within critical criminology, it is possible to explore and recognise more fully the potential for serious harms associated with counterfeiting which is contextualised within an understanding of the embedded nature of harm in consumer capitalism.

Counterfeiting, Harm and the Legitimate Industry

Of key relevance is the fact that the sustainability of illegal markets, such as that of counterfeits, is inherently reliant on the consumption of products (counterfeit or not). This is the case for counterfeit products consumers are deceived into buying, as much as is the case for counterfeits consumers knowingly buy. Yet, we remain in a situation where despite increased attention from criminologists towards understanding the *supply* of counterfeit goods, much of what is known about the consumption (or *demand*) of these goods tends to come from industry sources or outside of criminology. As a result, the consumption of counterfeit products tends to be understood as something outside of usual consumer behaviour, with an implication that the practice is deviant. However, it is more helpful to acknowledge the harms of leisure as something which is a 'transgression of the ethical duty to the other' rather than a rejection of social norms and values (Smith and Raymen 2016, 3). Thus, consuming counterfeits can be interpreted not as 'transgressing but conforming to capitalism's disavowed core "values" and practices, which are exploitative, acquisitive and socially irresponsible' (Hall and Winlow 2015, 51). In addition, as pointed out by Hobbs (2012, 265)

> [we] should not [be] blind to the attractions of market behaviour that makes nonsense of the often arbitrary distinctions between legal and illegal business.

Engaging with fashion can be considered as one of the primary modes of consumption in contemporary society. The acts of consuming products, as well as consuming shopping experiences as a leisure activity, are both relevant. Consumerism and leisure are central to everyday life (Bauman 2005) with status being ultimately best presented through consumption and leisure in contemporary capitalist society (Hall et al. 2008; Lloyd 2013). A continually evolving fashion industry, with daily updates of new 'must have's' (and of course by default the resulting effect of existing goods diminished to *must nots*) provides one of the most effective ways to engage with consumption. For Bauman (2007) this 'buy it, enjoy it, chuck it out cycle' (p. 98) coupled with the 'constant pressure to be *someone else*' (p. 100) reinforces the constant demand in neo-liberal capitalist societies for the consumption of fashion. As Lloyd (2013, 152) summarises:

> the genius of consumer capitalism reveals itself in the fact that these desires do not present themselves to us as desire, rather we are convinced that we *need* each specific consumer product. Creating *pseudo-needs* and then ensuring we can never satisfy them ensures the economy keeps going on the back of our thwarted desire.

The very nature of fashion relies on the process of 'introduction and imitation' (Yurchisin and Johnson 2010, 3); a process which is at the heart of stabilising capitalist global economies increasingly reliant on the consumption of products and leisure (Hoskins 2014). Whilst consumers are sold ideals of free choice and identity expression through fashion, the reality is that the nature of fashion is one which is structurally and systemically harmful. The ever-increasing pressure to consume perpetuated by the cycle of introduction and imitation combines with desire for immediate and emotional gratification. This takes place amongst a social and economic backdrop which is characterised with precarity, anxiety and insecurity (Hall et al. 2008; Lloyd 2013), not to mention an ever increasing consumer debt market (Horsley 2015). The very nature of fashion serves to exacerbate consumer anxieties in a way which goes far beyond buying clothing items due to the focus on the body (Entwistle 2000). A booming health and wellness industry with quick fix diets and its self-proclaimed 'lifestyle coaches' exists alongside an ever-growing beauty and cosmetics industry which enables consumers to manipulate their bodies into the latest fashionable craze. Of course with this comes further anxiety, insecurity and harm; not to mention a booming illicit pharmaceutical and cosmetic trade (see Hall and Antonopoulos 2016).

Further, the emphasis within the fashion cycle on *copying* in itself adds to the potential to blur the boundaries between products which are deemed as problematic, i.e. counterfeit, and those that are not. As Hilton et al. (2004, 345) argue: the 'problem' of counterfeiting 'partly lies in the industry itself'. The nature of the fashion 'cycle' is one which relies on designs being replicated to the mass market. Designers show their designs on the catwalk (runway) and styles, trends and designs become modified for the mass market and this is distributed to the consumer through fashion magazines, celebrities, advertising, online and, of course, in shops (Barnard 2007). Therefore, legitimate fashion goods are readily available on the high street with designs closely based on what has been shown on the catwalk at varying price points to attract the consumer. Part of the role of fashion magazines, vloggers and social media accounts is to perpetuate this onto the consumer—for example, features which include advice on how to recreate a particular look seen on celebrities or elsewhere. In essence, fashion relies on imitation for mass production—copying in this sense is accepted because it both publicises the fashion brand, and 'legitimates their designs as ones which are desirable and worth copying' (Hilton et al. 2004, 351). Copying is also legitimised by fashion brands themselves through ready to wear lines and franchising. At the same time, there is also the visible growth in value retailing and its 'disposable' fashion (shops such as Primark, H&M and Matalan which sell fashion goods at a low price point) and the popularity of 'fast fashion'. This essentially advocates purchasing cheaper items which are often much less durable to enable consumers to keep up with rapidly changing fashion trends. The demand for cheap, affordable and fast fashion is high with 'shoppers seeking something new to wear every week' (Morgan and Birtwistle 2009, 190), alongside a strong demand for more expensive branded products. The advent of fast fashion and its resultant speeding up of the fashion cycle (goods can go from production to consumption within a matter of days), coupled with ever-expanding modes and ease of consumption, generates a resounding success platform for impulse buying. 'The international mass consumer now wants the latest fashion posthaste, necessitating flexibility and turnaround at levels that disrupt all stable norms of industrial competition' (Ross 1997, 11) which will have inevitable harm attached. Thus, as well as encouraging consumers to buy cheap products, this can blur the boundaries between counterfeits and non-counterfeits. Discounting of goods, selling of factory rejects and parallel trading all add to compound the complex discussions around ethics, the fashion industry and counterfeiting (Hilton et al. 2004). Motivations for counterfeit products must therefore be caught up within motivation for legitimate products which goes considerably beyond simple rational economics of cost (Large 2011).

At the same time, in addition to the nature of fashion being one based on copying, Hilton et al. (2004) also raise important ethical concerns about the legitimate fashion industry, which they suggest must be considered in a discussion around the ethics of counterfeiting. This was notably apparent in the work of Large (2011) whose research with consumers found that many had real concerns not just about the ethical issues of manufacturing and producing counterfeits, but also with the manufacture and production of fashion goods more generally. Whilst fashion companies would be inclined to deny any poor procedure, there has been evidence of poor practice in the past (see Dickson 2005; Klein 2005; Panorama 2008; Ross 1997) and consumers certainly seem to be under the belief that this is still taking place.

It is often easy to point the finger at value retailers whose entire business model is based on high volume sales of cheap, disposable items such as Primark—especially as a result of the Panorama documentary aired in 2008 (Panorama 2008), which highlighted issues such as child labour and poor production practices. However, these issues are not necessarily exclusive to value retailers alone (Hoskins 2014; Siegle 2011). Poor production practices are commonly associated with unsafe working conditions. For instance, the collapse of the Rana Plaza, a factory in Savar, Bangladesh in April 2013 produced new calls for scrutiny on the global fashion industry. More than 1000 factory workers were killed and over 2000 more injured in a factory which collapsed only a day after it was ordered to be closed due to safety concerns.[2] (Jones 2016). Rana Plaza housed a number of popular global high-street fashion brands, a number of whom appear yet to take financial responsibility towards compensating victims' families (see Clean Clothes Campaign 2017a). In July 2016, 38 people were formally charged with murder following the collapse (Guardian 2016)—although it is not clear at the time of writing to what extent this case has progressed. However, this was not a one-off incident, only a few months prior to the Rana Plaza collapse was the Tazreen Fashions Factory fire, again in Bangladesh which killed 112 workers and injured scores of others. This fire was one of a number of clothing factory fires in the years preceding (Human Rights Watch 2015).

These high-profile events brought global scrutiny on the global fashion industry and generated questions about the working standards, conditions and safety of the workers employed to produce these

---

[2]Large cracks appeared in the walls and foundations of the building the day prior to its collapse and a government inspector ordered the building to be closed. However, workers were assured by managers that the building was safe and that they should continue to work. The building collapsed following a power failure in which a generator was switched on to provide power and caused the building to shake enough to collapse (Jones 2016).

fashion goods and a succession of contract stipulations from brands and national laws to formally address concerns. However, in common with existing zemiological work on the workplace (Tombs 2004; Tombs and Whyte 2007), the success of legislation and regulation is questionable. Human Rights Watch (2015) reported:

> consistent violations of worker's rights in factories including practices contrary to both national law and codes of conduct Western retailers insist suppliers use.

The report, based on research with workers from numerous factories across Bangladesh, found violations which included: physical abuse, sexual abuse, verbal abuse, forced overtime, failure to pay wages on time or in full, dirty drinking water and pressure to not use the bathroom (Human Rights Watch 2015). Despite a recognition that unions are one of the most effective ways to make a workplace safer (Tombs 2004), Human Rights Watch further found that attempts to set up unions often result in dismissals, pay refusal and assault. December 2016 witnessed mass dismissals of workers in factories supplying global brands such as H&M, Gap and Zara for protesting about low pay (Clean Clothes Campaign 2017b; Safi 2016). In addition, concerns remain about the exploitation of children. Quattri and Watkins (2016, 3) report that there is a 'high work incidence of children aged 6 –14' years old; children who are working 'beyond just a few hours a day'. Although Quattri and Watkins' report focused on child labour in Bangladesh generally, in terms of the fashion industry, it was found that the garment sector accounts for two-thirds of female child labour. Children therefore are exposed to the same dangers as adult workers in these environments, but are even more vulnerable due to their age. Most children who are working are, perhaps unsurprisingly, not in education (Quattri and Watkins 2016). These kinds of social harms are imperative to consider in recognition of their overwhelming exacerbation of social inequalities and impact on the economically disadvantaged (Hall and Winlow 2015; Pemberton 2016; Yar 2012). Given the seeming lack of progress against poor practices, labour exploitation, questionable ethics and physical safety of workers (see Ross 1997), this is a multi-billion pound industry which must be addressed in criminology and highlights the need for engaging with a social harm approach. In short; 'the fashion industry lays out in sharp relief all the ins and outs of capitalism' (Hoskins 2014, 9) and 'the organising features of capitalism are inherently harmful' (Pemberton 2016, 35). As argued by Tombs (2004, 177), there may be more value in 'critically dissect[ing] and ultimately shed[ding] the illusions of law' than arguing for expanding the reach of criminal legislation.

In addition to the concerns about workers, the relationship between the fashion industry and environmental harm is one which warrants further attention and advances in green criminology provide an important extension to the zemiological gaze (White and Heckenberg 2014). EcoWatch (2015) suggests that the fashion industry is 'the second dirtiest industry in the world' after oil. Ho and Choi (2012) note the 'negative ecological footprint' that the industry leaves behind—primarily due to high volume, low-value manufacturing and the complexity and speed of the supply chain. There are two issues of environmental concern here. First, the waste and pollution generated from manufacturing and supply—including production processes, transportation and energy consumption—which is evident at all stages of the supply chain. However, also of relevance is waste post-consumption, which as Hvass (2014) argues is a growing problem. Within the UK alone, in 2005 DEFRA (2007) estimated that 2 million tonnes of textile waste is generated every year, with more than half of that ending up in landfill. Issues of harmful waste disposal practices, whether legal or illegal, tend to affect the poorest in the world the most (White and Heckenberg 2014). The tendency for wealthy countries to export their waste to less developed countries is well documented, as is the tendency for waste disposal sites in communities to be located in the most disadvantaged areas (see White and Heckenberg 2014) again highlighting the structural harms of 'inequalities generated by neoliberalism' (Pemberton 2016, 51).

These issues are not just the problem of low-value and high-street fashion brands. As Hoskins (2014) argues, there is little value in separating 'high' fashion and 'high-street' fashion in any examination of the global fashion industry. This is because luxury fashion houses rely on mass production of items such as T-shirts, bags and sunglasses for profits in similar locations and manners to high-street or 'fast fashion' brands.

Further, on a wider conceptual level as Hoskins asks, 'why pretend over-consumption is a problem of only the cheapest brands?' (2014, 3). Whilst this discussion around harm has moved to focus on the legitimate fashion industry, all of these issues will be relevant to the shadow counterfeit fashion industry. Thus, on the one hand, whilst it is clear that attention needs to be afforded to the harms of the fashion industry, it is also likely that the harms of the shadow counterfeit fashion industry are likely to be exacerbated by the lack of any kind of scrutiny or regulation. Therefore, it is evident that if we move beyond binary definitions and a view of harm which is largely constructed in terms of crime, there is a need to examine closely the harms of the legitimate and illegitimate fashion industry. It is also evident, that the fashion industry is at least partly responsible for the shadow counterfeit fashion industry.

Conclusion

In conclusion, there is a clear need for the incorporation of zemiology to expand the criminological enterprise. The on-going problem of criminology is its focus on legally defined criminal acts, and further the tendency to devote more attention to those it considers most serious. However, these constructions are often based on problematic notions of crime, harm and victimisation. Therefore, if criminology is to understand illicit markets, we need to move beyond simply focusing on the illicit market as if it exists separately and provide a more critical understanding within the context of the parallel legal market. From a demand perspective, this is partly because consuming illicit goods is an extension of consuming licit goods. Within the example of fashion counterfeiting, there are further clear parallels between the legitimate and illegitimate market, and a difficult question of whether the fashion industry should shoulder some of the responsibility for the counterfeit industry. This should involve recognising the harms which are associated with the legal market and the overlapping relationship between the licit and illicit—particularly within the context of a globalised consumer market. Recognising a very broad array of social harms beyond those defined legally as crime is essential, as is recognising the role of the capitalist economic system (Hillyard and Tombs 2004). At the same time, thought must be given to how harm should be defined and addressed particularly within a competitive research agenda.

Since we could suggest that 'harm is invisible, embedded within the social organisation of consumer capitalism' (Raymen and Smith 2016, 402); as those interested in harm, we need to go beyond focusing on the *crime* problem (i.e. fashion counterfeits) and consider the real 'crime' problem as one which lies with the corrupt, abusive and harmful nature of the fashion industry. Are we, by predominantly focusing on the legal definition of criminality, missing the fundamental problem, the harm caused by the legitimate fashion industry? However, to what extent are these harms exacerbated by the illegitimate industry which is further deregulated and is associated with other forms of serious crime of which the harm should not be dismissed (Hall and Winlow 2015)? Counterfeiting is a topic which itself is an issue worthy of further attention, however the complexities of these kinds of consumer markets appear part of a bigger problem which transcends the legitimate and illegitimate marketplace. Therefore, fashion counterfeiting can be seen as a vehicle which allows us to examine these complexities, and by encapsulating a zemiological viewpoint, pushes beyond traditional criminological boundaries and highlights the importance of a more engaged critical discussion about crime and harm.

References

AACP. n.d. Proving the Connection. Links Between Intellectual Property Theft and Organised Crime. *Alliance Against Intellectual Property Theft (Formerly Alliance Against Counterfeiting and Piracy)*. http://www.allianceagainstiptheft.co.uk/downloads/reports/Proving-the-Connection.pdf. Accessed 10 Sept 2007.

AIM. 2005. Faking It: Why Counterfeiting Matters. Briefing Paper April 2005, *Association des Industries de Marque, European Brands Association*.

Anderson, John. 1999. The Campaign Against Dangerous Counterfeit Goods. In *International Criminal Police Review: Special Issue on Counterfeiting*, ed. Raymond Kendall, 56–59. Lyon: ICPO/Interpol.

Antonopoulos, Georgios A., Alexandra Hall, Joanna Large, Anqi Shen, Michael Crang, and Michael Andrews. 2018. *Fake Goods, Real Money. The Counterfeiting Business and its Financial Management*. Bristol: Policy Press.

Barnard, Malcolm. 2007. Introduction. In *Fashion Theory: A Reader*, ed. Malcolm Barnard, 1–13. Oxon: Routledge.

Bauman, Zygmunt. 2005. *Liquid Life*. Cambridge: Polity Press.

———. 2007. *Consuming Life*. Cambridge: Polity Press.

Bosworth, Derek. 2006. Counterfeiting and Piracy: The State of the Art. In *Intellectual Property in the New Millennium Seminar*. Oxford: Intellectual Property Research Centre. www.derekbosworth.com. Accessed 27 July 2011.

Christie, Nils. 1986. The Ideal Victim. In *From Crime Policy to Victim Policy: Reorienting the Justice System*, ed. Ezzat A. Fattah, 17–30. Basingstoke: Macmillan.

Clean Clothes Campaign. 2017a. *Rana Plaza*. https://cleanclothes.org/safety/ranaplaza. Accessed 6 Jan 2017.

Clean Clothes Campaign. 2017b. *Press Release 05.01.17: Bangladeshi garment workers face mass firings and criminal charges*. https://cleanclothes.org/news/2017/01/05/bangladeshi-garment-workers-face-mass-firings-and-criminal-charges. Accessed 6 Jan 2017.

Croall, Hazel. 2010. Middle-Range Business Crime. In *Handbook on Crime*, ed. Fiona Brookman, Mike Maguire, Harriet Pierpoint, and Trevor Bennett, 678–697. Devon: Willan.

DEFRA. 2007. *Maximising Reuse and Recycling of UK Clothing and Textiles*. London: Department for Environmental Food and Rural Affairs.

Dickson, Marsha A. 2005. Identifying and Profiling Apparel Label Users. In *The Ethical Consumer*, ed. Rob. Harrison, Terry Newholm, and Deirdre Shaw, 155–172. London: Sage.

EcoWatch. 2015. Fast Fashion Is the Second Dirtiest Industry in the World, Next to Big Oil. http://www.ecowatch.com/fast-fashion-is-the-second-dirtiest-industry-in-the-world-next-to-big–1882083445.html. Accessed 6 Jan 2017.

Entwistle, Joanne. 2000. *The Fashioned Body: Fashion, Dress and Modern Social Theory*. London: Polity.

Grossman, Gene M., and Carl Shapiro. 1988. Foreign Counterfeiting of Status Goods. *The Quarterly Journal of Economics* 103: 79–100.

Guardian. 2016. Rana Plaza Collapse: 38 Charged with Murder over Garment Factory Disaster. https://www.theguardian.com/world/2016/jul/18/rana-plaza-collapse-murder-charges-garment-factory. Accessed 6 Jan 2017.

Hall, Alexandra, and Georgios A. Antonopoulos. 2016. *Fake Meds Online: The Internet and the Transnational Market in Illicit Pharmaceuticals*. Basingstoke: Palgrave.

Hall, Steve, and Simon Winlow. 2015. *Revitalizing Criminological Theory: Towards a New Ultra—Realism*. London: Routledge.

Hall, Steve, Simon Winlow, and Craig Ancrum. 2008. *Criminal Identities and Consumer Culture: Crime, Exclusion and the New Culture of Narcissism*. Devon: Willan.

Heinonen, Justin A., Thomas J. Holt, and Jeremy M. Wilson. 2012. Product Counterfeits in the Online Environment: An Empirical Assessment of Victimization and Reporting Characteristics. *International Criminal Justice Review* 22: 353–371.

Hillyard, Paddy, and Steve Tombs. 2004. Beyond Criminology? In *Beyond Criminology: Taking Harm Seriously*, ed. Paddy Hillyard, Christina Pantazis, Steve Tombs, and Dave Gordon, 10–29. London: Pluto.

Hillyard, Paddy, Christina Pantazis, Steve Tombs, and Dave Gordon (eds.). 2004. *Beyond Criminology: Taking Harm Seriously*. London: Pluto.

Hilton, Brian, Chong J. Choi, and Stephen Chen. 2004. The Ethics of Counterfeiting in the Fashion Industry: Quality, Credence and Profit Issues. *Journal of Business Ethics* 55: 345–354.

Ho, Holly P.Y., and Tsan-Ming Choi. 2012. A Five-R Analysis for Sustainable Fashion Supply Chain Management in Hong Kong: A Case Analysis. *Journal of Fashion Marketing and Management* 16: 161–175.

Hobbs, Dick. 2002. The Firm: Organisational Logic and Criminal Culture on a Shifting Terrain. *British Journal of Criminology* 42: 549–560.

———. 2012. 'It Was Never About the Money': Market Society, Organised Crime and UK Criminology. In *New Directions in Criminological Theory*, ed. Steve Hall and Simon Winlow, 257–275. London: Routledge.

Horsley, Mark. 2015. *The Dark Side of Prosperity*. Farnham: Ashgate.

Hoskins, Tansy E. 2014. *Stitched Up: The Anti-Capitalist Book of Fashion*. London: Pluto.

Human Rights Watch. 2015. 'Whoever Raises Their Head Suffers the Most': Workers' Rights in Bangladesh's Garment Factories. https://www.hrw.org/report/2015/04/22/whoever-raises-their-head-suffers-most/workers-rights-bangladeshs-garment. Accessed 6 Jan 2017.

Hvass, Kerli K. 2014. Post-retail Responsibility of Garments—A Fashion Industry Perspective. *Journal of Fashion Marketing and Management* 18: 413–430.

IPCG. 2010. Intellectual Property Crime Report 2009–2010. Intellectual Property Crime Group. UK Intellectual Property Office. http://www.ipo.gov.uk/ipcreport09.pdf. Accessed 15 Aug 2011.

Jones, Reece. 2016. *Violent Borders: Refugees and the Right to Move*. London: Verso.

Klein, Naomi. 2005. *No Logo*. New York: Harper.

Large, Joanna. 2011. *Criminality, Consumption and the Counterfeiting of Fashion Goods*. Unpublished PhD Thesis, Leeds University.
———. 2015. 'Get Real Don't Buy Fakes': Fashion Fakes and Flawed Policy—The Problem with Taking a Consumer—Responsibility Approach to Reducing the 'Problem' of Counterfeiting. *Criminology and Criminal Justice* 15: 169–185.
Lavorgna, Anita. 2015. The Online Trade in Counterfeit Pharmaceuticals: New Criminal Opportunities, Trends and Challenges. *European Journal of Criminology* 12: 226–241.
Levi, Michael. 2007. Organised Crime and Terrorism. In *The Oxford Handbook of Criminology*, 4th ed., ed. Mike Maguire, Rod Morgan, and Robert Reiner, 771–809. Oxford: Oxford University Press.
Lloyd, Anthony. 2013. *Labour Markets and Identity on the Post-Industrial Assembly Line*. Basingstoke: Ashgate.
Mackenzie, Simon. 2010. Fakes. In *Handbook on Crime*, ed. Fiona Brookman, Mike Maguire, Harriet Pierpoint, and Trevor Bennett, 120–136. Devon: Willan.
Morgan, Louise R., and Grete Birtwistle. 2009. An Investigation of Young Fashion Consumers' Disposable Habits. *International Journal of Consumer Studies* 33: 190–198.
OECD. 2008. The Economic Impact of Counterfeiting and Piracy. *Organisation for Economic Co-Operation and Development*. http://www.oecdbookshop.org/oecd/display.asp?lang=EN&sf1=identifiers&st1=9789264045521. Accessed 27 July 2011.
OECD and EUIPO. 2016. Global Trade in Fake Goods Worth Nearly Half a Trillion Dollars a Year. *Organisation for Economic Co-Operation and Development and European Union Intellectual Property Office*. http://www.oecd.org/industry/global-trade-in-fake-goods-worth-nearly-half-a-trillion-dollars-a-year.htm. Accessed 22 Oct 2016.
Panorama. 2008. Primark: On the Rack. *Panorama, BBC One*, June 23. http://news.bbc.co.uk/1/hi/programmes/panorama/7461496.stm. Accessed 13 June 2011.
Pemberton, Simon. 2016. *Harmful Societies: Understanding Social Harm*. Bristol: Policy Press.
Quattri, Maria, and Kevin Watkins. 2016. Child Labour and Education: A Survey of Slum Settlements in Dhaka. *Overseas Development Institute*. https://www.odi.org/sites/odi.org.uk/files/resource-documents/11145.pdf.
Raymen, Thomas, and Oliver Smith. 2016. What's Deviance Got To Do With It? Black Friday Sales, Violence and Hyper-Conformity. *British Journal of Criminology* 56: 389–405.

Rojek, Chris. 2017. Counterfeit Commerce: Relations of Production, Distribution and Exchange. *Cultural Sociology* 11: 28–43.

Ross, Andrew (ed.). 1997. *No Sweat: Fashion, Free Trade and the Rights of Garment Workers*. London: Verso.

Safi, Michael. 2016. Bangladesh Garment Factories Sack Hundreds After Pay Protests. *Guardian*. https://www.theguardian.com/world/2016/dec/27/bangladesh-garment-factories-sack-hundreds-after-pay-protests. Accessed 6 Jan 2017.

Siegle, Lucy. 2011. *To Die For: Is Fashion Wearing Out the World?* London: Harper Collins.

Smith, Oliver, and Thomas Raymen. 2016. Deviant Leisure: A Criminological Perspective. *Theoretical Criminology*. Online First. https://doi.org/10.1177/1362480616660188.

Sullivan, Brandon A., Fiona Chan, Roy Fenoff, and Jeremy M. Wilson. 2016. Assessing the Developing Knowledge-Base of Product Counterfeiting: A Content Analysis of Four Decades of Research. *Trends in Organised Crime*. https://doi.org/10.1007/s12117-016-9300-5.

Tombs, Steve. 2004. Workplace Injury and Death: Social Harm and the Illusions of Law. In *Beyond Criminology: Taking Harm Seriously*, ed. Paddy Hillyard, Christina Pantazis, Steve Tombs, and Dave Gordon, 156–177. London: Pluto.

———. 2010. Corporate Violence and Harm. In *Handbook on Crime*, ed. Fiona Brookman, Mike Maguire, Harriet Pierpoint, and Trevor Bennett, 884–903. Devon: Willan.

Tombs, Steve, and Dave Whyte. 2007. *Safety Crimes*. Devon: Willan.

Treadwell, James. 2012. From the Car Boot to Booting It Up? eBay, Online Counterfeit Crime and the Transformation of the Criminal Marketplace. *Criminology and Criminal Justice* 12: 175–192.

UNODC. n.d. Focus On: The Illicit Trafficking of Counterfeit Goods and Transnational Organised Crime. *United Nations Office on Drugs and Crime*. http://www.unodc.org/documents/counterfeit/FocusSheet/Counterfeit_focussheet_EN_HIRES.pdf. Accessed 6 Jan 2015.

Vagg, Jon, and Justine Harris. 1998. Bad Goods: Product Counterfeiting and Enforcement Strategies. In *Crime at Work Vol. 2: Increasing the Risk for Offenders*, ed. Martin Gill, 185–200. Leicester: Perpetuity Press.

Von Lampe, Klaus. 2016. *Organised Crime: Analysing Illegal Activities, Criminal Structures, and Extra Legal Governance*. London: Sage.

Wall, David S., and Joanna Large. 2010. Jailhouse Frocks: Locating the Public Interest in Policing Counterfeit Luxury Fashion Goods. *British Journal of Criminology* 50: 1094–1116.

White, Rob, and Diane Heckenberg. 2014. *Green Criminology: An Introduction to the Study of Environmental Harm*. Oxon: Routledge.

Wilson, Jeremy M., and Roy Fenoff. 2014. Distinguishing Counterfeit from Authentic Product Retailers in the Virtual Marketplace. *International Criminal Justice Review* 24: 39–58.

Yar, Majid. 2005. A Deadly Faith in Fakes: Trademark Theft and the Global Trade in Counterfeit Automotive Components. *Internet Journal of Criminology.* www.internetjournalofcriminology.com.

———. 2012. Critical Criminology, Critical Theory and Social Harm. In *New Directions in Criminological Theory*, ed. Steve Hall and Simon Winlow, 52–65. Oxon: Routledge.

Yurchisin, Jennifer, and Kim K.P. Johnson. 2010. *Fashion and the Consumer*. London: Berg.

Author Biography

Jo Large is a Lecturer in Criminology at the University of Bristol, UK. Jo's research focuses on the connections between consumption and harm. This includes analysis of counterfeit markets and the overlapping nature of licit and illicit economies. More recently, Jo's interests have extended to examine the relationship between volunteer/charity based tourism and harm.

Serving Up Harm: Systemic Violence, Transitions to Adulthood and the Service Economy

Anthony Lloyd

Introduction

The emerging body of literature on social harm affords new opportunities to look critically at the social landscape in post-crash Britain (Yar 2012; Smith and Raymen 2016; Pemberton 2015). Zemiology offers new directions in fields such as crime (Hillyard and Tombs 2004), climate change (White and Heckenberg 2014) and leisure (Smith and Raymen 2016). Less frequently, the zemiological gaze has been brought to bear on the workplace (Tombs 2004; Tombs and Whyte 2007; Scott 2017). These works often highlight harmful conditions in relation to physical well-being and the absence of effective health and safety regulation (Tombs and Whyte 2007). This chapter presents a new contribution to harmful working by linking an emerging ultra-realist schema (Winlow and Hall 2016; Hall and Winlow 2015) with the structural conditions of employment and experiences of workplace culture within the service economy. The empirical data, which drives the harm discussion within

A. Lloyd (✉)
Teesside University, Middlesbrough, UK
e-mail: Anthony.Lloyd@tees.ac.uk

this chapter, underpins a number of other publications in relation to the service economy (see Lloyd 2012, 2013, 2017, 2018). Specifically, this chapter will identify a shift from job security towards job flexibility that has marked significance for employees within the service economy, including the erosion of stability. Within a realist framework, absences matter as much as presences; the absence of stability in employment conditions, working conditions and ontological security, impacts young people in their quest to locate a stable sense of purpose and place as they transition to adulthood.

A political-economic shift from production and manufacturing towards consumerism reconfigured Western landscapes from the 1980s onwards (Harvey 2005), and propelled the service economy from the periphery to the centre of UK labour markets. Between 1971 and 2008, Teesside in the UK (the site of the long-term ethnographic study of the service economy underpinning this chapter) lost 100,000 manufacturing jobs, largely in steel-making and petrochemicals, which were replaced by 90,000 jobs in service industries (Shildrick et al. 2012). This was indicative of a sweeping shift across the UK, USA and parts of Europe as burgeoning consumer markets presented opportunities for expansion in retail and leisure services, the night-time economy and other customer service functions (Lloyd 2013). In a culture that increasingly demonises those out of work (Shildrick et al. 2012), paid employment is today regarded positively, with scant regard for the actual conditions of employment. Media scrutiny has highlighted individual operators such as Sports Direct or Amazon as distinctly beyond the pale in terms of working conditions and management practices, yet those who direct their ire at Mike Ashley have often failed to let their gaze drift beyond their target. Sports Direct and Amazon are not rogue operators in an otherwise proficient and unproblematic stratum of the labour market but instead represent the *normal functioning of the late capitalist service economy*.

Ultra-realism and Social Harm

If zemiology is to carry weight as an explanatory frame, it must have solid foundations (Hall 2012). An emerging ultra-realist schema is venturing to thrust criminological and sociological thought beyond the ascendant empiricism directing the discipline, beyond the administrative and pragmatic wings of social science seeking efficient governance of the current political-economic order, and beyond the flaws within critical realism (Hall and Winlow 2015). Depth structures have causative effects on individuals and the socio-cultural logic of society (Bhaskar 2010); empiricism evidences what we can see but fails to contemplate the causal influence of the intransitive realm of deep structures upon the quotidian reality of individuals and communities (Winlow and Hall 2016). In this sense, critical realism offers a positive theoretical route towards grasping the relationship between concrete events, lived experiences and the deep structures of society (Collier 1994).

Ultra-realism follows this line of enquiry yet eschews the critical realist interpretation of subjectivity (Winlow and Hall 2016). Rather than endorse belief in a natural human essence, where the subject is inherently 'good', ultra-realism subscribes to the Lacanian-Žižekian explication of subjectivity (Žižek 2000). The subject is a non-essential void, an unconscious complex of pre-social drives and desires capable of both good and evil (Hall and Winlow 2015). This 'transcendental materialist' interpretation of subjectivity (Johnston 2008) suggests that the non-essential subject actively solicits an external symbolic order as a defence mechanism to provide internal meaning to external stimuli. The inherent plasticity of the brain ensures neuronal receptors adapt and reconfigure to equip the subject with the values, norms, language, comportment and symbolic framework necessary to exist in the world (Winlow and Hall 2013; Johnston 2008; Žižek 2000). In practical terms for this discussion, the symbolic order emanating from the depth structures of ideology and political economy influences the subject who possesses active agency to reproduce existing material and symbolic structures or to work to change them. In order to discern conditions within the service economy, an ultra-realist perspective contemplates the relationship between the individual, the workplace and the depth structures of political economy and ideology, which corresponds with Žižek's (2008) injunction to equate subjective and symbolic violence as symptoms rather than causes. The generation of harms, by virtue of the system and its normal functions, presents a constructive line for analysis. A critical facet of ultra-realism is its capacity to interpret absences as well as presences; in pursuit of the causative effects that generate harms within the service economy, the *absence* of something is just as causal as a presence (Winlow and Hall 2016).

Absences

Absences, within ultra-realism, have a probabilistic causal influence on our lives (Hall and Winlow 2015). Neoliberal restructuring does not mechanically cause harm, but the systemic violence at the heart of capitalism is visible through the subsequent absences of, for example, welfare regimes that forestall material deprivation or job security that provides a measure of stability. This negativity omits any form of *positive* transformation in material and social conditions but still retains the transformative potential to reshape interpersonal connections and working cultures. The post-war settlement enclosed a regulatory jacket around the generative core of capitalism to yield a degree of stability and durability at a material level; job security and propitious employment conditions were attained via legislation and union bargaining (Harvey 2005). Job security brought a modicum of compensation for stringent and often physically dangerous working conditions or mistreatment by management or other co-workers. This is not to romanticise industrial capitalism; harms were still inflicted at a systemic, symbolic and subjective level, yet the job security provided during the post-war settlement permitted the individual subject to situate their identity in a community, class or occupational culture (see Lloyd 2013).

The neoliberal 'restoration' (Harvey 2005; Badiou 2009), exemplified by ideological exhortations towards free-market principles of flexibility, freedom and choice represented a systematic puncturing of welfare's regulatory jacket (Whitehead and Hall forthcoming). Institutions previously exempt from market principles underwent a reorganisation of institutional culture and drivers that resulted in an ideological, symbolic and material shift in practice and the solicitation of market principles (Whitehead 2015). The faith in market mechanisms to efficiently order all facets of social life indicated the unshackling of capitalism's generative core. Economic stagnation in the 1970s was met with howls of derision at policy grounded in regulatory frameworks formulated to secure greater fairness and equality; by unleashing the free market, deregulating and re-regulating industries in order to facilitate market proliferation and autonomy, the social, cultural and economic landscape transformed dramatically. Since the financial crisis, neoliberalism has doubled-down. Despite its apparent flaws, market principles have diffused into the public sector whilst private firms maintain their pursuit of efficiency, productivity and growth. To further these ends, regulation on working environment and employment protections have been systematically reconfigured and eroded (Streeck 2016). Within the service economy, these absences are distinctly visible.

The Absence of Stability

The shift from job security to job flexibility is exhaustively recapitulated within the literature (Beck 2000; Standing 2011; Kalleberg 2009). Sennett (1999) articulates the 'corrosion of character' evident in the shift from established working environments and job security that affords the individual the long-term scope to mould durable character and identity, towards a variable pattern of working that focuses unreservedly on the short term. The absence of stability and security reconfigures labour markets and employment practices resulting in a reorientation of the subject in relation to work, career progression and company loyalty (Lloyd 2013). McDowell (2009) argues that interactive service work is flexible by nature; the direct service of consumer demand requires immediate delivery. As services cannot be stored and used later, the requirement for flexibility drives the sector, including the need for 24/7 service availability and provision. In Western Europe, North America and Australasia, the service economy accounts for three in four of all waged workers (McDowell 2009, 30). Given the recent proliferation of 'on-demand' working within the 'gig economy', the espousal of flexibility as intrinsically beneficial for both consumers and workers continues apace (Harvey et al. 2017). Consumer capitalism has embedded modes of leisure such as shopping, gambling and the night-time economy within its circuits (Smith and Raymen 2016), all of which require, to one degree or another, flexible customer service operations.

The character of service work may propel the demand for this flexibility yet it also reflects political, economic and ideological interests that rebalance the relationship between capital and labour (Harvey 2005). Systematic re-regulation of employment law has relocated power away from organised labour and the employee, which were ascendant in the middle third of the twentieth century, towards management and employers, seen as the innovators and wealth creators in an age of twenty-first century entrepreneurial capitalism. By autumn 2016, UK legislation and employment law exhibited minimum statutory rights for employees with notable loopholes that equipped employers with techniques to circumvent formerly statutory obligations. Statutory Sick Pay (SSP) is a guaranteed employment right across all variety of contract, but to qualify, employees must be absent for four or more consecutive days (Statutory Sick Pay, 1st September 2016). Workers off sick for one day can still be deducted pay, a regular practice observed in both retail and call centre work. Workers retain the right to request flexible working patterns that, according to the government, 'suit the employee's needs' (Flexible Working, 25th October 2016). The request to work part-time, compressed hours, flexitime, annualised hours or staggered shifts, however, must be made formally and only following 26 weeks' continuous employment with a company. As much of the literature on the service economy illustrates, employee turnover rates suggest that six months' continuous work is often elusive (Shildrick et al. 2012; Southwood 2011; Fenton and Dermott 2006). In the event the employee is eligible to submit an application, the employer can reject it on the grounds of business need. In observations and interviews with service economy workers, shifts affixed to weekly rotas became the responsibility of the employee to administer and change if required; managers habitually refused to accommodate shift changes and insisted the employee arranged to swap with a co-worker or perform the designated shift. Management refusal to bear responsibility for employee needs reflected an imposed so-called 'collegial ethos' in the workplace, which masked the shift in responsibility onto the employee and thus established an absence of security amongst employees expected to resolve their own problems, often without the support of superiors.

The reconfiguration of employment law dispenses freedom and flexibility for employers to navigate the circuits of consumer capitalism unencumbered by vociferous or onerous demands from labour. Firms can seize market opportunities without deferring to union voices. The flexibility agenda works almost entirely in favour of the employer; management practices that preach flexibility for workers in effect guarantee managers can employ staff on short-term contracts, zero-hours contracts, and part-time hours. Simultaneously, employees retain minimal rights and benefits, pay remains low, which enables management strategy and institutional practice to focus on 'just-in-time' service delivery or lean staffing models to maximise profit and demand higher productivity from employees. When retailers and food service industry representatives demand flexibility appropriate to the complexion of service work, they claim the right to employ working practices that best facilitate the bottom line. The inevitable reality of market-driven services beholden to shareholders or profit margins is the need to accumulate revenue; the *normal function of the service economy* requires employee relations and working conditions that may generate profit or growth but do so with disregard for job stability and security for service workers who engage in what Hatton (2011) calls the 'temp economy'.

An apparent acknowledgement of harms linked to job insecurity within the flexibility agenda engendered a reform movement headed under the term 'flexicurity' (see Wilthagen and Tros 2004). This 'theory-inspired policy model' not only promoted dynamism within competitive global markets through flexibility for employers but also ensured more and better jobs in a secure and socially cohesive labour market. The flexibility-security debate signals the poverty of left-liberal thought. It accepts the premise that dynamic, flexible, sustainable growth-led labour markets are essential and that any attempt to mitigate the harms of job insecurity must balance against the needs of the market.

Following the post-war settlement, a stable sense of working identity briefly appeared possible, sustained by a relative degree of job stability (Sennett 1999). The objective conditions of employment—job security, levels of pay, benefits, employment protections and skill level—ensured that the sense of historical progress felt through economic expansion and the proliferation of consumer markets was also recognised by the individual worker (Harvey 2005). Job security permitted one to plan for the future and furnished a durable sense of one's relative worth to society (Sennett 1999). Career paths and circumscribed routes from education into stable work were visible (Willis 1977). However, by the beginning of the twenty-first century, the sustained absence of job security erodes both an immediate sense of constancy for employees likely to change jobs repeatedly (Southwood 2011) and those durable patterns and transitional markers young people use in order to make sense of their place in the world (Silva 2014). Service economy jobs are commonly described as 'entry-level' or 'McJobs' and this indicates the conventional and now archaic presumption that low-paid service work, or 'Saturday job' is the first step on an occupational ladder. Young men and women traditionally entered into service work before they exhibited the social mobility valorised by neoliberals and moved on to better paid and higher skilled work. For many, this transitional stepping stone is now elusive. The labour market conditions in many parts of the UK and USA are severely limited; public sector retrenchment, a lack of inward investment from the private sector and low diversity within labour markets all serve to limit the choices available in post-industrial regions unable to entice capital investment (Lloyd 2013). Within this context, the pull of the 'hidden economy' offers opportunities to derive pecuniary advantage in the shadow of legitimate means of subsistence. From working cash-in-hand to outright illicit activity, the systemic harms of job insecurity can propel some individuals into various forms of illegal activity.

Much of the youth transitions literature encompasses debates concerning parameters and boundaries within the life course. Essentially, consideration of youth, adolescence and adulthood seeks clarification regarding the beginnings, endings and transitions between each phase of life (Furlong and Cartmel 2007; MacDonald and Marsh 2005; Arnett 2004; Hardgrove et al. 2015; Roberts 2011; Silva 2014). Some youth scholars emphasise 'fragmented transitions' (see MacDonald and Marsh 2005) that denote intrinsic labour market mutability, but this should connect to a shift towards emphasis on more 'profitable' avenues for identification such as leisure and consumer circuits (Smith and Raymen

2016; Winlow and Hall 2013; Lloyd 2012). Silva (2014) observes that young people mark transitions to adulthood subjectively rather than using objective conditions such as stable employment or parenthood. Indicative of what Cederstrom and Spicer (2015) call a 'wellness syndrome' that places responsibility for well-being on the individual, Silva's cohort exhibits a turn towards subjectivity. Instability marks objective conditions (Standing 2011)—'broken homes', poor educational achievements, inconstant and low-paid jobs in the service economy, addictions, failed relationships and criminal records, often gained through engagement in various forms of crime incentivised by the systemic harms which fracture legitimate labour markets. This ensures that objective conditions such as employment largely fail in the task of constructing a coherent sense of immutable progress through the life course. The absence of stability in, amongst other things, labour market conditions against which they can mark or recognise progression, results in the subject looking inwards for a sense of validation or achievement of adulthood.

The Impact on Working Conditions

Whilst the absence of job security engenders instability in the working lives of service economy employees, working conditions compound this anxiety. Management operation and organisational culture in late capitalist service work reveal capitalism's 'negation of the negation' (Winlow and Hall 2016). Taken from Hegel, the negation of the negation suggests that the gains made by labour noted above serve to negate the worst excesses of capitalism, as experienced in working practices. Capital's successful negation of the original negation is seen through the re-regulation of labour laws *and* the reorientation of working cultures and management practices that serve to create stressful, insecure and harmful conditions of employment.

McDowell's (2009) contention that service economy work is demand-driven proposes a working environment configured towards 'just-in-time' service and accommodating consumer requirements effectively and efficiently. In a culture of instant gratification and aversion to waiting (Crary 2013), consumer capitalism places additional emphasis on the prompt resolution of customer service enquiries. Management practice and organisational culture across service economy workplaces combine lean staffing models with profitability; performance management and targets are standard features of service economy work such as retail and call centres (Lloyd 2013) whilst efficiency and speed combine with customer satisfaction through emotional labour in the night-time economy and food services industries (Leidner 1993). Whilst 'shop-floor' culture and the interaction between customers and employees are not wholly shaped by management (Williams 2006), they certainly influence it either tacitly by accepting working practices and cultural norms or by actively endorsing certain behaviours that facilitate the achievement of targets and profitability.

Assisted by regulations supporting capital growth and profit as economically beneficial, the power imbalance between employer and employee fosters working conditions and management practices that best ensure profitability but frequently negatively affect employee well-being. Targets and performance management create a culture whereby employees face work intensification, either electronically as in the call centre (Taylor and Bain 1999; Lloyd 2013), or through management compulsion as in retail (Lloyd 2018). Pressure flows down corporate hierarchies: store managers must meet targets to ensure profit is achieved, team leaders must ensure teams hit targets and individual employees must suffer metrics-based performance management. This provokes an atmosphere whereby every customer is seen as an opportunity, every call a chance to improve figures, every table an opportunity for a tip. This application of affective, emotional or aesthetic labour (Hochschild 2003; Warhurst and Nickson 2007) suggests a vacuous or substanceless form of social interaction between two individuals, the customer and employee, focused on the self (Baudrillard 1993), and also creates a culture thoroughly compelled with the need to maximise profitability and achieve goals and targets.

The call centre literature establishes the work intensification and target-driven nature of an 'assembly-line in the head' as responsible for stressful working conditions and physical or emotional burnout (Lloyd 2013; Deery et al. 2010; Wegge et al. 2010). Many of these practices are also visible in retail; subjects attest to the target-driven culture underpinning management coercion to approach customers and deploy an extensive range of techniques and emotional labour to close a sale (see Lloyd 2018). Meanwhile, the demand-driven reality of service work inevitably creates slow intervals, experienced as mind-numbing periods of time where the 'tyranny of the clock' asserts itself; shifts are seemingly interminable. This dichotomy between intense work periods driven by management imperatives and intervals of slow, boring down time, characterise many service economy jobs. Of course, should the slow periods persist, for example, due to an economic downturn, management soon look to cut costs and conserve profit margins by reducing staffing levels.

Zero-hours and temporary contracts offer management the flexibility to staff according to customer demand and peak times, offering shifts during busy periods without any obligation to dispense shifts during quiet spells. The flexibility associated with these contracts works entirely in the employer's favour, while employees are seldom in the position to willingly refuse hours. Zero-hours contracts are also inadvertently divisive; an employee can suddenly find shifts available as a consequence of co-workers being ill, falling out of favour, someone being let go. In a culture of competitive individualism, zero-hours contracts reflect this as co-workers can become competition for vital resources. Temporary contracts afford flexibility to employers, as do employment agencies, nevertheless the employee experiences this as insecure and uncertain. Employers are often candid about the limited prospect of contract extensions but taking on staff to cover peak periods inevitably leads to hope for a permanent position. While some temporary positions do become permanent, many do not.

Stressful conditions, insecure contracts, targets and management pressure, coupled with customer-facing functions frequently accompanied by problematic interactions with dissatisfied customers, are the daily reality of service economy jobs. Levels of pay seldom reflect the hard work, stress and anxiety accompanying these insecure and difficult forms of employment. Employment law guarantees a national minimum wage to all employed on a contract (from permanent to zero-hours) but despite the UK government declaring commitment to a 'living wage', this is only available to over 25s. Pay levels are supplemented by bonuses derived from realisation of targets and performance management which ensures an instrumental, competitive individualism pervades the workplace as co-workers chase sales and targets in order to bolster meagre wages. Given policy analysis suggesting that the living wage still falls short of securing a reasonable standard of living, assuring bonuses through performance targets, overtime (often paid at basic rate), and working more than one job become normalised practice within the service economy.

Whilst the use of targets is not limited to the service economy, pay levels remain above the legal mandatory requirement and working conditions are often less physically hazardous than other forms of employment. However, exacting conditions, low pay and management practices devised to maximise revenue rather than well-being combine to produce difficult and harmful working environments. High levels of sickness, high staff turnover and mounting problems of mental ill health within low-paid forms of service work are manifestations of problematic employment conditions (Lloyd 2013). In today's service economy, employees lack any genuine protection from work intensification, management demand for targets, performance management, emotional labour, the insecurity and instability linked to flexible working patterns and low pay, but they *experience it as 'normal'*. In a culture of competitive individualism, co-workers offer little consolation against the drudgeries of work. The absence of protection from demanding working conditions engenders further harm, whilst this negativity transmutes the culture of the workplace and interpersonal relations between co-workers.

The Absence of Moral Responsibility

It is equally important to examine subjects willing to inflict harm on others (Hall and Winlow 2015). Those individuals are discernible across a range of contexts but are most noticeable in research conducted on violent and entrepreneurial criminals (Ellis 2016; Hall et al. 2008). Hall's (2012) concept of 'special liberty' delineates an individual embedded within the socio-symbolic structures of neoliberal ideology; epitomising the competitive individualism, envy and self-interest fuelling consumer capitalism, the individual possessing special liberty is convinced of their right to maximise their market share and keep rivals from threatening their position, using any means necessary. This is also evident within the service economy.

Some managers, team leaders and colleagues evince a willingness to visit harm on co-workers and subordinates in order to maximise an opportunity or preserve their position within the organisational hierarchy. Not all harm and violence is physical, although in the extended ethnography underpinning this chapter, physical violence did occur on occasion. The two most notable examples are 'stealing sales' and management bullying. Stealing sales is a practice that transpires frequently in retail. This occurs in several ways and essentially entails temporary or new and inexperienced sales people cultivating a sale, then experienced colleagues interjecting to 'steal' the sale and processing it under their employee number rather than the colleague originally responsible for generating the sale.

In the context of target-driven sales, performance management and bonuses linked to volume and quality of sales, the seemingly innocuous practice of 'stealing sales' becomes more invidious. Temporary sales personnel, usually employed over Christmas, compete for scarce permanent contracts and must display a positive attitude, willingness to sacrifice for the company, and good sales figures. Losing sales adversely impacts their sales targets and therefore their chances to secure permanent work. Those permanent colleagues in possession of special liberty seek to protect their own position and will deliberately harm temporary or inexperienced colleagues by stealing sales. Under pressure to meet their own targets, no justification is necessary for inflicting this harm. In a culture that actively encourages high-pressure, target-driven practices, management often approve of employees seen as proactive and capable and either accept or turn a blind eye to their harmful behaviour.

The second form of special liberty is perceptible in management practices within the service economy. Within this culture, team leaders and managers in possession of special liberty will exhibit behaviours that assert their authority over employees in a way that descends into bullying as a way to reinforce their own fragile position. Interviewees and observations highlighted instances where managers and team leaders victimised co-workers, often with the implicit acquiescence or involvement of other colleagues and managers either because of envy, fear of competition from high-performing sales-staff or simple personality clashes. With managers under intense pressure over targets, some inflict cruel and lasting harms on employees under the auspices of business need, but some inflict harms simply because they can. Employees, largely ignorant of the few rights they do possess, quietly accept this treatment until they leave or suffer emotional or physical damage (see Lloyd 2018).

The harms of special liberty reflect another absence, the absence of any sense of ethical obligation or moral duty to the other (Smith and Raymen 2016; Hall and Winlow 2015). The embedded ideological contours of consumer capitalism and neoliberal governance promote competitive individualism through social mobility, competition, meritocracy, self-interest, personal responsibility for well-being and a winner-takes-all attitude (Smith and Raymen 2016; Winlow and Hall 2013). Popular culture exhibits these values. This libidinal energy propels consumer capitalism and advances a culture increasingly devoid of the pro-social; the idea of an ethical obligation or any sense of moral duty to a co-worker or employee is perceived as naive. For *some* subjects, possessing special liberty allows them to navigate the insecure and unstable waters of contemporary capitalism, maximising their relative position by inflicting harms on others, acting as a bailiff, using their position to secure material, symbolic and emotional sustenance by removing it from co-workers. The absence of an ethical duty to the other signals a wider negative transformation of the workplace; absence is not merely a causative component of harm but also creates space filled by negativity—a negativity that reconstructs workplace culture, management practice and interpersonal relations.

Conclusion

An ultra-realist account of the service economy pinpoints the harms that emanate from a multitude of crucial absences. The absence of stability in service economy labour stems from the political-economic turn associated with neoliberal restructuring of labour markets inclined towards capital and the employer and at the expense of employee protection. The ideological change from 'security' to 'flexibility' reveals the generative core of capital eroding employee protections and benefits secured since the post-war settlement. In the absence of well-paid, secure, skilled and stable employment, the service economy is an insecure, low-paid and 'flexible' form of labour where employees have few rights and little recourse to challenge the imparities and injustices of the workplace. Work intensification strategies, relentless pressure to discharge successful emotional labour, and targets linked to performance management epitomise organisational practices that fill the voids which stem from these absences. The use of insecure, temporary and zero-hours contracts helps to keep costs low and ensures maximum flexibility for employers while the employee is left with insecurity and anxiety over the possibility of finding a steady, stable career path in order to pay bills and feed families. The absence of stability erodes the consolations that make difficult working practices bearable. Capital's 'negation of the negation' (Winlow and Hall 2016) ensures that service economy employees are embedded within its circuits; immediate pressures of bills and mortgages take precedence over time-consuming struggles to secure fair practices and pay rises, particularly in light of inadequate employee protection and rights. Meanwhile, capitalism offers consolations in the very consumer markets that service economy employees facilitate. Finally, the absence of an ethical duty or moral obligation to the other leads some to clothe themselves in a special liberty (Hall 2012) which prefigures a willingness to impose harm on co-workers in order to maximise market shares, boost sales figures and reach targets in order to achieve pay rises. The competitive individualism endemic in consumer capitalist culture plays out on the sales floor, either visibly or surreptitiously, as employees jostle for limited position and rewards. These harms are multitude and visible across the service economy, not simply in the most notable examples raised in media reports.

Perhaps the most problematic absence relates to the symbolic efficiency of neoliberalism (Winlow and Hall 2013). After decades of deep structural change reconfigured political economy, transposed and restructured organisational culture and working practices, redefined employment law in favour of employers and created vast numbers of low-paid insecure jobs that facilitate consumer capitalism's material and symbolic realities, neoliberalism's symbolic efficiency diminished significantly following the financial crisis (Žižek 2010). No longer a consistent set of signs and symbols, markers to root the individual within the social and afford a measure of sense and meaning to the world, the limits of neoliberal ideology become palpable and viscerally felt within marginalised communities, those stuck in the sorts of work described here, and the increasingly imperilled middle class. The fantasy of neoliberalism, upward social mobility for the hard-working, has vanished for a large section of the population. Years of low-paid, stressful, insecure work in service jobs marked by instability, targets and management demand fails to yield any sort of stable, meaningful existence or equitable standard of living (Lloyd 2013) and brings the intransitive realm of depth structures within the practical knowledge and realities of a significant segment of the population who realise that political narratives and ideological exhortations no longer speak to their experience of the social world. The absence of a symbolically efficient ideology begets further instability and harm at the material, symbolic and psycho-social level. This is the fundamental harm, the systemic violence of capitalism.

References

Arnett, Jeffrey J. 2004. *Emerging Adulthood*. New York: Oxford University Press.
Badiou, Alain. 2009. *The Century*. Cambridge: Polity Press.
Baudrillard, Jean. 1993. *The Transparency of Evil*. London: Verso.
Beck, Ulrich. 2000. *The Brave New World of Work*. Cambridge: Polity Press.
Bhaskar, Roy. 2010. *Reclaiming Reality*. London: Routledge.
Cederstrom, Carl, and Andre Spicer. 2015. *The Wellness Syndrome*. Cambridge: Polity.
Collier, Andrew. 1994. *Critical Realism: An Introduction to Roy Bhaskar's Philosophy*. London: Verso.
Crary, Jonathan. 2013. *24/7: Late Capitalism and the Ends of Sleep*. London: Verso.

Deery, Stephen J., Roderick D. Iverson, and Janet T. Walsh. 2010. Coping Strategies in Call Centres: Work Intensity and the Role of Co-workers and Supervisors. *British Journal of Industrial Relations* 48: 181–200.

Ellis, Anthony. 2016. *Men, Masculinities and Violence: An Ethnographic Study*. London: Routledge.

Fenton, Steve, and Esther Dermott. 2006. Fragmented Careers? Winners and Losers in Young Adult Labour Markets. *Work, Employment & Society* 20: 205–221.

Flexible Working. 2016. *The Crown Copyright*, Oct 25. https://www.gov.uk/flexible-working/overview. Accessed 17 Feb 2017.

Furlong, Andy, and Fred Cartmel. 2007. *Young People and Social Change: New Perspectives*, 2nd ed. Maidenhead: Open University Press.

Hall, Steve. 2012. *Theorizing Crime and Deviance: A New Perspective*. London: Sage.

Hall, Steve, and Simon Winlow. 2015. *Revitalizing Criminological Theory: Towards a New Ultra-realism*. London: Routledge.

Hall, Steve, Simon Winlow, and Craig Ancrum. 2008. *Criminal Identities and Consumer Culture*. Cullompton: Willan.

Hardgrove, Abby, Linda McDowell, and Esther Rootham. 2015. Precarious Lives, Precarious Labour: Family Support and Young Men's Transitions to Work in the UK. *Journal of Youth Studies* 18: 1057–1076.

Harvey, David. 2005. *A Brief History of Neoliberalism*. Oxford: University Press.

Harvey, Geraint, Carl Rhodes, Sheena J. Vachhani, and Karen Williams. 2017. Neo-villeiny and the Service Sector: The Case of Hyper Flexible and Precarious Work in Fitness Centres. *Work, Employment & Society* 31: 19–35.

Hatton, Erin. 2011. *The Temp Economy*. Philadelphia: Temple University Press.

Hillyard, Paddy, and Steve Tombs. 2004. Beyond Criminology? In *Beyond Criminology: Taking Harm Seriously*, ed. Paddy Hillyard, Christina Pantazis, Steve Tombs, and Dave Gordon, 10–29. London: Pluto Press.

Hochschild, Arlie R. 2003. *The Managed Heart*. London: University of California Press.

Johnston, Adrian. 2008. *Žižek's Ontology: A Transcendental Materialist Theory of Subjectivity*. Evanston: Northwestern University Press.

Kalleberg, Arne L. 2009. Precarious Work, Insecure Workers: Employment Relations in Transition. *American Sociological Review* 74: 1–22.

Leidner, Robin. 1993. *Fast Food, Fast Talk*. London: University of California Press.

Lloyd, Anthony. 2012. Working to Live, Not Living to Work: Work, Leisure and Youth Identity Among Call Centre Workers in North East England. *Current Sociology* 60: 619–635.

———. 2013. *Labour Markets and Identity on the Post-Industrial Assembly Line*. Basingstoke: Ashgate.

———. 2017. Ideology at Work: Reconsidering Ideology, the Labour Process and Workplace Resistance. *International Journal of Sociology and Social Policy* 37: 266–279.

———. 2018. *The Harms of Work: An Ultra-realist Account of the Service Economy*. Bristol: Policy Press. Forthcoming.

MacDonald, Robert, and Jane Marsh. 2005. *Disconnected Youth: Growing Up in Britain's Poor Neighbourhoods*. Basingstoke: Palgrave Macmillan.

McDowell, Linda. 2009. *Working Bodies: Interactive Service Employment and Workplace Identities*. Chichester: Wiley-Blackwell.

Pemberton, Simon. 2015. *Harmful Societies: Understanding Social Harm*. Bristol: Policy Press.

Roberts, Steven. 2011. Beyond 'NEET' and 'Tidy' Pathways: Considering the 'Missing Middle' of Youth Transition Studies. *Journal of Youth Studies* 14: 21–39.

Scott, Sam. 2017. *Labour Exploitation and Work-Based Harm*. Bristol: Policy Press.

Sennett, Richard. 1999. *The Corrosion of Character*. London: WW Norton & Company.

Shildrick, Tracy, Robert MacDonald, Colin Webster, and Kayleigh Garthwaite. 2012. *Poverty and Insecurity*. Bristol: Policy Press.

Silva, Jennifer M. 2014. *Coming Up Short*. Oxford: Oxford University Press.

Smith, Oliver, and Thomas Raymen. 2016. Deviant Leisure: A Criminological Perspective. *Theoretical Criminology*. https://doi.org/10.1177/1362480616660188.

Southwood, Ivor. 2011. *Non-stop Inertia*. Winchester: Zero.

Standing, Guy. 2011. *The Precariat*. London: Bloomsbury.

Statutory Sick Pay (SSP). 2016. *The Crown Copyright*, Sept 1. https://www.gov.uk/employers-sick-pay. Accessed 17 Feb 2017.

Streeck, Wolfgang. 2016. *How Will Capitalism End?* London: Verso.

Taylor, Phil, and Peter Bain. 1999. 'An Assembly Line in the Head': Work and Employee Relations in the Call Centre. *Industrial Relations Journal* 30: 101–117.

Tombs, Steve. 2004. Workplace Injury and Death: Social Harm and the Illusions of Law. In *Beyond Criminology: Taking Harm Seriously*, ed. Paddy Hillyard, Christina Pantazis, Steve Tombs, and Dave Gordon, 156–177. London: Pluto Press.

Tombs, Steve, and Dave Whyte. 2007. *Safety Crimes*. Cullompton: Willan.

Warhurst, Chris, and Dennis Nickson. 2007. Employee Experience of Aesthetic Labour in Retail and Hospitality. *Work, Employment & Society* 21: 103–120.

Wegge, Jürgen, Rolf van Dick, and Christiane von Bernstorff. 2010. Emotional Dissonance in Call Centre Work. *Journal of Managerial Psychology* 25: 596–619.

White, Rob, and Diane Heckenberg. 2014. *Green Criminology: An Introduction to the Study of Environmental Harm*. London: Routledge.

Whitehead, Philip. 2015. *Reconceptualising the Moral Economy of Criminal Justice*. Basingstoke: Palgrave Pivot.

Whitehead, Philip, and Steve Hall. Forthcoming. Generative Core and Regulatory Jacket (Work in Progress).

Williams, Christine L. 2006. *Inside Toyland*. London: University of California Press.

Willis, Paul. 1977. *Learning to Labour*. Farnham: Ashgate.

Wilthagen, Ton, and F.H. Tros. 2004. The Concept of 'Flexicurity': A New Approach to Regulating Employment and Labour Markets. *Transfer: European Review of Labour and Research* 10: 166–186.

Winlow, Simon, and Steve Hall. 2013. *Rethinking Social Exclusion*. London: Sage.

———. 2016. Realist Criminology and Its Discontents. *International Journal for Crime, Justice and Social Democracy* 5: 80–94.

Yar, Majid. 2012. Critical Criminology, Critical Theory and Social Harm. In *New Directions in Criminological Theory*, ed. Steve Hall and Simon Winlow, 52–65. London: Routledge.

Žižek, Slavoj. 2000. *The Ticklish Subject*. London: Verso.

———. 2008. *Violence*. London: Profile Books.

———. 2010. *Living in the End Times*. London: Verso.

Author Biography

Anthony Lloyd is Senior Lecturer in Criminology and Sociology at Teesside University. His research looks at reconfigured labour markets under neoliberal global capital and thus far has focused on call centres and the service economy. The connection between the sociology of work and labour markets, identity and subjectivity, and the field of zemiology and social harm forms the basis of his current research.

Harm and Transforming Rehabilitation

David Temple

Introduction

This chapter will focus on the connection between crime and harm within a probation setting. Indeed, in many ways the links between probation, crime and harm are synonymous. Historically, there have been calls for a move away from criminology towards zemiology in order to focus upon the study of a broader range of harms not legally defined as criminal (Hillyard et al. 2004; Hillyard 2015). A number of criticisms of criminology that inspired the development of zemiology are valid, particularly the numerous limitations of administrative criminology. Additionally, there is certainly a need to address state and corporate harms more thoroughly (Hillyard and Tombs 2007). However, creating divisions between critical criminology and zemiology is problematic

D. Temple (✉)
Teesside University, Middlesbrough, UK
e-mail: D.Temple@tees.ac.uk

given the overlapping interest amongst these areas of study (Friedrichs and Schwartz 2007; Rothe and Kauzlarich 2014).

Here, specific focus will be placed on the blurred lines of crime and harm caused by 'Transforming Rehabilitation'. This new bureaucratic strategy has markedly changed, some might even say revolutionized, the management of offenders in the community in three key ways: the creation and sale of 21 Community Rehabilitation Companies (CRCs) based upon 'payment by results', the extension of statutory rehabilitation to those serving prison sentences of fewer than 12 months, and the introduction of a 'new' resettlement strategy called 'through the gate'. The probation service has historically aimed to reduce crime and the risk of harm to the public, victims and offenders. However, the service has recently undergone significant changes in line with Transforming Rehabilitation meaning that the way the service will achieve these goals is less clear.

This chapter will focus on the splitting of probation into the National Probation Service (NPS) and 21 CRCs nationwide, and the increased numbers of offenders placed under probation supervision. The aim is to spotlight harm caused to a variety of actors as a result of Transforming Rehabilitation, namely probation officers, offenders and victims. The extent to which these harms (both present and potential) could, or should, be considered not only harmful but also criminal is assessed. This is not to call the Transforming Rehabilitation agenda itself criminal, but rather the potential for it to lead to an increase in criminality. Whether or not this will be reflected in official statistics is unclear (and unlikely for reasons that will be addressed), nevertheless the potential for increased harm is alarming. This not only has implications for the actors noted above, but for the general public. Furthermore, a number of harms outlined here were immediately evident to probation staff and academics nationwide. Despite this, the proposals moved forward at significant speed (Whitehead 2015a, b; Robinson et al. 2016).

The data presented throughout this chapter is based upon research undertaken in a probation setting. The period this research took place (July 2013–February 2015) is significant, as it occurred prior to, during, and after the dissolvent of the NPS and the subsequent implementation of the 21 CRCs. Following the implementation of these 21 companies on June 1st 2014, the research shifted its analytical lens towards one local CRC. It is for this reason that I focus only on two of the three key changes linked to the Transforming Rehabilitation agenda. It is also for this reason that the chapter focuses on the themes of harm and crime based exclusively upon changes to the CRC as this reflects the data collected. The data presented here comes from discussions with probation officers at various levels whilst conducting semi-structured interviews, each of whom would go on to work in CRCs. This chapter addresses their references to harm, criminality and fear for the future of the service.

The Splitting of Probation

The ways probation has aimed to reduce crime and harm have changed considerably since its inception over a century ago. With valuable analysis already in place (see Whitehead 2015b), it is worth simply noting that the initial principles of 'advise, assist and befriend' have been systematically dismantled by successive neo-liberal governments for over three decades (Burke and Collett 2016; Annison et al. 2014). Furthermore, the managerial principles of 'accountability', 'efficiency', 'competition', 'contestability' and 'managerialism' have become core to the organization of probation. These principles have been compounded by the plans to implement the Transforming Rehabilitation programme. As Burke and Collett (2016, 122) clarify, 'most importantly, under the Offender Management Act of 2007, the legislative provisions for dramatically different delivery mechanisms were in place for the Coalition administration to carry on where New Labour had left off'. However, these mechanisms were based upon the unproven perception that the private sector extolls far greater efficiency and effectiveness than any public sector institutions could hope to (Whitehead 2015a, b).

Nonetheless these delivery mechanisms have hollowed out the NPS. The NPS is still a public sector organization, however it is now primarily responsible for 'the management of high risk of harm offenders, as well as offender risk assessment, advising the courts and Parole Board and handling most breach cases' (Evans 2016, 156). There are now 21 CRCs in control of the supervision of low to medium risk offenders nationwide in exchange for 'payment by results'. This reflects not only the principles above, but a further withdrawal of the state from the public sector including reduced government expenditure in line with contemporary austerity measures (Annison et al. 2014; Whitehead 2015a, b). These private and voluntary sector organizations now supervise most offenders, around 70% (Burke and Collett 2016). Probation officer Andrew noted the harmful effects that the split between NPS and CRC can have upon offenders:

> It's made it difficult for offenders to understand, it's separated them even further. So the NPS, you are the ones that we really need to keep an eye on, you are the worst bunch of the lot. Then you get stuck there, if you are supervised by the NPS regardless of whether your risk reduces, you make good progress, you remain within the NPS. It's bureaucratic, it's risk management focused. It stops that opportunity to be able to be in mainstream society… It worries me around, the dangers as to why it has been split. How difficult it is to then increase people to high risk. The processes you then have to go through to get them into the NPS. It's just cumbersome and ridiculous; it's crazy, for the public and for staff. I really would like to be a bit more optimistic about it, but I can't see that much of a positive in it.

Of course, this does not sound like a particularly efficient dynamic, especially with increased efficiency being a key driver of Transforming Rehabilitation's considerable momentum. In addition, the transition to CRCs has also led to existing probation officers moving to the CRC, an experience Andrew and other probation officers have encountered. In total 'just over half of the population of probation staff—more than 9,000 workers—joined CRCs under TUPE regulations' (Robinson et al. 2016, 162). This created considerable uncertainty prior to the splitting of probation as staff members did not know what organization they would work for, and who would own the CRC.

Payment by Results

The ideology underpinning Transforming Rehabilitation suggests the probation service will reduce crime and re-offending based upon free market principles. The underlying rationale being that private and voluntary sectors are supposedly better placed to reduce crime re-offending in exchange for 'payment by results'. Payment by results is perceived to be more efficient, although 'empirical claims for its effectiveness are somewhat scarce and certainly insufficient to support such a radical policy shift' (Burke and Collett 2016, 124). When such organizations are successful in reducing crime and re-offending, they receive financial rewards from the government. As such, 'the awarding of governmental contracts and associated financial rewards will no longer support good intentions, rejected as passé because its ideology belongs to the unreformed public sector, but clear, demonstrable, and quantifiable results' (Whitehead 2015a, 292). This ideology was continually questioned by probation officers who did not feel that probation work should be based on profit making. This point was made explicit by Chris, who spoke at length on this point:

> I think it is absolutely horrible. As a member of the public, if I have become a victim of crime, I don't think it is fair that another company is making a profit out of me being a victim. It is a social and moral thing, it should be held in the government. It should be a public sector thing. Crime can hurt anybody and affect anybody. I think it is wrong, ethically and morally wrong to sell justice for profit.

Paul also believed that privatization was fundamentally wrong:

> It is as if we have done something wrong, when we know we haven't. I don't want anybody to be a victim of crime, but crime happens. To be privatized, it is wrong. It is wrong and I find it really demotivating, awful really.

Graham similarly highlighted his cynicism towards payment by results, and the quest for efficiency:

> It just seems really strange to break down such a large organisation without running something through to see if it is going to work or not. The reasons obviously are cost-cutting; I just can't see how it is going to work. I'm looking to get out.

Graham, Paul and Chris's comments show they took privatization personally. Trevor also noted similar themes when he stated that 'knowing what we do makes a difference, makes it even harder to swallow'. As Robinson et al. (2016, 171) recently noted Transforming Rehabilitation was harmful for staff, 'themes of loss, separation, status anxiety, insecurity and mistrust all point toward the pains of Transforming Rehabilitation (TR) from the point of view of probation workers in the CRC'. These were common themes amongst probation officers including those introduced above. Chris and Graham's comments also indicate a belief that the motivation for Transforming Rehabilitation was purely financial rather than a clear initiative to reduce crime and harm. We can clearly see scepticism towards payment by results, but why is this important within the context of this chapter? The crucial point here is that this scepticism amongst probationers was based upon a belief that this quest for efficiency would not benefit offenders, victims or the public. Graham points this out bluntly:

> If it is payment by results with these agencies (CRCs), people can fiddle the books and the government can make things look like everything is working perfectly well with certain agencies (CRCs), because it just depends on how you record stuff. The important stuff is just lost, if it is all just a numbers game and it all looks good on paper, because it can be made to look good on paper then agencies who are getting there money for doing that, are going to do that. I think as staff (members) who have worked in a completely different way, we're going to really struggle with that.

Indeed if success is judged on ability to meet targets, then statistics can potentially be manipulated. Under New Labour, meeting targets became a foundation of probation practice, an aspect expanded through the Transforming Rehabilitation programme. This has a real impact upon people's lives. Certain types of offenders will be dealt with in a way not conducive to the reduction of harm or crime. Evans (2016, 157–58) recently noted payment by results is 'expected to encourage companies to 'cherry pick' the less prolific offenders, who could more easily contribute to the reoffending targets and 'park' harder to help groups'. Paradoxically, it could lead to less support for offenders deemed likely to re-offend, such as those in Integrated Offender Management (IOM). Such offenders have deeply entrenched and multidimensional problems that could be ignored in order to generate better statistics (Evans 2016). By extension this impedes harm and crime reduction, increasing risk of harm to the offender, those around them and other members of the public. This leads us to question the rationale and aims underpinning newly formed CRCs.

Increased Numbers Under Supervision: Loss of Core Values and Deskilling of the Role

Here it is useful to highlight the second key change; increased numbers of offenders supervised by CRCs. Staff believed privatization would lead to more offenders being supervised by fewer members of staff. Not only would this place increased strain on staff, it is likely to lead to lower wages, increased use of technology and likely to involve the use of volunteers. As George questioned, 'Given the changes, where cost is going to be paramount, isn't it? Can we afford to take on new staff, or do we just give work to volunteers for nothing?'

Experienced members of staff left due to the introduction of the Transforming Rehabilitation agenda, because of their extreme discomfort around the new trajectory of the service. An important factor here is the values of the former public sector institution geared towards helping people gets lost. Indeed, as experienced members of staff leave, the core values grounded upon helping offenders reduce the harm they commit to themselves and others diminish. This is particularly apparent when the emphasis on efficiency and meeting targets becomes even more prominent. As George points out:

> It's going to be more in and out reporting, as fast as possible, trying to keep track of a ridiculous amount of people and not really building relationships with them (offenders) because there's going to be so many of them.

It should be noted that limitations on time spent with offenders also has foundations in New Labour's attempt to 'modernise' the Criminal Justice System. A clear concern was that this dynamic would become more pronounced owing to Transforming Rehabilitation. Graham highlighted the constraints this places on staff:

> The worry is that the core values of what we've always been about are just going to get lost, and it will purely be a paper exercise. People reporting in and going, and then just pass them onto an agency. That's the worry that we lose the relationships we have built up. The work that we normally do will just be lost.

Andrew also explained 'the whole process has been awful at times, you feel sort of deskilled'. This deskilling of the probation officer role was stated bluntly by Chris when commenting on Transforming Rehabilitation a couple of months after the split between NPS and CRC, 'you used to be able to give a fuck, sorry, you used to be able to care (about people). Now you are not, don't you think?' Furthermore as Paul points out, he needs to meet these targets:

> I am going to have to make sure that I am up to speed, I'll have to. Otherwise, you could end up down the capability route and without a job, which is not what you want. Will it benefit the offender? We will have to wait and see.

Paul notes staff will need to meet targets to keep their jobs. This not only means having to adapt how they work, it also adds pressures of failing to meet targets. Whitehead (2015b, 66) recently stated that immanent to Transforming Rehabilitation 'there is the problematic of efficiency targets swamping moral questions, and restructuring and rebalancing, unbalancing the dialectics of criminal justice by eroding historical, cultural and ethico-cultural conventions'. He goes on to clarify that 'practical reason, as in cognitive ability and intellectual curiosity, human feeling and empathy, are the constitutive elements of *relationships* in the people-facing professions. They are good in themselves and effective at reducing re-offending' (Whitehead 2015b, 80). It seems that such values, insofar as they still exist within staff members (having been diluted by 'Modernisation'), will diminish even further as staff leave (whether voluntarily or via redundancy).

New staff members coming in will inevitably be hired for lower wages (or perhaps no wages in the case of volunteers) in line with the need for efficiency; they will come in with different ideology, potentially a different understanding of the probation officer role. As Evans (2016, 157) notes, declining quality of staff is a concern because 'there is no requirement for the employees of the CRCs to be trained probation officers'. This is worrying given the dying ethos underpinning probation appears to solely exist within staff rather than as a clear organizational identity (Whitehead 2015b). Whilst not considered criminal, declining quality of service can be harmful to the officer–offender relationship that George, Graham and Chris noted earlier. On a wider scale, the sustained decline of the 'moral economy' of probation relates to zemiology, and its emphasis placed upon social, psychological and emotional harm (Whitehead 2015b; Hillyard et al. 2004; Hillyard and Tombs 2007). Furthermore, harm is caused directly by the state, through its physical and ideological withdrawal from the service. This point is made clear by Andrew in his distinction between personal and organizational values within probation. On Transforming Rehabilitation he comments:

> It's just crazy, it just seems crackers. I don't think anybody would ever say it's the best idea in the world. It is an ideological thing based on a decision which is not underpinned by any knowledge about the job that we do. That is the crux of it. I work with it, you've got to because it is your job. Most people who come into this job, do so because they have a value based on wanting to help people. I think that is what is keeping people going through this… Now it is purely about people. That is the thing that keeps me going. I have no loyalties to the government who have made this. If it was a pure drawing a wage thing, I wouldn't put as much into the job as I do… over time, I have seen a difference in the way that people work with people depending on your values. The difference between people who do it to draw a wage, and who do it because they actually care is so different.

We can see a serious concern as to the values of CRC staff. This decline in values is harmful to existing staff and offenders. The implication here is that the quality of supervision is lowered when the job is done 'simply to draw a wage'. Even if these values remain, the ability of staff members to adhere to them will become even more problematic.

Trevor similarly noted that deskilling was a real issue due to the increased numbers under supervision. Indeed it has been estimated that 50,000 more people will be subject to supervision each year (Evans 2016). Paradoxically this limits the effectiveness of supervision with offenders. Paul also stated 'we're going to get all these short term releases from prisons as well. We're going to be bombarded with them… there's just going to be so many of them'. This 'bombardment' will inevitably increase the amount of work for probation officers. George likened probation supervision to a factory operation several months after privatization:

> It's definitely not how it was set out one hundred years ago, 'advise, assist and befriend'. It's not like that at all is it? You might as well be a cardboard cut-out now with telephone numbers… I'm doing no more than (signposting) because I don't have time… these people are coming through on a conveyer belt and they're seeing them and seeing them.

The demotion to signposting offenders to alternative services and resources has become a common concern (Robinson et al. 2016). This reflects the reduction in services offered by the probation services that have been contracted out (such as education, training and employment and accommodation), as part of sustained retrenchment of the public sector synonymous with neoliberal policy. George expanded on the deskilling of probation officers:

> Now it is just touch base, you don't get to know the person, you come in, 'what's your problem?' and off you pop. There is no relationship really because you don't have time because you don't see them enough to build on that relationship. The relationship I have with particular offenders is historic, where they've been around a long time, they're usually the heavy end offenders… it's not personal anymore, it's almost clinical now… there is nothing there now, there is no guidance in terms of (what type of organization we are).

This increased workload raises serious questions about the efficacy and effectiveness of probation in reducing harm and crime. Within a climate of efficiency and cost-cutting, redundancies, etc., the ability to develop relationships, to be effective, will undoubtedly become even harder. As Evans (2016, 156) recently noted this problem has already come to fruition, as 'the most recent inspection of TR by HM Inspectorate of Probation which reports that fewer than half of CRC managed cases inspected had their first appointment with an offender manager within five working days of sentence'. Paul made this point clear:

> I wonder how the victim would feel about that, how we are managing the (offenders) order. I think in the future we are going to be encouraged, or we are going to be told that we have to see offenders less, because we have more people. Due to the changes in the law, with the sentencing of people with more than a day, less than a year's custody, they will end up under supervision. They will be at risk of enforcement or recall. I think we will be left with a bigger caseload, with less time to maybe be effective with our time with them.

Increased Risk of Harm, Decreased Public Safety?

This potential lack of effectiveness is extremely serious and will have a direct impact upon crime and harm reduction. Graham explains that:

> We do a lot that people don't know about… (the general public) don't know about the risk that we do contain on a daily basis and the potential of that risk not being contained with privatisation is a worrying thing.

It is useful to make clear at this juncture how Transforming Rehabilitation can impact upon the safety of the population in ways that may not be immediately clear to the public. Andrew clarifies the importance of quality probation work:

> I think that what we do works. I think overtime people might see the impact of it. They might see more crime. They might see more people begging on the streets, violent, agitated. I believe that might be the impact. People don't realise it because what we do is quite silent. It's a nightmare, I don't like it.

George also noted Transforming Rehabilitation is likely to increase risks to offenders and by extension the public:

> The risk is about the volume, the risk is about the lack of confidentiality, people are not going to open up because of the environment they are working in. Lots and lots of risk issues that are around and you think oh my God, what if?... It's all these what if's all the time, when you're talking volumes of people you daren't think of the risk... it is frightening.

The lack of confidentiality to which George is referring pertains to the locations CRC supervision takes place in. George supervises his offenders primarily in community centres, or occasionally on home visits (this is not the case for all CRCs nationwide). Although supervision in community centres is segregated from the public, there is still potential for other offenders or probation officers to be in the same room. This might prevent offenders from disclosing important information because they feel other people are listening. This information, or rather lack of it, could have an impact on them harming themselves or others. As George explains:

> If they have got issues, they aren't going to bring them up. You are perpetuating that revolving door because they aren't going to solve their issues, maybe in terms of ETE (education, training and employment) or accommodation... you're not going to pick any risk issues up. Somebody with accommodation issues, you refer them to that agency and hope that that agency is going to pick them up. But you've got no time to track and monitor the progress, so you're not doing them a lot of favours really. It might be mass reporting, but it's all superficial, you're not getting any deeper. Although it is payment by results, I wouldn't be surprised if the re-offending rates did go up. We are not going to affect any change, we don't have time.

The use of community centres is predominantly a cost-cutting measure, enabling more offenders to be supervised in less time. Supervision by numbers is not well equipped to assist with the complex and chaotic nature of offenders' lives. George believes this 'mass supervision' will allow offenders to go under the radar, and that it would become even harder to develop effective relationships. He notes this will also benefit offenders who have no intention of reducing re-offending:

If you've got somebody who is dodgy, who doesn't want to sit and talk, they can be in and out unnoticed and go under the radar... (offenders) who you know are still dealing, are up to no good, and they're going to go under the radar... if you've got the time to sit and have a chat with somebody, there is always something that you can pick up... but you don't have time, there's no time for that. The wheel will come off because there are too many people, too many inexperienced staff... but we have to make it look good on paper.

The Future for CRCs

George's comments above show there is considerable risk of harm related to Transforming Rehabilitation. The governmental programme could lead to an increase in offending because offenders will find it much easier to 'go under the radar', for serious issues not to be picked up, for offending to continue unnoticed. These issues relate to a number of social harms beyond criminality: mental health, substance misuse, health and well-being, homelessness/accommodation and unemployment. Similar points were made by numerous staff members when contemplating the future of the probation service. As Paul questioned, 'will we be effective, will our communities, will the public benefit? I do worry about that'.

To restate, a number of concerns outlined in the staff testimonies above are not specific to Transforming Rehabilitation. Rather the concern, with the loss of relationships, of bureaucracy, of efficiency, of superficiality, of reduced state involvement, of the decline in 'social work', is that these influences will become more pronounced. The ultimate conclusion of this form of working, a process sped up by the Transforming Rehabilitation agenda, is the lack of human contact and a movement towards supervision by machines. This dynamic was clearly a grave concern of staff, given that 'work with offenders is a *morally significant activity* that cannot be reduced to technical gimmicks for achieving efficiency and effectiveness' (Whitehead 2015b, 63). This is seemingly the endpoint of an organization now concerned with economic over social need. As George explains:

We know in London they're looking at bringing in finger print recognition. So somebody goes to something similar to an ATM machine, puts their finger on and it asks three questions. One of them is do you need to see an Offender Manager, are you still living at the same address? I can't remember the other one. That's bizarre isn't it, and that's about supervision by numbers. It's not supervision is it? It's not supervision at all, that's just saying this is where you are. It's a ridiculous situation to be in where people are monitored by machines. We could be in exactly the same position, so the people that we worry about in terms of mental health, the heavy end drug users. You can't supervise people like that, it's not right, there is no respect, there is no interaction. We're talking about people getting money out of machines, that's what it is about isn't it, it's terrible. To spend public money prosecuting somebody to ultimately go and put their finger on a machine (laughs), ridiculous! (long sigh) it doesn't bear thinking about does it?

Graham also noted a similar development whilst reiterating a lack of public awareness:

There's been all sorts of different worrying developments that they've tried… using machines to report to instead of using Offender Managers, clients just had to go and swipe a card into a machine and that was their supervision session, and they've tried that. So knowing, they've thought of call centres, phoning call centres as their reporting for that week. So knowing, that that's the kind of thinking behind these big agencies, it does worry you. Because it is something the public don't know about, the public aren't being informed of the potential risk of all of this. It's just worrying; it's all been kept very quiet.

George states similar themes emphatically, and it is worth ending with the following quote as it encapsulates a wide range of themes discussed above:

I think that people now, especially offenders, are treat like scum. You are not worth the effort of having a face to face conversation with somebody, it's appalling. I hope I'm never around to see that actually come to fruition because I think it's absolutely appalling. The worst thing is, the general public have no idea, they have no idea what is going on. I think ultimately everything we do should be about respect, where is the respect? The heavy-end offenders are going to love it because they are going to continue to offend.

It'll make no difference to them, well it will, they'll be able to get away with it because you won't see any signs… the vulnerable are going to be at risk. It's only suitable for a few, but then you think the whole thing is a joke.

Conclusion

We can see through this excavation of concerns surrounding CRCs that a number of changes have caused (and could further cause) harm on numerous levels. The organization will suffer a loss of identity and further loss of its core values as they become replaced by a focus on meeting targets. Given the 21 CRCs do not necessarily have any common ground; the core values of these disparate companies are unclear. The organization has been dismantled without any clear evidence of benefits beyond saving money and opening up another avenue for private profit (Burke and Collett 2016; Whitehead 2015a, b). The service is also at risk of complete dissolution, of existing without any human contact which will compound the potential harms noted above. As Burke and Collett (2016, 131) presciently argue, 'the introduction of ATM style reporting kiosks by at least one of the new owners as part of their cost cutting plans (Travis 2016) hints at a potentially dystopian future in which the complexities of human interactions are reducible to a series of impersonal processes'.

We have seen in detail the harmful effects of Transforming Rehabilitation on probation staff. This includes: insecurity, uncertainty, deskilling of their roles, lower wages, unmanageable caseloads, lack of time with offenders and limitations on effectiveness of work with offenders. This is related to a potential decline in the quality of support available to offenders due to an increase in the use of cheaper and inexperienced staff. Ultimately, this means that supervision is by and large provided by staff who now have even less time to give offenders help with problems and issues they experience, and who maybe do not hold the traditional values of the probation service, an organization historically geared towards helping people. This will impact upon vulnerable offenders in need of support, who may also be negatively impacted by a lack of confidentiality. At the other end of the scale, offenders will find these dynamics make it easier to go under the radar, to continue offending. We have seen the impact on offenders whose risk of harm will likely be manipulated for profit (Evans 2016). Thus, we can see that crime and harm are interconnected at various levels. With this in mind, an attempt to distinguish between the two becomes extremely difficult. This is precisely because of the crossover in interests between critical strands of criminology and zemiology (Friedrichs and Schwartz 2007; Rothe and Kauzlarich 2014).

Again, this is not to disagree with the critique of criminological studies that do not take harm seriously (Hillyard and Tombs 2004; Hillyard 2015). The aforementioned systemic harms associated with Transforming Rehabilitation are vitally important. None the least because such radical change can also clearly have a harmful impact upon victims of crime: who are at increased risk of further victimization, whose victimization is being profited from, and who do not receive justice in terms of effectiveness of punishment. By extension, the general public will be at increased risk of victimization. It is on this point particularly that the distinction between crime and harm, between criminology and zemiology becomes complex, and to an extent unnecessary.

Zemiology seeks to move beyond punishment, legality and the criminal justice system, to a broader understanding of harm (Hillyard 2015). But what next, what is the end goal besides drawing attention to these things (which agreeably is important); wouldn't the end goal ultimately bring us back to criminology, namely criminality and punishment as is the case here? Of course, this is not to suggest that this requires a movement towards administrative criminology. To clarify this point, it is of value to re-quote Graham:

> If it is payment by results with these agencies (CRCs), people can fiddle the books and the government can make things look like everything is working perfectly well with certain agencies (CRCs), because it just depends on how you record stuff. The important stuff is just lost, if it is all just a numbers game and it all looks good on paper, because it can be made to look good on paper then agencies who are getting there money for doing that, are going to do that.

At the core of what is now a 'reorganised' probation service, an organization tasked with reducing criminality and harm, lays an extreme paradox that could ultimately lead to heightened risks to public safety. That this forms part of a criminal justice system suggests that with regards to the future of CRCs, distinguishing between crime and harm will become increasingly difficult. Particularly, because the variety of harms outlined above highlight the potential for increases in criminality in distinction to the stated aims of reducing re-offending. This reflects the process noted earlier of a retrenchment of public sector institutions and the adoption of the perceived efficiencies of free market capitalism, 'rather than pursuing the substantive value of personal social service and responding to social need' (Whitehead 2015a, 302).

The harms outlined here were foreseeable, particularly by probation staff that could see few ways in which the Transforming Rehabilitation agenda would reduce harm or crime. Andrew noted that it is seemingly based on ideology rather than evidence. As such, the potential harms emanating from this bureaucratic reorganization have been disavowed. In brief, this term reflects that various actors *knew* about these potential harms, but they *acted* as if they did not (see Hall et al. 2008; Winlow and Hall 2013). In the same way that we are told of economic growth and economic recovery seemingly divorced from the lived experience of many, changes related to Transforming Rehabilitation could lead to increased levels of harm and crime even if this is not reflected in statistics. As Graham notes it can be made to look as though this move has been successful, that targets have been met, that levels of crime and harm are officially reduced. But will this be the real legacy of Transforming Rehabilitation?

References

Annison, Jill, Lol Burke, and Paul Senior. 2014. Transforming Rehabilitation: Another Example of English 'Exceptionalism' or a Blueprint for the Rest of Europe? *European Journal of Probation* 6: 6–23.

Burke, Lol, and Steve Collett. 2016. Transforming Rehabilitation: Organizational Bifurcation and the End of Probation as We Knew It? *Probation Journal* 63: 120–135.

Evans, Emily. 2016. The Expected Impacts of Transforming Rehabilitation on Working Relationships with Offenders. *Probation Journal* 63: 153–161.

Friedrichs, David, and Martin Schwartz. 2007. Editors' Introduction: On Social Harm and a Twenty-first Century Criminology. *Crime, Law & Social Change* 48: 1–7.

Hall, Steve, Simon Winlow, and Craig Ancrum. 2008. *Criminal Identities and Consumer Culture: Crime, Exclusion and the New Culture of Narcissism*. Cullompton: Willan Publishing.

Hillyard, Paddy. 2015. Criminal Obsessions: Crime Isn't the Only Harm. *Criminal Justice Matters* 102: 39–41.

Hillyard, Paddy, and Steve Tombs. 2004. Beyond Criminology? In *Beyond Criminology: Taking Harm Seriously*, ed. Paddy Hillyard, Christina Pantazis, Steve Tombs, and Dave Gordon, 10–29. London: Pluto Press.

———. 2007. From 'Crime' to Social Harm? *Crime, Law & Social Change* 48: 9–25.

Hillyard, Paddy, Christina Pantazis, Steve Tombs, and Dave Gordon (eds.). 2004. *Beyond Criminology: Taking Harm Seriously*. London: Pluto Press.

Robinson, Gwen, Lawrence Burke, and Matthew Millings. 2016. Criminal Justice Identities in Transition: The Case of Devolved Probation Services in England and Wales. *British Journal of Criminology* 56: 161–178.

Rothe, Dawn, and David Kauzlarich. 2014. A Victimology of State Crime. In *Towards a Victimology of State Crime*, ed. Dawn Rothe and David Kauzlarich, 3–14. London: Routledge.

Travis, A. 2016. May Wants Police Commissioners to Set Up Free Schools for 'Troubled Children'. *The Guardian*, 4 February.

Whitehead, Philip. 2015a. Payment by Results: The Materialist Reconstruction of Criminal Justice. *International Journal of Sociology and Social policy* 35: 290–305.

Whitehead, Philip. 2015b. *Reconceptualising the Moral Economy of Criminal Justice: A New Perspective*. Basingstoke: Palgrave Pivot.

Winlow, Simon, and Steve Hall. 2013. *Rethinking Social Exclusion: The End of the Social?* London: Sage.

Author Biography

David Temple In 2016, David Temple was awarded his PhD at Teesside University. His thesis, entitled '*News from Nowhere: Reconceptualising Desistance*', focused on the desistance attempts of older male offenders in North East England. David is currently a research associate on the 'Challenging Youth Racism' project at Teesside University.

Index

A
Absences 89, 98, 100, 102, 139, 246–249, 258, 259
Absence of security 250
Administrative criminology 4, 147, 190, 191, 196, 265, 280
Anxiety 110, 232, 253, 255, 259
Artificial boundaries 101
Asphyxiation 168, 169, 176
Asylum systems 201

B
Bearers of harm 66
Beyond Criminology 1, 5, 12, 13, 16, 18–21, 23–25, 33, 35, 85–87, 94, 95, 148, 196
Borders 86, 91, 92, 100, 129, 130, 139, 183, 184, 188–193
Brexit 120, 185

Bureaucracy 189, 277

C
Caricature of criminology 95
Catastrophes 152
Centrality of harm to crime 58, 91
Cisnormativity 153
Civilising process 107, 108
Class 15, 44, 69, 70, 110–113, 115, 122, 152, 158, 248, 260
Collaborative integration 93
Community Rehabilitation Companies (CRCs) 266–268, 270–273, 275–277, 279–281
Competitive individualism 111, 255, 256, 258, 259
Conceptual linkages 91
Concrete universals 119

Consequentialist 60, 61, 72
Consumer capitalism 225, 230, 231, 238, 249, 251, 254, 257, 258, 260
Consumer culture 109, 116, 117, 126, 225, 226
Continuum of sexual violence 134
Corporate 12–14, 21, 26, 27, 63, 66, 92, 111, 119, 129, 130, 149, 171, 184, 191, 192, 196, 204, 207, 254, 265
  allies to control immigrants 191
  crime 12–14, 21, 26, 27, 63, 66, 92, 119, 130, 149, 192, 204
  harms 14, 26, 63
  interests 12, 130, 171
  responses to refugees 184
Counterfeit 223–233, 237, 243
Counterfeit fashion 225, 229, 237
Counterfeiting 5, 223–230, 232, 233, 237, 238
Crime 1, 2, 4–7, 11–21, 25–27, 33–35, 37–42, 44–46, 49, 50, 57–67, 72, 74–77, 84–87, 90–93, 96–102, 108, 119, 122, 123, 126, 130, 131, 137–141, 147–149, 154, 159, 166, 169, 173–176, 178, 179, 184, 187, 188, 190, 192, 203–205, 207, 208, 211–213, 223–226, 228–230, 237, 238, 245, 253, 265–267, 269, 270, 274, 275, 280, 281
Crime-control policy 58, 67, 68, 75, 76
Crime Harm Index 63, 67
Criminal harm 45, 48, 88
Criminalisation 1, 6, 14–18, 58–61, 67, 72, 73, 75, 90, 99, 148,
149, 167, 168, 170, 171, 173, 177–179, 184, 185, 187–190, 193, 195, 196
Critical criminology 4, 5, 7, 19–22, 25, 35, 36, 47, 57, 94, 95, 113, 114, 132, 230, 265
Critical realism 123, 247
Cultural harm 6, 167, 168, 170, 171, 173

D

Dangerousness 168, 171
Deaptation 107, 114, 117
Decline in social work 277
Depth structures 247, 260
Deskilling of probation officers 274
Deviant leisure 94, 120
Diametric opposites 87, 101
Disavowed harms 114, 231, 281
Dyad 90, 91

E

Eco-eco disaster 152
Emotional harm 273
Emotional labour 254–256, 259
Empirical domain 92
Environmental harm 204, 206–210, 213, 214, 236
Experiential reality of crime 92

F

False alternatives 97, 98, 102
False dichotomies 91, 96, 101
Fashion cycle 232, 233
Fashion industry 6, 225, 231, 233–238

Fast fashion 233, 236
Fetishistic disavowal 115, 117
Foucault, Michel 168, 173, 174, 176
Functionally aggressive 109

G

Gender 5, 6, 15, 16, 43, 44, 112, 122, 130–132, 136, 139, 145–149, 152, 153, 155–160, 170
Germany, Cologne 136
Greece 2, 90, 137, 153, 187, 188
Green criminology 6, 204, 208, 209, 211, 215, 236

H

Harm 1, 2, 4–7, 12, 13, 15, 18, 20–27, 33, 34, 36–45, 47–52, 56–70, 72–76, 85–89, 91–93, 96–102, 107, 108, 111–114, 119, 121, 122, 130, 133, 139–141, 147–149, 151–157, 159, 160, 165–168, 170–172, 177–179, 184, 191–197, 201, 203, 204, 207, 208, 211, 213, 223–225, 227, 228, 230, 232, 233, 237, 238, 243, 245, 248, 256–260, 265–267, 270, 271, 273–275, 279–281
Harm assessment framework 5, 58, 66, 68
Harm and crime reduction 271
Harmful conduct principle 61, 73
Harmfulness 60, 72–74
Harm prevention principle 61, 73
Hegemonic heterosexuality 148, 171
Heteronormativity 153

Heterosexism 16
Hidden economy 99, 252
Hidden victimage 97

I

Ideology 6, 108, 114, 116, 122, 247, 256, 260, 269, 273, 281
Illicit markets 225, 229, 237
Imaginary 115, 116, 177
Imaginary dualism 97
Imaginary penalities 148
Injustice 2, 3, 26, 58, 75, 76, 89
Insecurity 118, 122, 232, 256, 259, 270, 279
Institutionalised altruism 109
Integrated approach 98, 100, 102
International crime decline 120
Intransitive realm 247, 260

J

Job flexibility 246, 249
Job insecurity 251, 252
Job stability 251
Jurisprudence 2, 22–24, 90

L

Labour exploitation 134, 235
Leisure 94, 194, 225, 231, 232, 245, 246, 249, 252
Lexical diversity 90
Libidinal energy 110, 111, 258
Licit economy 225
Little evils 113, 119
Loss 2, 3, 27, 65, 75, 87–91, 118, 122, 196, 207, 212, 224, 270, 271, 279

Loss of relationships 277

M
Mass supervision 276
McJobs 252
Moral economy of probation 273
Moralist 60, 170

N
Negation of the negation 253, 259
Negative rights 108, 114, 121, 123
Neoliberalism 99, 111, 113, 116, 118, 119, 236, 249, 259, 260
Neural plasticity 116, 247
Non-safety critical counterfeits 224, 225, 227

O
Objectless anxiety 117, 118
Organised crime 63, 67, 84, 111, 139, 226, 228, 229

P
Payment by results 266, 268–270, 276, 280
Permanent managed deaptation 110
Political catastrophism 121
Political economy 177, 225, 247, 259
Pornography 6, 165–168, 170–173, 176–179, 182
Positivism 141
Post-war settlement 248, 251, 259
Privatisation 7, 270, 274, 275
Probation 7, 265–270, 272–277, 279–281

Profit making 269
Proportionality 64, 74, 90
Proto-subject 116
Pseudo-pacification process 108, 110
Punishment 2, 3, 38, 59, 61, 64, 65, 76, 87, 89–91, 96, 101, 102, 148, 159, 280

Q
Queer criminology 147

R
Racism 157, 282
Real 13, 26, 46, 52, 92, 98, 107, 110, 111, 114–120, 151, 213, 214, 230, 233, 238, 270, 274, 281
Rendezvous subjects 95
Re-offending 269, 272, 276, 281
Restorative justice 59, 65, 66, 74, 75, 123, 131
Retaliatory procedures 90
Risk of harm 147, 266, 268, 271, 275, 277, 280
Ritualised punishment/penalty 64, 90

S
Safety critical counterfeits 223, 228
Semantic analysis 88
Serious crime 62, 228, 238
Seriousness 26, 62–64, 74, 76
Service economy 5–7, 245–259
Sex-gender 145, 159, 160
Sexuality 5, 138, 146, 147, 158, 166, 170–172, 177, 178
Shop-floor culture 254

Index

Social harm 2–5, 11–13, 15–20, 22–26, 33–41, 43–45, 47–50, 57, 67, 88, 89, 94–96, 159, 170, 184, 193, 205, 212, 224, 225, 236, 245, 246
Social justice 4, 15, 21, 22, 27, 58, 75, 109, 209
Social recognition 111, 112
Socio-symbolic aggression 107, 108
Special liberty 111, 112, 122, 256–259
Status anxiety 270
Stressful working conditions 254
Structural harms 34, 147, 156, 159, 160, 167, 171, 177–179, 195, 236
Subjective harms 7
Subjective violence 247
Subjectivity 115, 122, 247, 253
Supervision by numbers 276, 278
Symbolic 43, 111, 112, 115–117, 151, 247, 248, 256, 258, 260
Symbolic efficiency 116, 119, 259, 260
Symbolic inefficiency 110
Symbolic Order 116, 117, 247
Symbolic violence 247
Systemic harms 97, 99, 100, 119, 122, 252, 253, 280

T

Target-driven culture 254
Teesside, North East of England 246
Telemorphosis 147, 149–153, 157, 159, 160
Tension 33, 34, 36, 40, 49, 51, 85, 86, 107, 114
Textile waste 236
Topical guardianship 100

Transcendental materialism 107, 113–115, 118, 123
Transforming Rehabilitation 266–273, 275–277, 279–281
Transgender 146, 149, 158, 190

U

Ultra-realism 93, 94, 123, 246–248
Un-criminalised harms 92, 96–100, 102

V

Victimology 65, 66, 140, 147
Visual representations of harm 149

W

War 5, 6, 119–121, 129–136, 139–141, 179, 188
Work intensification 254, 256, 259

Y

Youth transitions 252

Z

Zemia 1–4, 6, 86–91, 96, 97, 100–102
Zemiology 2, 4–7, 12, 16, 18–25, 33–40, 44–52, 56–58, 86–88, 91–98, 100–102, 108, 132, 134, 139, 140, 147, 148, 159, 160, 167, 168, 171, 179, 185, 191, 192, 196, 208, 209, 213, 230, 237, 245, 246, 265, 273, 280
Zero-hours contracts 251, 255, 259

Printed by Printforce, the Netherlands